THE
POPE'S
WAR

Other Titles by Matthew Fox

THE POPE'S WAR

Why Ratzinger's Secret Crusade Has Imperiled the Church and How It Can Be Saved

MATTHEW FOX

FOREWORD BY BRUCE CHILTON

STERLING ETHOS

New York

STERLING ETHOS
New York

An Imprint of Sterling Publishing
387 Park Avenue South
New York, NY 10016

STERLING ETHOS and the distinctive Sterling logo are registered trademarks of Sterling Publishing Co., Inc.

Library of Congress Cataloging-in-Publication Data

Fox, Matthew, 1940-
 The Pope's war : why Ratzinger's secret crusade has imperiled the church and how it can be saved / Matthew Fox ; foreword by Bruce Chilton.
  p. cm.
 Includes bibliographical references (p.   ) and index.
 ISBN 978-1-4027-8629-7
 1. Benedict XVI, Pope, 1927- 2. Church controversies—Catholic Church—History—20th century. 3. Catholic Church—History—20th century. 4. Church controversies--Catholic Church—History—21st century. 5. Catholic Church—History—21st century. I. Title.
 BX1378.6.F69 2010
                                                                    282.09'045—dc22

10 9 8 7 6 5 4 3 2 1

Picture Credits

COURTESY WIKIMEDIA COMMONS: 28 Leonardo Boff, 2005/Hermínio Oliveira: Agência Brasil, 107 St. Josemaria Escriva: Communications Office of Opus Dei

GETTY IMAGES: [STF/Staff]AFP/Getty Images: 3

CORBIS: 125 © TONY GENTILE/Reuters/Corbis, 130 © Bettmann/CORBIS

ARTISTS: 33 © Ingrid H. Shafer, 55 © IHU/Unisinos, 145 © Michael Amsler

Tyrants are more afraid of good people than of bad people.
—Thomas Aquinas

✠

Great Spirits have always encountered violent opposition from mediocre minds.
—Albert Einstein

✠

every day I am afraid
that he died for nothing
because he is buried in our churches,
because we have betrayed his revolution
in our obedience to and fear of authority
—Dorothee Soelle

✠

This book is dedicated to all those Great Spirits, many of them martyrs in our time, brave and good souls in Latin America, who have fought the good fight and often paid the ultimate price to render the message of Jesus about love and justice incarnate in today's history and culture and are birthing another way of being church. With special thanks to Oscar Romero, Sister Dorothy Stang, Penny Lernoux, Bishop Casaldáliga, Cardinal Arns, Leonardo Boff, and thousands of others known and unknown who remind all of us of the link between courage and Spirit.

CONTENTS

FOREWORD

✠

PROPHECY INVOLVES CONFRONTING PAIN and encountering beauty, both for the prophet and whoever listens attentively. For forty years, Matthew Fox has been America's principal prophet to the Roman Catholic Church.

Conventional authorities have never shown a liking for prophets; they typically try to silence them by any expedient means. Matthew Fox has been silenced. He obeyed an order not to speak or teach for a year, which then stretched on to fourteen months. Then he opened a conference address by saying, "As I was saying fourteen months ago when I was so rudely interrupted. . . ." His Dominican order expelled him under pressure from the Vatican.

Rejection of that kind brings loneliness, compounded when friendships dissolve in the fear that showing concern for a silenced colleague might bring repercussions. But Matthew Fox's steady focus on his vision has enabled him to attract thousands of disciples and tens of thousands of readers, to pioneer some of the most productive programs of theology in recent years, and to nurture a loyal circle of sympathizers and friends.

What is it that provokes extreme reactions to prophets? Why can't they just have their say and go about their business—and let their listeners go about theirs? The prophet Jeremiah said that he tried not to voice his message, but that the word of God consumed him from within like a fire (Jeremiah 20:9). Matthew Fox's good faith effort to obey his superiors resulted only in his deepening commitment to the message that they did not wish to hear.

Three millennia ago, the prophet Elijah insisted that when God chose an entire people to be his own, that choice was incompatible with rule by leaders who arrogated royal power to themselves. Either the sheep were for the shepherds, as kings and their entourages believed, or the shepherds were for the sheep under the guidance of God, the true shepherd. Any prophet who has insisted that God's preference is clear has found himself or herself in trouble, sometimes deep trouble. Jeremiah spoke of the fire within him after he had been beaten and sequestered in stocks by Pashur, a priest in charge of the temple. Matthew Fox's voice broke out with increased prophetic clarity after he had been silenced by Cardinal Joseph Ratzinger, at the time the prefect of the Congregation for the Doctrine of the Faith, known until recent years as the Office of the Inquisition.

Cardinal Ratzinger, of course, became Pope Benedict XVI, and much of Matthew Fox's book is taken up, as its title suggests, with the question of Joseph Ratzinger's purpose in all his roles during his ascent within the Vatican's hierarchy. The story of the suppression of Liberation theology is told, with many examples of how its exponents were silenced by Rome, and sometimes harassed, tortured, and killed by local paramilitaries. Fox is not concerned with Joseph Ratzinger himself, but with how the present governance of the Roman Catholic Church favors a particular temperament.

In many bureaucracies, concern for watching one's own back causes bureaucrats to prefer colleagues who keep the team together and do not mount radical challenges. The more enclosed the bureaucracy, the more mediocrity and conventionalism will be elevated. So what would we expect of the curial system in the Vatican, where cardinals selected by popes select new popes, without regard to or consultation with lay people, priests, or even bishops? It is a system without mooring in its base.

The rules that control the election of popes and the place of cardinals are comparatively recent, and have in fact been changed from time to time. They might have been shaped in a progressive direction, and the Second Vatican Council, convened by Pope John XXIII—the good pope, as Matthew Fox sees him—held out some hope for that. But instead, Pope Paul VI appeared ambivalent about the impetus of the Council, Pope John Paul I did not survive long enough to put his progressive principles into practice, and Pope John Paul II deliberately set about moving back to a pre-Council model for the papacy. His active collaborator in a view of the papacy as a monarchy was Cardinal Ratzinger (then known by the nickname of the pope's Rottweiler), who is continuing the process of undermining key aspects of the Council as Pope Benedict XVI.

So far, that story of power shifts between democratic and monarchial claims of authority might sound like simple politics, and politics is naturally involved. But something fiercer and more troubling lies beneath the surface. Matthew Fox's book brings this factor out. The doctrinal claim that the pope can be infallible is a comparatively recent invention. When infallibility is attributed to the head of a bureaucracy, the result is to seal off the operation from criticism and self-examination.

Matthew Fox sees the extraordinary power of denial working out in the scandal of pedophilia and in the scandal of how that behavior has been concealed—and even enabled—by the Vatican, including Joseph Ratzinger. The spectacle of the Congregation for the Doctrine of Faith silencing theologians for their opinions while letting priests accused of pedophilia take charge of children is difficult to understand at all, unless Matthew Fox's analysis of this denial is accepted. He compares the behavior of Vatican bureaucrats to an addiction, where the abused substance is their power.

The analogy of the Vatican monarchial pretensions to an addiction goes deeper. Matthew Fox sees that we are living in an era in which behaviors of addiction and codependence are increasing. Literal substance abuse is an obvious example, but the same analysis applies to the rise of fascism and to its replication in neo-conservative movements, to the increase of fundamentalism in Protestant theology, and to the growing violence of Muslim jihads. In all these cases, self-selecting groups claim that they alone have the authority to guide their communities, and to suppress any dissent. They are addicted to a self-serving ideological definition of what their communities should be, and find ways to dismiss and relegate anyone who disagrees. Matthew Fox calls this "integralism," which he identifies as the sickness of our time.

But there is no reason for which this sickness should be unto death. Matthew Fox is not merely a pundit, content to analyze the gravity of our predicament. As a prophet he sees the way forward and articulates that way. What has been repressed, after all, by the Vatican's bureaucracy is not merely a political alternative to its rule by denial, but the movement of Spirit through men and women who have willingly paid the price for speaking and acting on behalf of their vision of a genuinely apostolic Christianity, where care for the poor and embracing diversity are once again virtues.

The very word "apostolic" means "sent" by God; every person who has had an encounter with the divine knows this fresh sense of purpose in the world. Mystical engagement with God is not an unusual or arcane activity for Matthew Fox, but literally comes naturally to people. This is because, in his theology, there was original blessing before there was original sin: God's loving companionship with the man and woman who God made in the divine image and likeness. For investigating and applying this profound principle, derived from the Bible (Genesis 1:27), Cardinal Ratzinger wanted to silence Matthew Fox. He failed. All such efforts will fail in the long run, because part of the beauty of prophecy is that, through all the pain it endures, its resources lie much deeper than human pretensions to power.

Bruce Chilton,
Bernard Iddings Bell Professor of Religion,
Bard College

TUMBLING DOWN . . . JUST LIKE THE BERLIN WALL

✠

THE LATE FATHER BEDE GRIFFITHS, an English Benedictine monk who ran an ashram in southern India that married Christian and Hindu ways, and who authored many deep books, said to me shortly before he died, "Don't worry about the Vatican. Don't even think about them. Continue to do what you are doing, planting new shoots for a new Christianity. The Vatican will all come tumbling down some night, just like the Berlin Wall."

These wise words from a saintly Christian monk seem to be coming true right in front of our eyes. The mythologies that have kept Roman Catholicism going for many centuries, including but not limited to priestly celibacy, are melting before our eyes as more and more facts come out not only about pedophile clergy but above all about the hierarchy that allowed these predators to move from parish to parish and diocese to diocese. But this news of child sex abuse is just the tip of the spear in the war for the soul of the church that Pope Benedict XVI and his predecessor, Pope John Paul II, have been waging for decades.

For close to forty years a religious collapse has been going on in our midst. The Roman Catholic Church, a Western institution at least 1,800 years old, has been bleeding profusely. In great part the press has ignored what is going on, preferring as it too often does to focus on popes in pretty clothing ("Is he wearing Prada shoes and sunglasses?") and counting the babies they kiss in front of television cameras, feeding the temptation to render the pope a celebrity. Recently, however, the pedophile crisis that so wracked American and Canadian churches eight years ago is arising again in Ireland, Switzerland, Italy, Belgium, and the pope's home country, Germany. Indeed the pope stands at the heart of the crisis.

But it is important to know that clerical sexual abuse of minors is only a symptom of a deeper struggle, a structural shift, a *coup d'eglise*, that has been occurring for forty years. According to some of the best minds in the church, a schism has been occurring. The church itself is disintegrating before our eyes, and there is one man more than any other who, with the full support of the previous pope, John Paul II, has led that disintegration. His name is Joseph Ratzinger.

For twenty-four years preceding his papacy (1981–2005) Ratzinger was the chief inquisitor under Pope John Paul II, serving as the prefect, or head, of the Congregation for the Doctrine of the Faith (formerly known as the Holy Office or the Office of the Inquisition). The buck stopped with him when it came to clerical abuse since his congregation was responsible for dealing with errant clergy. Starting his career as a theologian, he first came forward as reform-minded. From his appointment as archbishop of Munich and Freising in 1977 by Pope Paul VI, Ratzinger rose in the hierarchical ranks and was eventually made dean of the College of Cardinals in 2002. There are those who maintain that Ratzinger actually became pope in violation of the rules of the game, since he campaigned for the job—giving speeches and publishing a book just before the papal election—something that canon law, an archaic legal system that is the only code by which this massive global institution governs itself, forbids. Interestingly, he hardly had to go to that length since he had had a strong hand in the appointment of 113 of the 115 cardinals who voted in the election. He went to great lengths to ensure that he was not forgotten in the conclave that would elect him.

History will record about Joseph Ratzinger that his most memorable accomplishment was to bring the Inquisition back into being. That is no exaggeration whatsoever. I recall when I was a teenager and quite self-conscious about my Catholic faith in the public high school I attended in Madison, Wisconsin, questions about the Crusades and the Inquisition (no one was talking then about the witch burnings, but that history would gradually be uncovered by women scholars as well). I went to our parish priest and asked about the Inquisition since none of my Catholic education had taught me about it. The priest said, "Oh, that's all in the past." I actually believed him. And when the good Pope John XXIII appeared like a bolt from heaven in 1958 and called the Second Vatican Council (1962–1965) to update the church and to rehabilitate theologians who had been silenced and abused under the previous pope, Pius XII, I and millions of others were cheered to hear that the Index of Forbidden Books and other relics of Inquisition spirit would be dismantled and replaced with the light of critical thinking and genuine dialogue over differences.

Even Father Joseph Ratzinger himself was swept up into this powerful movement of renewal. For example, he wrote in 1962 that the meaning of prophecy is "in the prophetic protest against the self-righteousness of the institutions . . . God, throughout history, has not been on the side of the institutions but on that of the suffering and persecuted."

But that was then and this is now. After Pope John XXIII came Pope Paul VI (1963–1978), who tried to carry on the spirit of Vatican II and brought the council to its conclusion. Pope Paul VI took it upon himself to deal with the issue of priestly celibacy and reiterated the familiar teaching in his encyclical *Sacerdotalis Caelibatus*. His biggest move, however, turned out to be the sharp put-down of birth control that he set out in his lamentable encyclical *Humanae Vitae*, which forbade birth control even in these times of population explosion. Contrary to his commission, which included laypeople and even women who recommended easing restrictions for Catholics on birth control, Pope Paul VI ensured the preservation of the old line in the end. An uproar followed. Comments Catholic historian Garry Wills: "The Pope was stunned. He would spend the remaining ten years of his pontificate as if sleepwalking . . . He was increasingly melancholy and prone to tears." Pope Paul VI complained that he was a "prisoner" in the Vatican, and he never wrote another encyclical. These two encyclicals became the rallying flag and litmus test for the curial forces in the Vatican for years to come: Either get on board with priestly celibacy and with no birth control or you are not a true member of the church.

Following Pope Paul VI was another forward-thinking pope, Cardinal Luciani or Pope John Paul I (elected in August 1978), who lasted only one month in the job before he died very suddenly one night. The most serious detective work done on his untimely death concluded that he was murdered and that the murder may have been at least in part an inside job. This same investigator concludes that some cardinals had to be involved. Significantly, Pope John Paul I was about to launch an investigation into the financial situation of the Catholic Church when he met his sudden demise. Also, he had been on the birth control commission and voted with the majority, a vote that Paul VI ignored, and it was widely anticipated that he would change course regarding the birth control issue. In his brief tenure as pope, John Paul I actually congratulated the first couple to give birth to a test tube baby even though *Humanae Vitae* had condemned in vitro fertilization. Wills comments: "This was the kind of warm pastoral statement John XXIII was known for, and Luciani disturbed some in the Curia with the fear that they were in for another Johannine papacy." Moreover, shortly before his death, Luciani declared in a public pronouncement, "God is Father, but even more Mother."

The one who followed was no balancer of the male and female sides to God's nature. Pope John Paul II, for all of his piety to the Virgin Mary, mother of Jesus of Nazareth, was hardly a champion of women or the feminine side of God. He was seemingly rushed onto the papal throne by clerics of the right and the CIA (one former CIA agent told me John Paul II, formerly Cardinal Karol Wojtyla, the archbishop of Krakow, was "their man" in Poland for decades). The second John Paul did not carry on the traditions of Vatican II or of Pope Paul VI or Pope John Paul I. When John Paul II entered the papacy, one of his first acts was to name Cardinal Ratzinger the head of the Holy Office or Inquisition—known in our day as the Congregation for the Doctrine of the Faith (CDF).

The story of the historical Inquisition technically began in 1232 with the appointment of Dominican and Franciscan inquisitors—investigators and enforcers of the Catholic faith—but reached a high point of wantonness in the Spanish Inquisition under Torquemada. I hold that it has reached another high point in our own time under the direction of Cardinal Ratzinger, now Pope Benedict XVI (who became pope on April 19, 2005).

It is rare for an inquisitor to become pope. One such person was Gian Pietro Caraffa, who became Pope Paul IV (1555–1559). His accomplishments included ratifying the Statute of Toledo, which forbade persons with Jewish blood to hold office. This pope forbade Jews to possess any religious book except the Bible and abolished Hebrew printing in Rome, which had become the capital of Hebrew printing in the Renaissance. He forbade Jews to own any real estate or attend any Christian university or to hire any Christian servants. He increased Jewish taxes and insisted Jews wear distinctive badges and address Christians as "sir." He put the Talmud on the Index of Forbidden Books, and, above all, he created the original Jewish ghetto in Rome one mile from the Vatican. In one month all Jews were rounded up and relocated to an area one mile square with only one entrance. The Jews had to pay for constructing the enclosure. As many as ten thousand persons lived there at one time. Says Cardinal Edward Cassidy, "The ghetto, which came into being in 1555 with a papal bull, became in Nazi Germany the antechamber of the extermination."

In Torquemada's day, Rome was envious of the power he wielded in Spain, being as close to Ferdinand and Isabella as he was. But Rome could do nothing about it. At least they kept him at arm's length from the Vatican itself. Interestingly, Ratzinger and John Paul II actually tried to canonize Queen Isabella, the patron of Torquemada, a saint. Since Torquemada and Isabella, among other things, expelled at least eighty thousand Jews from Spain and confiscated their property and belongings—and killed more than two thousand people at the stake—this canonization effort never quite yielded the results Ratzinger and John Paul II sought.

Nevertheless, over the course of twenty-four years, the two of them proceeded to dismantle all the thinking and creativity that had been unleashed by Pope John XXIII in the church—thinking that included liberation theology and the creativity of base communities in Latin America and beyond, along with their lively liturgies and rich theological exploration and courageous stand against injustice. In the dying days of the Cold War, liberation theology was a convenient political target. In Holland a renaissance of liturgical creativity ensued after the Council. I remember visiting Holland in 1969 and attending liturgies in which the Credo was put to gospel music (sung in Dutch) and the "Beatles Mass" in which great drumming and dancing was encouraged and priests were writing poetry and songs. All that vitality was snuffed out by Rome. The pope and Cardinal Ratzinger also went out of their way to shut down Creation Spirituality movements in North America and beyond.

In his role as head of the revived Inquisition, Ratzinger silenced, and in many cases dismissed, more than ninety-one theologians or pastoral leaders. I was among those silenced and ultimately dismissed, after a twelve-year battle with Ratzinger that began in 1983. A theologian's job is to think—to think through the inherited legacy of the Christian faith and to attempt to apply it to contemporary issues. But Joseph Ratzinger was bent on ending such critical and creative thinking in the Catholic Church. One professor from my alma mater, the Institut Catholique de Paris, came to a dialogue I did several years ago in the Midwest with a scientist, and she said to me afterward: "There is nothing like this happening in all of Europe. Pope John Paul II and Ratzinger have ended all thinking in theology faculties on the continent. Theology is dead there." When one ends all thinking, silences theologians, condemns books, and rouses the faithful to utter slogans instead of thinking, one invites trouble.

And trouble the Catholic Church got. The law of the church, over which the pope is the supreme arbiter, has been too long turned toward a medieval pursuit of heresy while ignoring real evil in its own ranks. Among the troubles that happen when you dumb down an organization over the course of three decades is that dumb people hold positions of power and control decision making, and are never held to account. I recall my Dominican master general once telling me, during the trials I was having with the Vatican, that "everyone in Rome knows that only third-rate theologians occupy the Congregation for the Doctrine of the Faith office." And yet this office, contrary to the stated documents of the Second Vatican Council, holds the keys to condemning theologians and theological movements. The man who said this to me dismissed me when he was leaving office as master general by putting my dismissal papers on a boat between Rome and Chicago, thus ensuring that the Dominican chapter meeting in Mexico City that summer would not hear of the dismissal until well after they disbanded. This man, an Irish Dominican, will not be remembered for his courage. But that is another story.

The world is awakening now to these troubles of the Catholic Church, and in particular to those of priestly pedophilia. Such troubles, along with the old-boy network that perpetuates them and resists all efforts at reform—including bringing women into the tight all-male system—have only grown since first being covered broadly in the 1990s by author Jason Berry and others, and then as they surfaced in an unrelenting way in Cardinal Bernard Francis Law's fiasco in Boston in 2002. Cardinal Law fought the state, prosecutors, and media on a daily basis in his efforts to resist telling the truth of an ugly and sordid story that implicated him, since he passed serially abusive priests from parish to parish and to other dioceses knowing full well what was at stake. He hid eleven thousand pages of documents from investigators. Is Law in prison for these crimes today? No. After stonewalling for two and a half years he was promoted to a plush position as an archpriest in Rome, where he will not be extradited. There he looks over a serene fourth-century basilica while the church teeters on the brink of disaster from neglect.

The day that the news of Boston pedophile priests countenanced by a cardinal first emerged, I was teaching a class in a doctor of ministry program in Oakland, California, and we had a discussion of the events. One woman spoke up and said, "As a business executive I can tell you this: When this happens in business the CEO is gone in twenty-four hours, no questions asked." That was a telling comment. First, such things happen in business. They happen everywhere. Wherever humans gather there is the potential for abuse. But the other lesson is this: Leaders must lead, and when business leaders fail to lead, they are gone *toute de suite*. One wonders why the Catholic Church and its leaders are not held to the same standard of ethics as CEOs in business. The bishop is after all the CEO of the local church. How rare it has been for bishops who learned about priestly pedophilia to tell the truth, remove the priest, and get him help or send him to jail, or leave his post if he fails to do those things. Once again, an old-boys club seems to prevent such honesty.

The victims of priestly abuse never really get over it. Sexual predation is like that. It creates scars on the soul that are very hard to erase and at best can be ministered to over a long time. I have listened to stories of sexual abuse, and I know how serious an offense that can be. The wounds are deep. Many victims end up drinking or taking drugs and falling into addictions of many kinds, their souls wandering and lost. Often marriages and relationships are almost impossible to hold together. Suicide is another common outcome of childhood abuse. In recent revelations of clerical abuse in Belgium, which included the sordid story of a prominent churchman named Bishop Roger Vangheluwe who abused his nephew for many years, we have learned that thirteen young people committed suicide because of clerical abuse.

There is a profound relationship between the dumbing down of the church and the pedophile crises precisely because only a churchman who is ignorant, or without conscience, or both, would pass offenders from parish to parish or from diocese to diocese or from country to country. Another less obvious part is the sanctioning of pyramids of power that ensure that not just one victim is abused but the entire community, and ultimately the entire church. The support of anti-intellectual and ultraright movements such as Opus Dei, the Legion of Christ, and Communion and Liberation are at the heart of Pope John Paul II and Ratzinger's strategy to displace the traditional religious orders with so-called lay groups that prefer ideology—"the pope is always right, obey the pope"—to theology and gospel values. A dumbed-down church is a yes-man church. No intellectual questioning or conscience is allowed to emerge without being swiped down. A dumbed-down church becomes an immoral church, a church whose only virtue is loyalty and obedience and that turns a blind eye to justice.

This is what has happened on Chief Inquisitor Cardinal Ratzinger's watch.

On the day that the pedophile revelations came out in Boston, my twenty-eight-year-old nephew and his wife were driving their car from their home in Salem, Massachusetts, to their local Catholic church. They were en route to baptizing their newborn baby when they heard the news on the radio. Salem, after all, is part of the diocese of Boston. When they heard the news they stopped the car and asked, "What are we doing? We are taking our baby to be baptized in a Catholic church that passes pedophile priests around but condemns liberation theologians and prophetic priests like our uncle." With that, they turned their car around and drove home.

There is great meaning in this story. It is about an entire generation that is not buying the mythology of celibacy any longer. It is not buying into the lies and hypocrisy of organized religion any longer. It helps to explain a situation a few years later, when I was conducting a retreat in northern New York State (a generally conservative area). I asked the participants on our first gathering on a Friday night what religious traditions they came from. Of 150 participants, about 100 were Roman Catholic. "Okay," I said. "And how many of you are practicing?" About sixty raised their hands. "And now," I asked, "how many of your kids are practicing?" Every hand went down. One hundred percent of the younger generation had left the church—and this in conservative upstate New York. I recently received a letter from a very intelligent Irishman who spoke about the younger generation's attitude toward religion in Ireland. Said he, "for the younger generation . . . religion is seen as being run entirely by old men who have a complete detachment from reality and who belong to a secretive fraternity in which child rape is tolerated and facilitated."

Welcome to the church of the Inquisition redux. This is Pope Benedict XVI's church.

Cardinal Joseph Ratzinger has envisioned a smaller church, one existing in "small, seemingly insignificant groups that nonetheless live an intense struggle against evil." As Pope Benedict, he is overseeing a shrinking church. Whether supporting the kind of church sects that I discuss in Section Three, or forcefully expelling theologians like myself (I've been warmly embraced by the Anglican communion for sixteen years), or allowing heinous sexual abuses to go unchecked so as to alienate young adults like my nephew and his wife, a smaller church is what Ratzinger is achieving.

It is not just the pedophile victims who are hurting in the Catholic Church today. Many laypeople and church workers and good priests are hurting badly. The emptiness of the Catholic churches is clearly evident in Western countries. During Pope John Paul II's reign, thirteen churches were closed in San Francisco alone. One person wrote to the *San Francisco Chronicle*: "This is a mismanaged corporation. Instead of selling off their assets and closing churches they should be asking: 'Why doesn't anyone want what we have to sell any more?'" One diocese on the East Coast has been busy closing forty-two parishes this season.

I call what is happening to Catholicism in this book a "tragedy," and I use that term advisedly. *Merriam-Webster's Collegiate Dictionary* defines "tragedy" as "a medieval narrative poem or tale typically describing the downfall of a great man." We are talking here about the downfall of a great institution, a great movement in history that admittedly contributed to some very negative events, such as inquisitions and crusades and witch burnings and empire building and racism and sexism and homophobia. But it is also an institution that, in its better days, gave us the monastic orders that kept scholarship alive during centuries of cultural darkness; that offered education and uplifted the poor at times; that inspired artists and musicians as great as da Vinci, Michelangelo, Mozart, and Beethoven; that left us models of spiritual and intellectual depth and heroism in persons like Francis of Assisi, Hildegard of Bingen, Thomas Aquinas, Dorothy Day, Oscar Romero, Teilhard de Chardin, Pope John XXIII, Thomas Berry, and countless more. It is tragic that we are watching this legacy melt away before our eyes.

Another definition for "tragedy" is "a disastrous event or a calamity." It is a calamity that Ratzinger/Benedict's "New Inquisition" has brought about in history and the Catholic Church. Today, when leadership is so needed in areas ranging from ecological devastation and climate change, to war and peace, to population control and educational needs, to peace among warring religions, to awakening people to sexism and homophobia, the Catholic Church has lost most of its credibility and much of its intellectual resources. In its present form it has very little to offer at this critical time in history.

Yet it has not always been so. There is much in Catholicism's rich and varied traditions that is wise, challenging, uplifting, and even adventurous. But adventure is not something that stirs the souls of today's inhabitants of the Vatican palaces and those yes-men they appoint to carry out their visionless intentions. The destruction of base communities in Latin America, the "elevating" of little men to places of influence and power—this is not a contribution to history. I know one archbishop who had a fine record of struggle on behalf of justice who actually put his head down and cried on the lap of a friend of mine, saying, "There is not one bishop they have appointed in twenty years that I can admire." The great project of dumbing down the church has succeeded, perhaps beyond the wildest expectations of its grand inquisitor.

In this book I will tell the story of what has been going on and of the principal players in the calamity/tragedy in hopes of taking lessons from all this sad history. We should not underestimate the power of the Spirit to make things new and to start over and to truly bring about a New Creation—once the deadwood is cleared away. The denuding of the church that is occurring today, the separation of so many young people from its traditions, won't stand for long. The Spirit of creativity steps into vacuums very nicely. Deep ecumenism and the drinking from the wells of all the world's spiritual traditions is an appropriate next step for humankind. After the deconstruction comes the reconstruction.

But still the story needs to be told so that we understand what we are moving from and who can and cannot inspire us for the new spiritual era that humanity is called to, an era when blind institutions must change or suffer great losses and truly "die" (to use Jesus' word) just like a seed dies in the earth so that life might emerge. Yes, the story needs to be told so that something new can truly happen.

There are three legs to the scandal we are considering, a scandal whose secrets are now being told: There is the once secret but now much publicized sexual scandal and its cover-ups; there is the financial scandal, which is giving simony a new name, that is coming out in the open now; and there is the theological scandal—some would call it a schism—that has stripped the decisions of Vatican II so all collegiality is gone and theologians are gagged and what is left standing is the pope and his Curia and those who take vows to obey only them and to think only their thoughts. What does all this have to do with Jesus?

I tell this story in four parts. Section One deals with Ratzinger's life story as a youth and an upcoming theologian at the Second Vatican Council, and then his "conversion" from progressive thinker to ecclesial climber and chief inquisitor. Section Two deals with his chosen enemies, whom I call the "Silenced Ones." Of course I can only treat some of the theologians and activists he silenced and denounced in a book this size (a fuller list is found in the Appendix). It is important to let the Silenced Ones speak. What wisdom are they carrying secretly in their hearts? Why did their thinking and actions put so much fear and dread into the minds at the Vatican?

Section Three deals with Cardinal Ratzinger's allies. Just as we learn a lot about a person by his enemies, so too we learn a lot from one's friends and allies. We deal with Opus Dei, the Legion of Christ, and Communion and Liberation, three of the special groups that Ratzinger has praised and protected for years while attacking theologians and spiritual movements that did not fit his criteria of über-right politics and religiosity. The fact that sordid characters like Father Josemaria Escriva, Father Marcial Maciel, and Cardinal Bernard Law were champions of these same movements cannot go unnoticed.

Section Four deals with the silver lining and the good news in this sad story, for here we take a look at the devastation wrought by the past two popes (over more than thirty years) and we realize that maybe the Holy Spirit had a plan in all this destruction. Maybe the forms of religion and Catholicism as we have come to rely on them in the modern era needed a great dying, a great tumbling down, just like the Berlin Wall.

If so, then the obvious question that arises is this: Where do we go from here? What is the future of Christianity and of Roman Catholicism as we know it? In these chapters I explore the surrendering of certain myths that needs to happen as well as the nurturing of others, saving treasures from the burning building of the institutional Catholic Church, and what a truly *catholic* Christianity and a post-Vatican and more grassroots Catholic*ism* would look like. In short, we take up the challenge to push a restart button on a two-thousand-year attempt, often flawed, to carry on the teaching and the spirit of Jesus of Nazareth.

When I pounded ninety-five theses at the Wittenburg doors in 2005 shortly after Ratzinger was made pope, I did so knowing that this man and his minions were a dangerous team to turn the church over to. I did not know the depths of the perversity there—for example, in the depth and breadth of pedophile scandals or in all the extreme sects that they championed. I had not yet read Jason Berry or heard of Father Maciel or of Sister Jane. I did know something of the theological abuse and financial abuse and sexual lies being played out behind the scenes. Great are the media voices and powers that will prefer to distract from the issues at stake in this book by painting me as an imperfect messenger (which I am). This book is not about me, but about the history of Christianity (and indeed religion) as it is being played out in our time. Greater still is the anguish and brokenheartedness, the disgust and moral outrage of the "faithful," including good lay people and priests, at the scandalous "leadership" of the Church the past forty years. It is their anger and willingness to take back the Church and create it in new forms that counts. It is rising out of denial that matters. It is their willingness to build grass roots communities and start a global lay ecumenical council and reinvent how we do church that will reinvent church. Hopefully this book may assist that important process. And Spirit may have the last word as it had the first.

THE MAKING OF AN INQUISITOR: RATZINGER'S LIFE STORY

✳

"The first thing you have to know about Cardinal Ratzinger is that he is not a Christian." These words were spoken to me by a white-haired priest and respected canon lawyer who worked for years in Rome during the pontificate of John Paul II. (It is the job of a canon lawyer to know the intricacies of Church law. Canon lawyers tend to be conservative people, sort of legal accountants.) After this man left Rome, he took up residence in a major American city to work as a canon lawyer in the diocese. I had approached him to advise me at the time I was being attacked by Ratzinger in his twelve-year effort to shut down my master's program at Holy Names College, Oakland, and to get me to cease writing theology. He succeeded in shutting down a program famous for its deep ecumenism, its marriage of science and spirituality, its draw of serious students from all over the world, and its recovery of our own Western mystical tradition with special emphasis on the works of Meister Eckhart, Hildegard of Bingen, Thomas Aquinas, and contemporary mystic-prophets, liberation theologians, and feminist writers.

What made Ratzinger—Pope Benedict XVI—who he is? And just what kind of a man is he? Recently, a forty-year-old man who is a Roman Catholic asked me the following question in light of the scandals emerging about priestly pedophilia and hierarchical cover-up: "How can a man like Ratzinger make it to the top of the church?" Perhaps this section will shed some light on his journey.

CHAPTER I

THE YOUNG RATZINGER

✠

J OSEPH RATZINGER WAS BORN ON
April 16, 1927, in the small town of
Marktl am Inn in Bavaria, Germany,
and he grew up in a series of small vil-
lages in Bavaria. He was the third child
of a policeman and his wife, who was a
stay-at-home mother. Urban life was not
a part of his experience. A slight child,
he resented those who played sports or
were physically robust. In 1939 he entered the minor seminary, but he disliked living at school because "he was
compelled to spend two hours every day
on the playing field. Ratzinger, who was
no good at sports and was smaller and
weaker than most of the older boys, said
he got tired of being a drag on his team
day after day." While Ratzinger disliked sports, he was drawn to music and
the arts and experiences in nature in the dramatic foothills of the Alps. And
he loved the Catholic liturgy, with its Gregorian chant, its sense of mystery
and antiquity, and the smell of beeswax in the air. Ratzinger writes: "It was
a riveting adventure to move by degrees into the mysterious world of the
liturgy, which was being enacted before us and for us on the altar."

Young Ratzinger in Hitler Youth uniform

Catholic journalist John Allen, who has interviewed Ratzinger on
several occasions, observes that "when Ratzinger wants to strike an auto-
biographical chord, he always looks back to his early days in one of four
small Bavarian towns. Those memories are of intimate moments shared
with his family; of the rock-solid Catholic ethos of Bavaria, expressed in
the liturgy and the simple faith of the people regarding liturgy." Adds the

same journalist: "Childhood memories are the ones most closely tied to his understanding of who he is and what he believes. Listening to him and reading him today, it is striking that Ratzinger rarely makes reference to his mid-twenties through mid-forties, the years as a professional theologian during which he achieved wide fame."

Other lacunae also abound in Ratzinger's telling of his own story. Rupert Shortt of the *Times Literary Supplement* comments on the Cardinal's memoir *Milestones*, which appeared in 2000: "This book leaves a sour taste in the mouth all the same, because it fails to mention either the Jews or the Holocaust a single time. Given an ideal chance to deplore a catastrophe in which he had been a blameless bystander, the then Cardinal chose instead to emphasize Hitler's persecution of Catholics . . . [H]is discussion ignored the largely supine response to the Nazis of both clergy and laity. Secondly, he drew the highly contentious lesson that the Church can only resist dictatorships effectively when run as a very tight ship. Alert reviewers of *Milestones* pointed out that on the contrary, German Catholics were hamstrung by a tradition of docile obedience to authority during the 1930s, and that only Protestant Denmark provided a largely unsullied record of anti-Nazi resistance."

Ratzinger's uncle had been a well-known priest who was progressive insofar as he opposed excessive Roman influence in the German church, but he was also notoriously anti-Semitic. Ratzinger has expressed pride in his uncle but has never once criticized him for his anti-Semitism.

Ratzinger joined the Hitler Youth movement at fourteen years of age, and later he was conscripted into the army. Apparently by 1941 youth were required to join the Hitler Youth.

In 1943 Ratzinger was conscripted into the German anti-aircraft corps and then he joined the German infantry. In 1945 he deserted the army and returned home, but he was captured by the advancing Allied army and was put in a POW camp for a few months. When the war ended he entered the seminary along with his older brother and was ordained a priest in 1951.

It is striking to compare Ratzinger's lessons from the war years to those of Father Bernard Haring, for example, who as a priest was also conscripted into the German army and who spent time in a Russian concentration camp. Haring, who became a moral theologian of great stature, declares that the number one lesson he drew from living through the war was that of resistance and the need for civil disobedience. Haring expresses remorse that so many Christians in Hitler's Germany went along on the basis of obedience. Indeed, he tells us that he constructed his entire moral theology on the theme of "responsibility" in contrast to the blind obedience that so many German Christians exhibited. (Haring, as we shall see later, was one of the many theologians attacked by Ratzinger.)

On the other hand, "Ratzinger's reading of the war omits what many people would consider its main lesson, namely the dangers of blind obedience. Millions of Germans like the Ratzingers who passed Nazi prisons on their way to school and work, who watched Jews driven out of their communities, who knew that political opponents of the Nazis such as Hans Braxethaler died for their resistance, nevertheless did little to stop what was happening." As Ratzinger rose the ecclesial ladder, he more and more built his theology on obedience.

Curiously, Ratzinger seems to think to this day that the Catholic Church did a good job of standing up to Hitler. In light of more and more documents that are gradually emerging, in such studies as John Cornwell's *Hitler's Pope: The Secret History of Pius XII* and James Carroll's *Constantine's Sword: The Church and the Jews: A History*, this position becomes stranger and more and more difficult to defend. When the Nazis came to seize Jews in Rome in 1943, the Jewish ghetto was located within eyesight of the Vatican, and Pope Pius XII did nothing overtly to save them. Yet had the pope spoken up strongly and acted decisively, chances are strong that Hitler would have backed off, because a backlash would have unleashed a movement throughout Italy "that might have seriously hindered the Nazi war effort. And thus even Hitler came to acknowledge what Pacelli appeared to ignore: that the strongest social and political force in Italy in the autumn of 1943 was the Catholic Church, and that its scope for noncompliance and disruption was immense." No protest came from the pope.

Only one Roman Jew survived the deportation, and in an interview on the BBC in 1995 she said: "I came back from Auschwitz on my own. I lost my mother, two sisters, a niece, and one brother. Pius XII could have warned us about what was going to happen. We might have escaped from Rome and joined the partisans. He played right into the Germans' hands. It all happened right under his nose. But he was an anti-Semitic pope, a pro-German pope. He didn't take a single risk. And when they say the pope is like Jesus Christ, it is not true. He did not save a single child. Nothing."

John Allen, in his well-researched study of Ratzinger's Germany, points out that the German bishops did not stand up to Hitler as had, for example, the Dutch bishops who in May 1943 forbade Catholic policemen from hunting down Jews even if they lost their jobs over it. Some German bishops, such as Konrad Grober of Freiburg, were enthusiastic supporters of the Nazis. And he was not alone by any means. Recently I saw the film *Constantine's Sword*, which showed a large Nazi rally in which a Catholic bishop sharing a large stage with Hitler applauded with gusto and gave an enthusiastic Nazi salute. It was chilling. The clergy helped smuggle many Nazis into Argentina and other places after the war. Comments Allen, "In this light, Ratzinger's appraisal seems one-sided and even distorted in its emphasis on the moral courage of the church, at the expense of an honest reckoning with its failures." One of Ratzinger's current goals as pope is to see that Pope Pius XII is canonized a saint.

Many of the Catholic hierarchy were openly and proudly pro-Hitler (and pro-Mussolini in Italy, and pro-Franco in Spain). We know that the papal nuncio to Berlin throughout the war, Archbishop Cesare Orsenigo, was a Nazi sympathizer, as was the rector of the German College in Rome, also an archbishop. Many members of Hitler's government, such as Ernst von Weizsacker, the ambassador to the Vatican, professed to be good Catholics. He bragged how in 1943 the papal limousine that took him to an audience with his long-time acquaintance, Pope Pius XII, flew the papal flag and the swastika side by side "in peaceful harmony."

Nor is the issue of the role of the Catholic Church under Hitler an unimportant issue in the mind of Ratzinger. Why? Because, I believe, for him this is what drives his compulsion to centralize the Catholic Church in the Vatican today. This is the reason he gives for broaching no creativity or "dissent" from theologians—because in his worldview the Catholic Church must be "a bastion against totalitarian derangement."

Allen comments: "Having seen fascism in action, Ratzinger today believes that the best antidote to political totalitarianism is ecclesial totalitarianism. In other words, he believes the Catholic Church serves the cause of human freedom by restricting freedom in its internal life, thereby remaining clear about what it teaches and believes. It is a position he defends ably, but it is strikingly different from the conclusions of many of Ratzinger's German theological peers who also lived through the Nazi era." And what if the Church itself becomes a totalitarian derangement in the process? That issue is not addressed by Ratzinger. His constant call against "relativism" is also a code word for his beloved centralization. If it smacks much more of Hitler than of Jesus that may be partially because

Ratzinger was so traumatized by Marxist activists during the events of 1968 in his teaching days. And his village, when he was a child, also underwent a Marxist trauma of sorts.

In 1919, a communist uprising created a short-lived Soviet Republic of Bavaria, the only such Soviet government ever erected in Western Europe. It was brutally suppressed by the German army, but the bloody days of 1919 "loomed large in the political imagination of Bavarians for many years to come." Ratzinger was born eight years following this uprising. Today Bavaria is known as "one of the most culturally traditional and politically conservative pockets of the country." There is little urbanization—even today more than half of the people live in towns with populations smaller than five thousand. Bavarian Catholics not only resented the communists but also harbored their share of resentment toward Germany as a whole and the modern world of the Enlightenment culture, because in the nineteenth century Bismarck in his *Kulturkampf* tried to wipe out Catholicism because he saw it as a threat to the stability of the Prussian state—and in the process he suppressed religious orders, took over Catholic schools, and withdrew public funding from Catholic institutions. The result was "a strong Catholic reaction against modern secular culture" in Germany. Jews also were blamed for the actions Bismarck took, and so the whole project fanned anti-Semitism in Bavaria as well. This anti–secular culture motif runs through Ratzinger's entire worldview today, whether he is attacking liberation theology, feminism, or homosexuality.

When Ratzinger talks today about his youth, one hears much sentimentalizing about the beauties of growing up when he did in the town of Traunstein, Bavaria. But he leaves out something else that was going on in Germany at large and in his beloved "rock-solid Catholic ethos of Bavaria." He never talks about the Nazis who were welcomed in Bavaria. Life was more than reading great literature, playing Mozart, going on trips to Salzburg with his family, attending Mass, and studying for exams—all experiences he loves to recall. "The truth, however, is that the horrors of the Reich were right there in Traunstein, staring Ratzinger in the face, just outside the door of the gymnasium or across the seminary playing field." Wrote a local historian: "This was once a calm, small city of the picturesque Voralberg at the foot of the Bavarian Alps. The war and its consequences transformed it into an over-populated lunatic asylum of hopeless inhabitants." Included was fierce anti-Judaism.

On Kristallnacht, November 9, 1938, Brownshirts attacked homes of Traunstein's few Jewish citizens, smashing windows and threatening to deport them if they did not leave. The best-known Jewish family in town, the Hozers, left the next day for Munich. They were arrested and sent to Dachau in 1941. Jewish homes were confiscated. Some people tried to help the Jews. One Jewish woman committed suicide rather than accept deportation. Three days later—by November 12, 1938—Traunstein was declared free of Jews. Maybe the rock-solid Catholicity of Bavaria that Ratzinger to this day loves to rhapsodize about was not so healthy after all. Perhaps his memory is hyperselective.

In recalling those days, Ratzinger makes a strong point about how anti-Nazi his father, a local policeman, was because he belonged to the Center Catholic Party and not the Nazi Party. One wonders if his father objected to the events of Kristallnacht and arrested anyone responsible. Ratzinger admits that his father took no overt steps in opposition to the Nazis. "He made no public opposition; that wouldn't have been possible even in the village." But in fact, resistance was possible. In Traunstein there were examples of it, among people known to Ratzinger and his family. Granted such resistance was risky, and a few Traunsteiners paid the ultimate price for it. Still, for Ratzinger to declare that it was not possible is profoundly telling. One response to the Nazis was to hide under the radar, be as apolitical as possible, and immerse oneself in art, literature, science, or religion. Most Germans who disapproved of the Nazis chose this option. The communists in his hometown did resist. John Allen comments that "in light of Ratzinger's later conclusions about the intrinsic connection between Catholicism and resistance to the Nazis, it is interesting that the most spectacular acts of resistance in his own hometown were committed by Communists, not by the Catholics." And what about the country as a whole? Many priests stood up to Hitler, and one thousand priests were put to death in Dachau.

There was some resistance by some bishops, but by no means the whole Catholic Church, as Ratzinger argues when he says that Catholicism presented the only real challenge to the authority of National Socialism inside Germany. To say such a thing, which Ratzinger does to this day, Allen believes, is "based on a selective reading of the historical evidence. The truth is that during the Third Reich Catholicism was every bit as much a fellowship of sinners as it was a communion of saints."

First, Hitler came to power on the back of Catholic support. Catholic leaders never supported the Weimar experiment with democracy, which they saw as a legacy of the Enlightenment and the *Kulturkampf.* The "Enabling Act" that allowed Hitler to take power was passed with the help of the Catholic Party and bishops in 1933, and four days after signing on, the German bishops rescinded the ban on Nazi Party membership that they had declared earlier. The concordat that Pacelli (the future Pope Pius XII) arranged with Hitler spoke volumes to the faithful, accompanied as it was with a photo of Hitler and the papal nuncio smiling with each other. It showed that coexistence was possible and encouraged at the highest level of the Catholic hierarchy. Hitler said that the concordat meant that from now on "the Reich members of the Roman Catholic confession will put themselves without reservation at the service of the new National Socialist state." One commentator notes that the concordat bound the Catholic Church in Germany "to silence on outrages against the Jews" and "on any issue the Nazi regime deemed political."

May Day celebrations, which had been forbidden in Traunstein for Catholic trade associations because they smacked of communism, were now acceptable. Catholics could march with the Nazis because they were not communist. And there was plenty of open anti-Semitism in Catholicism. In addition, there were a number of "Brownshirt bishops" who fully supported Hitler.

Near the war's end, as the Allies were approaching on May 2, 1945, the SS emptied the concentration camps and drove victims into Hufschlag, the village where Ratzinger had moved to with his family. There they executed sixty-one inmates at the edge of the forest. Only one person survived, by playing dead. Local children discovered the bodies. Comments Allen: "It is striking that Ratzinger leaves out any mention of these upheavals. In a city of fewer than 12,000 people, even allowing for the chaos and confusion, Ratzinger must have known what was happening . . . One gets the impression that the Third Reich has meaning for Ratzinger today primarily as an object lesson about church and culture, and only the details consistent with that argument have passed through the filter of his memory." A kind of memory loss and a romanticizing of his childhood seems to have overtaken Ratzinger—along with a romanticizing of what the Catholic Church actually did and did not do vis-à-vis Hitler.

What I learn from this recounting of Ratzinger's story are seven important lessons about the man.

He is a champion of denial and adept at it. He chooses to remember what he wants to and represses or conveniently forgets the rest—for example, his Jewish neighbors and their treatment at the hands of local Nazis—and the facts that Catholic Bavaria sported many local Nazis and that his hometown participated in Kristallnacht. One wonders how many of these participants attended Sunday Mass that weekend.

Denial is fed by lies and distortions about church and Catholicism. Denial and lying make a volatile mix as when, for example, Pope Benedict journeyed to South America and actually said in a speech that the Indians of South America welcomed the Christian missionaries from Spain. He was practically booed off the stage and derided on the front pages of newspapers the next day. It is as if he can believe whatever he wants about history. Denial gives a person that kind of mind-set and control over the truth.

Sentimentalism is everywhere integral to Ratzinger's spiritual temperament. But, as Ann Douglas has revealed in her weighty study on the subject, the essence of sentimentalism is "rancid political consciousness." Sentimentalism is feelings without care for justice. Nazi concentration camp hierarchy would torture prisoners during the day and return home at night and weep listening to Beethoven. "Scratch a sentimentalist and you find a violent person," Carl Jung warned. Lurking behind sentimentalism is pent-up rage. Ratzinger whenever he can substitutes the word "charity" for the word "justice."

One can see how Ratzinger appears so easily to dismiss the sexual predations of pedophile priests, including his and the late pope's champion in Latin America, Father Maciel of the Legion of Christ, whom Ratzinger refused to investigate for years even though nine ex-seminarians sent him documentation of their abuse at his hands. Because Maciel hewed to the party line of right-wing activism he was "supporting the church too much" to be criticized. It also explains Ratzinger's support of Cardinal Bernard Law of Boston, the champion of pedophile priests in America who is now safely ensconced in Rome. Denial is conveniently selective.

There is a real banality in Ratzinger. His theological writings, when not sentimental, are filled with his private interpretations of past theologians. But they say nothing. In my reading, they are utterly lacking in originality or creativity. This and academic envy help explain his attacks on theologians, all of whom are more creative than he. Envy, hatred, and war make good bedfellows, as I demonstrated in my book on evil, *Sins of the Spirit, Blessings of the Flesh.*

What is the role of women in Ratzinger's life? He dreads the feminist movement very much (he calls it the "radical feminist and lesbian" movement)—that is clear. But what is a woman to Ratzinger? She is someone not worthy to be a priest or to be listened to in his church hierarchy. The only woman mentioned in Ratzinger's biography other than his mother is his sister. What did she do with her life? She was a devoted housekeeper to his brother, who was also a priest.

I look in vain for any sign of moral courage in Joseph Ratzinger's story. It was not present when his Jewish neighbors were being deported, it was not present in his joining the Hitler Youth as an adolescent, nor was it present in his war record. It is not present in his work as a theologian. Sentimentalism is not about courage. Nor is bullying, which is about carrying on a fight while hiding behind the power of others or behind institutional power.

I am struck by how much of Joseph Ratzinger's life story consists of tapes he has continued to play out throughout his life. Consciously or unconsciously, playing throughout his childhood we see lack of compassion, hiding one's eyes from the poor and suffering (a necessary trait for an inquisitor who chooses to attack heroes such as Oscar Romero, Bishop Pedro Casaldáliga, Leonardo Boff, and others supporting the poor in Latin America), violence, power for power's sake, denial (and creating an illusory heroic Catholicism that "stood up" to Hitler), fear of women, fear of gays, fear of theologians, and fear of ideas. Where does it stop?

Ratzinger is not a man of peace; he is a man of war. He is filled with rage. Long before the events of 1968, he was filled with rage. A young American priest who was studying biblical studies in Rome in the early 1960s was telling a story at the table in his house of studies in Rome when Ratzinger was present. It seems that Cardinal Bea, one of his professors, told a joke about how Pope John XXIII was presented with biblical scholarship that concluded that Jesus never said, "Thou art Peter and upon this rock I will build my church." Pope John jumped up from his papal throne and said playfully, "Well, I guess you better take this throne away." "Everyone at the table laughed—except Father Ratzinger. He looked at me with steely eyes. He didn't speak. He didn't have to . . . Pope John could laugh about it because he felt so secure in his own faith; he didn't care if Jesus had said those words or not. Joe Ratzinger couldn't laugh. He stared at me and I knew what he was thinking. The rest of the room seemed to fade away, and the sound of laughter and clinking glasses was muted."

Many people sense a bully operating in Ratzinger the inquisitor. A friend of mine, a lawyer and a practicing Catholic, calls Ratzinger "the Bavarian bully." One wonders if perhaps this characteristic dates back to his frustrated youth when he could only watch other boys play rough-and-tumble sports and was continually left out or wishing he was left out of their games. Ratzinger's brother, who is also a priest, has recently confessed to physically abusing boys in his choir. Perhaps they grew up in a household with a certain maltreatment from their policeman father. Surely the Nazi times must have made it very difficult to grow up even without such harassment. Like many boys neglected or picked on in the schoolyard and never chosen to join the team, Joseph grew up to become a bully. (I am even reminded of the Columbine High School youths who, in 1999, having been excluded by the jocks like Ratzinger was, resorted to acts of supreme violence against their classmates. Does this shed light on Ratzinger's move from being a theologian to being a killer of theology and theologians?)

In the 1970s psychologist Dan Olweus began to study the phenomenon of bullying among Norwegian schoolchildren. Bullying led to suicides by the victims then as it does today in the United States. "Bullies go for admiration, for status, for dominance," René Veenstra, a sociologist at the University of Groningen in the Netherlands, comments. Bullying is not just teasing, but long-term and unwanted intimidation, and it rarely takes place between social equals. It may well be that Ratzinger's hangover from his early days prods him to be more than a social equal—and being at the upper rungs of ecclesial hierarchies guarantees that role of dominance for him. Yet bullies, despite their aggressive behavior, do want affection and approval—from their own in-group. Maybe this is one reason Ratzinger puts so much value on loyalty and silence in his all-male celibate clerical club. There, among his own in the Curia, he garners his daily approval. To allow women in would render bullying unproductive.

Therein lies the next part of his story: his theological and vocational journey from priest and theologian to antitheologian and, as I posit, "killer" of theology.

Chapter 2

RATZINGER'S CONVERSION

✠

A GREAT CHURCH EVENT OCCURRED IN 1962; indeed it has been called "the most important religious event of the twentieth century." That was the year Pope John XXIII's Second Vatican Council began. He had called the council to "open up the windows of the church," which had been for a long time nailed shut under the dour and lengthy papacy of Pius XII. Many of the finest Catholic theologians had been held suspect in those years or silenced, among them Father M. D. Chenu of France, active in the worker priest movement after the war; Father Teilhard de Chardin, poet, scientist, and priest; the German Jesuit Karl Rahner; Father Bernard Haring; Dominican Father Edward Schillebeeckx from Holland; and Jesuit Father John Courtney Murray from the United States. The council would prove to be a moment of reconciliation and of release for the pent-up thinkers in the Catholic Church, most all of whom were vindicated by the conciliar debates and documents that followed. More than 2,500 bishops from around the world participated, and they were invited to bring their *periti,* or theological advisers, with them.

Joseph Ratzinger was invited to attend as the *peritus,* or theologian, to Cardinal Josef Frings of Cologne, who was considered by council observers to be a moderate more than a progressive. Ratzinger was only thirty-five years old at the time the Second Vatican Council opened.

Frings was an accomplished biblical scholar and had close ties with Third World bishops, since his diocese was very wealthy and he often supported the church in the Third World. At seventy-six years of age and with failing eyesight, he depended on his *peritus* to read many of the documents to him. Nevertheless, he rose to considerable prominence in the council since he was a leader among the German bishops, and the German-speaking bishops "represented undoubtedly the single most influential block in the council."

Ratzinger on more than one occasion was the spokesperson for the German bishops, which put him, young as he was, very often in the limelight. The document that Ratzinger most contributed to was that on revelation, and he worked on that document with Karl Rahner, who was older than he. (Many years later, in 1984, just a few months before he died at age eighty, Rahner wrote Ratzinger a scathing letter for his refusal to allow Johann Metz to teach at a university. But that was an older Ratzinger, "Ratzinger Two," not the younger Ratzinger, "Ratzinger One," who was out front in 1962.)

At the council it was Cardinal Frings himself who brought down the house one day for attacking the Holy Office, calling it "a cause of scandal to the world." He added: "No one should be judged and condemned without being heard, without knowing what he is accused of, and without having the opportunity to amend what he can reasonably be reproached with." The bishops broke into loud applause (which was against the rules), and this moment came to be recognized as a "defining moment in the Council." In 1964 Ratzinger himself said that the Holy Office should take lessons from secular democracies regarding protection of individual rights. "The age of absolutism gave the Holy Office its rules . . ." he proposed. How different a view he would promulgate later when he took over the Holy Office, renamed the Congregation for the Doctrine of the Faith.

The first document to emerge from Vatican II was the Constitution on Sacred Liturgy (*Sacrosanctum Concilium*). Changes included turning the altar around so the priest faced the people, taking down communion rails, communicants standing instead of kneeling, replacing Latin with vernacular languages, connecting liturgy to issues of social justice, and activism beyond church buildings. As one commentator put it, "Perhaps most important for average churchgoers, everyone became participants, and not simply passive observers, in the Eucharistic celebration." Or, as Benedictine Father Godfrey Diekmann of St. John's Abbey in Collegeville, Minnesota, put it (he was one of fifty-five international liturgists who helped compose the document), "it was a Magna Carta of the laity."

At the time Ratzinger very much signed on to this reform and wrote positively of the "decentralization of liturgical decision-making." In addition, he commented that the first chapter of the document on liturgy "contains a statement that represents for the Latin Church a fundamental innovation." What was that innovation? A new independent authority for national conferences of bishops. He went on: "Perhaps one could say that this small paragraph, which for the first time assigns to the conferences of bishops their own canonical authority, has more significance for the theology of the episcopacy and for the long-desired strengthening of episcopal power than anything in the Constitution on the Church itself."

Neither Pope John Paul II nor Pope Benedict XVI have followed this teaching. That is just one reason many church thinkers talk about their being in schism from the church as expressed in Vatican II. The council set up a process for translations of sacred texts in worship, and for thirty years scholars and translators employed those processes. But in 1997 a reform of the reform was instigated in secret at the Vatican. Eleven men met to overhaul the readings of Scripture for liturgy. They short-circuited a six-year debate about inclusive language and retained uses of masculine vocabulary. As one observer put it, "powers in Rome handpicked a small group of men who in two weeks undid work that had taken dozens of years." A Georgetown University professor saw this as a "partisan" attack on liturgists and communities. "They don't listen to liturgists and they don't listen to local communities."

In 1968, Ratzinger himself signed on to a statement signed by 1,360 Catholic theologians from fifty-three countries. The Nijmegen Declaration said, "Any form of inquisition, however subtle, not only harms the development of a sound theology, it also causes irreparable damage to the credibility of the church as a community in the modern world." The same document made it clear that the teaching office of pope and bishops "cannot and must not supersede, hamper and impede the teaching task of theologians as scholars."

At the council the Declaration on Religious Freedom (*Dignitatis humanae*), which was strongly influenced by the work of the American Jesuit John Courtney Murray, stated the following:

The Vatican Council declares that the human person has a right to religious freedom. Freedom of this kind means that all men should be immune from coercion on the part of individuals, social groups and every human power so that within due limits, nobody is forced to act against his convictions nor is anyone to be restrained from acting in accordance with his convictions in religious matters in private or in public, alone or in association with others. (sec. 2)

Ratzinger One signed off on this. Ratzinger Two would have nothing to do with it.

When one considers the work of Father Ratzinger at the council—including this Nijmegen Declaration that he signed in 1968—and holds it up to his statements and actions since 1968, one can see a remarkable shift. The Ratzinger of the council and the Ratzinger that follows after 1968 hardly seem like the same person at all. Theologically, they were not. What explains that difference? Did the events of 1968 so traumatize him that he needed to retreat to his make-believe version of his Catholic faith in the bucolic foothills of the Alps? Did he have to associate anew with "brownshirt" bishops and founders of sects such as Josemaria Escriva to find his true community? Did he choose to take the road of power rather than the road of inner transformation?

The year 1968 was a tumultuous one around the globe. In the United States two assassinations roiled the country—that of the Reverend Dr. Martin Luther King Jr. in April, which set off riots all through urban America, and then the shooting of Senator Robert F. Kennedy on the day of his presidential primary campaign victory in California. The war raged in Vietnam, and so did students marching in opposition to it in Europe as well as the United States. In the spring of 1968, student rioters in Paris dug up stones on Boulevard Saint Michel and used them as weapons to hurl at the police. Tear gas was everywhere. Students created barriers from felled trees and cars to defend themselves from the police. With strikes freezing public transportation, gasoline stations, grocery stores, and more shut down; businesses closed and the student uprising brought down the government of President Charles de Gaulle. I was there. I lived through the powerful dynamics of it all.

I was also receiving letters from friends in Chicago who were beaten up in Grant Park by the police at the tumultuous Democratic Convention, which took the Democrats decades to get over and gave the 1968 election to Richard Nixon. My Dominican provincial was sitting in Mayor Daly's box at the convention while his police were beating up protestors, including my brother Dominican activists, in Grant Park. Turmoil was in the air. Vietnam was an issue that split fathers from sons. But so too was education itself.

In the Catholic Church, 1968 will be remembered as the year of Pope Paul VI's notorious encyclical that reinforced birth control prohibitions, *Humanae Vitae*. The acceptance or rejection of this teaching has marked a line in the sand between progressive and conservative Catholics ever since. Theological protestations arose, petitions signed by thousands of theologians were disseminated, and quasireligious riots broke out around the globe. (A bus driver in Brazil, when told of the encyclical, remarked, "Why did anyone bother to inform the pope about condoms in the first place?")

Students were protesting in Germany as well as in Berkeley, Madison, and Paris. The German educational system that students were rioting about in 1968 left much to be desired. Only 7 percent of German youth in 1968 qualified for a university-level education, and only 3 percent enrolled. The student-teacher ratio in German universities at that time was three times as high as in the United States and four times as high as in England. The boomer generation was growing by leaps and bounds.

"Under the strain, university service broke down in many places, creating a general mood of frustration . . . Student activists described the relationship in Germany as resembling that of a feudal lord to his serfs; there was an almost unbridgeable gap between the lordly professor and the lowly students. This, too, sparked outrage in a generation already disposed to question the integrity of its elders." The fact is that most of the violence in the streets of Tubingen, where Joseph Ratzinger taught, came from the police, not the student protesters. Marxist philosopher Ernst Bloch taught at the University of Tubingen also, and Protestant theologians Juergen Moltmann and Ernst Kasemann were teaching a "theology of hope" and stressing the role of political responsibility. Indeed, Kasemann's daughter had been murdered by the military junta in Argentina on account of her political involvement.

Some students in the University of Tubingen took over lecterns during lectures by theologians. One day a group of students barged into a meeting of the theology faculty and demanded to be listened to. While other faculty patiently hung around to listen to the student rants, one professor rose up and stalked out. It was Ratzinger. People who were there say when he came back another day he was a different person. Said one theologian: "A young, friendly, communicative scholar turned in on himself and became very dogmatic. Some people, of course, continued to see him as a model of courtesy. This is because he seems to be the kind of person who will really open up to others if he feels they are on his wavelength, but finds it harder to get on with a larger range of characters." Observers saw "a shift in character. An earlier openness was supplanted by intolerance and gloom." A former student of Ratzinger in Tubingen named Wolfgang Beinert told *Time* magazine in 1993 that the events of 1968 had "an extraordinarily strong impact" on Ratzinger. Before then he had been "very open, fundamentally ready to let in new things. But suddenly he saw these new ideas were connected to violence and a destruction of the order of what came before. He was simply no longer able to bear it." It was too much for him.

We should not forget, however, the story told previously of the steel-eyed look Ratzinger gave the young biblical student when he recounted the "Thou art Peter" joke. This may have been a warning of another, more threatened person lurking inside Ratzinger even before the student rebellions of 1968.

In 1969 Ratzinger left Tubingen and joined the faculty of Regensburg University, which was forming in his home district of Bavaria. Regensburg was a brand new school and Ratzinger's move was a dramatic one, or, as Allen put it, "it was as if a senior editor at the *New York Times* left at the height of his career to start up a small regional newspaper in Albany." A number of Ratzinger's students were dismayed by his obvious fear and change of perspective and quit studying with him to study instead with Hans Kung or Johann Metz (both of whom were later attacked by Ratzinger when he was head inquisitor). Ratzinger's own words on the Tubingen experience tell us something of his fears when he says the experience taught him "an instrumentalization by ideologies that were tyrannical, brutal, and cruel. That experience made it clear to me that the abuse of the faith had to be resisted precisely if one wanted to uphold the will of the council . . . I did see how real tyranny was exercised even in brutal forms . . . anyone who wanted to remain a progressive in this context had to give up his integrity."

Why was Ratzinger so ill at ease with chaos? Why was he so afraid of what was going on at the university? In contrast, a professor of mine who had played a significant role at the Second Vatican Council and especially in shaping the Pastoral Constitution on the Church in the Modern World (*Gaudium et Spes*), the French Dominican M. D. Chenu, lived through the events of 1968 with a very different attitude than Ratzinger. Though far older than Ratzinger, he was far from frightened by the closing down of the University of Paris by students or by rioting in the streets against de Gaulle's riot police. Chenu came to class one day and led us in a discussion of the twelfth century renaissance and ended class this way: "We have been discussing history. Here is your chance to contribute to it. Go out and join the revolution and don't come back next week. Come back in two weeks and tell me what you have contributed." Chenu was seventy-five years old at the time. His path to theology was markedly different from Ratzinger's.

Was Ratzinger's new path a path of personal will to power? People who know him best seem to feel that that was the truth. Hans Kung, who originally invited him to join the faculty at Tubingen, says simply that "he sold his soul for power." A former student of Ratzinger's, an American who went to Rome to confront him in the 1990s, came to the same conclusion. "It's all about seeking the purple," he reported after spending a few hours with him. It is said that in the brief period in which he was archbishop of Munich, Ratzinger had "rocky relations with the priests in his archdiocese." They did not find him to be a good listener in the least. Three years after he advanced up the ladder to his post in Rome, the priests wrote that "those who, like Ratzinger, exalt themselves in such a triumphalistic manner above every thing . . . exclude themselves as dialogue partners." Biographer John Allen puts it this way: "As Ratzinger took on an increasingly conservative stance, he was rewarded with greater access to power and privilege, culminating in his 1997 appointment as archbishop of Munich. Ratzinger's altered stance was certainly in line with where the political winds in the German bishops' conference were blowing during the 1970s as the staunchly conservative cardinal Joseph Höffner of Cologne eclipsed the moderate but aging cardinal Julius Döpfner, archbishop of Munich. It is also indisputable that after Ratzinger's appointment to Rome, his revised positions on collegiality, on the theological status of bishops' conferences, on the role of the doctrinal congregation, and on development in the tradition all bolstered his career." Allen goes into considerable length to demonstrate how Ratzinger changed positions on all of these matters including on liturgy and ecumenism. A 180-degree shift is evident.

The council invoked a more horizontal Catholicity wherein the bishops and their conferences played a role to balance the power of the pope that the First Vatican Council (1869–1870) stressed. The Dogmatic Constitution on the Church (*Lumen gentium*) tried to balance Vatican I and papal infallibility with the bishops and collegiality. Ratzinger One contributed to that document. But Ratzinger Two rejected what Ratzinger One had approved. Ratzinger One called bishops' conferences "the best means of concrete plurality in unity." Ratzinger Two said, "Truth is not arrived at by majority vote" and proceeded to marginalize and defang bishops' conferences around the world in favor of submitting to whatever Rome has to say about any subject whatsoever whenever Rome has to say it. Allen comments that "most of the reforms he urged in 1968 have been ignored during his twenty-year tenure" as prefect of the CDF.

The schizophrenic shift from the old to the new Ratzinger shows in the students he trained as well. In Bonn and Munster from 1959 to 1966 he trained "theologians who were reform-minded and interested in expanding the boundaries of theological inquiry; after 1969 Ratzinger at Regensburg trained theologians who emphasize orthodoxy, submission, and patrolling the borders between church and world."

Today, decades after the council, Ratzinger, as Pope Benedict XVI, often goes into denial in his recollections about Vatican II and actually contradicts what he wrote at the time. One biographer comments about Ratzinger's memoir *Milestones,* "His attempt to present his thinking as a seamless garment probably constitutes the greatest piece of legerdemain in the memoir." His denials are enough to provide a whole new chapter in Garry Wills's aptly titled book *Papal Sin: Structures of Deceit.*

To understand Cardinal Ratzinger and his rise to prominence it is important to understand the German Catholic Church and how different it is from other European churches or from the Catholic Church in North America. As Penny Lernoux points out, "while only a minority of German Catholics practice their faith, all are forced to pay a religious tithe as part of their taxes." The result is that the German Catholic Church holds considerable financial resources, second only to the American Catholic Church. But because the money comes from the state, the German hierarchy rarely has to listen to the Catholics in the pew. This, Lernoux feels, helps to explain "the attitude of Cardinal Joseph Ratzinger, head of the Vatican's CDF, and other German bishops who think numbers less important than absolute obedience. So long as the money continues to flow, they can afford to ignore statistics that show a church in decline." Contrast this to France, where the church is not state-supported and is in no way fat or lazy. The German church is very well-heeled.

Another dimension to German Catholicism that struck me in the late 1960s when I spent a semester in Munster was the great divide between German theology and the preaching in the parish church. I found the preaching to be in great part out of touch with theology and in fact quite sentimental. Karl Rahner, Johannes Metz, and biblical studies seemed to hardly penetrate the pulpit at all. It was just the opposite in the French church where, for the most part, even poor parish priests often gave a solid sermon from decent scriptural and theological sources. This division between theology and parish may well affect Ratzinger, who so often talks about the "little people" and the "simple believer" whose faith he does not want to rock. For example, he gave the following reason for condemning the theology of Hans Kung (once his colleague and indeed the professor who invited him to the faculty at Tubingen) in a sermon delivered on December 31, 1979: "The Christian believer is a simple person: bishops should protect the faith of these little people against the power of intellectuals." A deep condescension, if not insult, to the intelligence of laypeople is revealed here.

There are other ways in which the German Catholic Church differs from the American Catholic Church. "The Germans know how to use their financial muscle" with Rome, Lernoux points out, and money is "a major source of the Germans' power in Rome." In contrast, American bishops give millions of dollars annually to the Holy See "without asking for an accounting or an occasional favor in return." It was a German cardinal, Höffner of Cologne, very conservative and very close to Cardinal Ratzinger, who oversaw Vatican finances until his death in 1987. The German church sponsors its own aid agencies, Adveniat and Misereor, who hold great sway, especially in Latin America. They resisted liberation theology and base communities strongly. "Höffner and Ratzinger were the big guns in the German hierarchy," and they teamed up to condemn theologians Hans Kung as well as Johann Baptist Metz, whose appointment to a chair of theology at the University of Munich they blocked. They also went after the Jesuit Karl Rahner, who defended his brother theologians and is considered one of the greatest Catholic minds of the twentieth century.

Cardinal Höffner also teamed up with Reagan's White House to attack both the Brazilian bishops and the American bishops when their pastoral letter on nuclear warfare questioned the Reagan administration's arms buildup. In 1982 Höffner wrote to the president of the National Conference of Catholic Bishops, accusing the American bishops of selling out to the Russians. Meeting in Rome at a gathering arranged by Ratzinger, the Catholic bishops acquiesced, and "the Catholic leadership of one of the most powerful countries in the world bowed to the German-Polish foreign policy."

Meanwhile, Höffner also attacked the Brazilian church. He went to São Paulo to investigate the theological faculty where most of the Brazilian seminarians were trained. When he returned to Europe he wrote a "violent condemnation of the theological faculty." The Brazilian bishops held together and met with the pope in 1986 and parlayed the attack on their theologians—at least for a while. "Perhaps because the Brazilian bishops knew better the ways of the Vatican, or perhaps because they were more courageous, they were better than the Americans at defending their beliefs."

The conservatives in the German church hierarchy very much influenced the thinking of the pope even before he became pope. John Paul's feelings about communism were fed by the German bishops, who, even before Cardinal Karol Wojtyla's ascension, had been fulminating against the "socialist" tendencies of some churches in South America. The Germans preferred right-wing governments that were strongly anticommunist and pro-capitalist, even though such regimes frequently persecuted local Catholic churches. Unable to understand that capitalism had produced one standard of living in Germany but quite another in Latin America, they were horrified when some South American bishops, most notably the Peruvian and Brazilian hierarchies, denounced the voraciousness of foreign capitalism. Liberation theology and the Christian base communities were blamed for such radicalism, although the communities were only seeking the same basic rights that were taken for granted in Germany. The German-Polish alliance in the Vatican interpreted protests against right-wing regimes and their foreign multinational allies as proof of Marxist tendencies among the churches.

This also fed into the hands of Washington. Rome and Washington were on the same page in opposing liberation theology in South America. In June 1982, Ronald Reagan met with Pope John Paul II in Rome, and the discussion centered on Poland and Eastern Europe. Carl Bernstein wrote a cover story for *Time* magazine ten years later with the bold headline: "Holy Alliance: How Reagan and the Pope conspired to assist Poland's Solidarity movement and hasten the demise of Communism." Prior to that 1982 meeting, advisors to Reagan met in Santa Fe to discuss a pressing question: What to do about liberation theology in Latin America? They produced a document that came to be known as the Santa Fe Document, which stated: "American foreign policy must begin to counterattack (and not just react against) liberation theology." They also recognized that they could not just eliminate base communities, which were too strong, too much supported by the bishops, and too inspired by the many martyrdoms occurring in efforts to bring about social justice. What they could do was split the church.

Events in Iran and Nicaragua convinced them of the importance of not ignoring the religious factor. The Institute for Religion and Democracy (IRD) was set up to counterattack liberation theology. The attack to come from Ratzinger against liberation theologians was very likely a quid pro quo for the support Solidarity received from the CIA. The teachings of Vatican II had gotten Latin American Catholics to engage in the struggle for justice, and the Church was the strongest institution in Latin America and had the most credibility. Says Lernoux: "No matter how many priests and nuns were murdered, or how often the bishops were threatened, the seeds of popular democracy continued to spread. Only Rome could make any impact on a Catholic rebellion, and it therefore fell to Cardinal Ratzinger to deal with a major source of the problem—the Latin American theologians."

Reagan and the pope were also on the same page regarding the Philippines. Both Rome and Washington supported the Marcos dictatorship to the bitter end—even though it was priests and nuns and liberation theologians in the Philippines who helped to support the nonviolent protests that brought down the detested Ferdinand Marcos dictatorship. Ronald Reagan and Pope John Paul II shared several similarities. Both were very stubborn men and both "revealed a parochial view of the world's diverse history and cultures." Just as John Paul's political vision was "stuck in the Cold War fifties" and that was the formative period for Reagan's politics as well. "Neither man could understand the nationalistic yearnings of the Third World, which were inevitably attributed to Marxist influence." Both were "skilled showmen," actors or aspiring actors who used crowds and television cameras to their great advantage.

In a personal interview I had with Penny Lernoux she told me that it is the "German mafia" who are making the decisions in the Vatican and that Ratzinger (then only a cardinal) is their "front man." Getting rid of Ratzinger would not change things, she commented. She also pointed to a table in the hotel restaurant where we were meeting in downtown Oakland. "See those three men. They are CIA," she said. "They and people like them follow me wherever I go. But actually, they are so stupid. I can ditch them just about whenever I please. It's kind of insulting, how they put such silly men on my tail," she remarked with a laugh.

People who have known Joseph Ratzinger a long time say that his life changed forever in 1968. Regarding his appointment as prefect of the Congregation for the Doctrine of the Faith by Pope John Paul II, a former colleague of Ratzinger's comments: "This Polish pope decided to rely very much on a well-known German theologian to interpret modern thought for him. This selection came at the very time, however, that Ratzinger had actually withdrawn from modern thought." Not only had he "withdrawn" from it, he had decided to go to war over it. And the greatest of the wars he was bent on initiating was that against liberation theology in Latin America.

In addition to the events of 1968 that we have considered, there was a very significant gathering that year in Medellin, Colombia. There the Latin American bishops convened to discuss the movement of liberation theology. They gave their blessing to the movement. To Ratzinger, "Medellin must seem like another ripple effect of the great wave of leftist radicalism that gripped the world in that year." His objections to this grassroots movement of response to the poverty and centuries of oppression in Latin America went way back for Ratzinger: "His effort to break liberation theology was not a course of action he settled upon after taking office; it was something he came into the office ready to accomplish."

In 1984 Ratzinger attacked liberation theology in a journal published by the Communion and Liberation movement (which we will consider later). The fact that he chose this group to wage his war against liberation theology is telling in itself and it demonstrates how in league he is with them. (They are also a group to which he spoke when he was campaigning for the job of pope after John Paul II died. Canon law forbids such campaigning, but that did not deter him.)

Ratzinger calls liberation theology a new kind of heresy. "The essay amounted to Ratzinger's formal declaration of war, because now his assessment was clear—liberation theology is not just dangerous or unorthodox, it is heretical . . . He warned that in liberationist thinking, the 'people of God' is opposed to the 'hierarchy,' thus setting up a class struggle inside the church." He used liberation theology as a foil for his own agenda: Advance the hierarchy, advance the Vatican as the only teacher of faith. He continues. He calls theology of liberation "a perversion of the Christian message as God entrusted it to His church."

A tidal wave of reaction followed. "Around the world, many Catholic leaders reacted with outrage. English Dominican theologian Nicholas

Lash said Ratzinger had 'made up a system which does not exist.'" Father Edward Schillebeeckx of Holland observed, "The dictators of Latin America will receive it with joy because it will serve their purposes." It was in this context that, just a few days later, Father Leonardo Boff of Brazil had his encounter with Ratzinger at the headquarters of the former Holy Office of the Inquisition. (We discuss this in the next chapter.)

While many Latin American bishops and cardinals supported liberation theology at this time, over time Ratzinger appointed a hierarchy who fought it tooth and nail. Franciscan Cardinal Juan Landazuri of Peru defended liberation theology, but in 1989 Ratzinger appointed Jesuit Vargas Alzamora, who had strong ties to Opus Dei, as archbishop of Lima. This is part of the overall strategy that we saw earlier. The Vatican, as long as it chooses the hierarchy, can outlast any particular movement; by arousing suspicion and keeping the heat on long enough for its sponsors to die off, it then can step in and appoint church leaders to their liking. "This transition demonstrates that as long as the selection of bishops is reserved exclusively to Vatican officials, there is no defeat they cannot eventually reverse."

The same holds for its attacks on theologians. By censoring their books, by whipping up hysteria against them, by accusing them of heresy or suspected heresy, by making them spend their time defending themselves against unjust attacks and ignorant attackers, they lose their focus and time for study, research, and writing. As Allen points out, "as the social reality in Latin America was shifting, the liberationists should have been engaged in creative thinking; instead their time was largely consumed by defending themselves from Ratzinger's inquests or engaging in self-censorship to ward off a new round of scrutiny."

Some theologians withdraw from the public eye or they huddle in quiet and demure places while time and culture pass them by. Some have died of heart attacks under the pressure, and some have actually died of depression. Theology itself becomes less and less a dialogue with culture and more and more an argument carried on within church confines. This way theology dies and is replaced by ideology. Not only do the reputations of theologians become sullied, but the very task of theology sours as it becomes less and less relevant. Then only what the church hierarchy decides is a religious agenda makes the media. Theologians as well as theology fade away. Eventually both die.

How important were Ratzinger's attacks on liberation theology? "Ultimately he alone had both the power and the conviction to stop the movement in its tracks," notes Allen. By 1980, more than eight hundred priests and nuns had been martyred in Latin America, but rather than draw inspiration and courage from the valor of these prophetic witnesses to justice, Ratzinger and the extreme right-wing groups he preferred in Latin America went after the very values of social and economic justice that these Christians shed their last drop of blood to defend. Allen admits that his "fight against liberation theology is at the heart of Ratzinger's legacy." Key to Ratzinger's position against liberation theology was his effort to link it to state terror in Eastern Europe—a distant stretch indeed since liberation theology grew from the experience of poverty in Latin America and not from Soviet ideology in Eastern Europe. It also draws from the prophetic tradition of the Hebrew Bible and of Jesus' teachings in the Gospels.

Ratzinger wrote in 1984 that millions of people behind the iron curtain lost their "basic freedoms" because of "totalitarian and atheistic regimes which came to power by violent and revolutionary means precisely in the name of the liberation of the people." Then he applies this to base communities in Latin America—a huge jump indeed—when he continues: "Those who, perhaps inadvertently, make themselves accomplices of similar enslavements betray the very poor they mean to help." It is difficult to follow the logic of this—unless of course Ratzinger is baring his soul here about what happened to him in the 1968 student movement in his university and the buttons it pushed about fear of chaos. Indeed, as part of his patronizing attitude toward Latin America, Ratzinger does not even give the founders of liberation theology credit for what they have done. He believes even liberation theology began in Germany with theologians like Johann Metz, and not in Latin America. Colonial thinking? One Latin American archbishop would complain years later that the Vatican "cannot accept that anything new or inventive could come out of the Third World."

Actually, liberation theology got its initial inspiration from the Second Vatican Council, which insisted on joining the struggle for social justice in the Pastoral Constitution on the Church in the Modern World (put together by theologian Father M. D. Chenu more than by any other single theologian). But it was truly born in a 1968 assembly of Latin American bishops in Medellin, Colombia, in which they endorsed a "preferential option for the poor" by the church in Latin America. Among the theologian advisors at that conference was Gustavo Gutierrez (who studied with

Chenu in Paris); his book *A Theology of Liberation*, published in 1971, first used the term that became so infamous in Rome under Ratzinger and Pope John Paul II.

Archbishop Oscar Romero of San Salvador, El Salvador, was a particular thorn in the side of the Vatican because he took a clear stand on behalf of the poor in his country. In January 1979, he excommunicated the president of El Salvador for his failure to stop the killing of priests and laity. In Rome, they called Romero a "Marxist" and a "subversive." In his diary Romero says that the real issue is that many priests were striving to be faithful to Vatican II "translated for Latin America by Medellin and Puebla." (Puebla was a second gathering of Latin American bishops that endorsed a "preferential option for the poor.") In Rome there was a plan to remove him from his position as archbishop, but the military beat them to it when, on March 24, 1979, Romero was gunned down by right-wing military henchmen while saying Mass in a church in downtown El Salvador. To this day, Rome has not bothered to declare him a saint even though Catholic theology teaches that martyrs for the faith are saints. Instead, Ratzinger and others pushed to canonize extreme right-wing fanatics such as Opus Dei founder Josemaria Escriva, whom we will meet later.

In 1981, John Paul II did an extraordinary thing when he intervened with the Constitutions of the Jesuit order to impose his own leadership on their religious order. The pope did not like the leadership of Father Pedro Arrupe, who encouraged Jesuits to embrace liberation theology and base communities. When Arrupe had a stroke in 1981, the pope appointed his own man to head the order and forbade the Jesuits to elect their own leader for two years.

In 1984, Ratzinger attacked liberation theology in an article in the Communion and Liberation journal *30 Giorni* in which he complained that the movement of liberation theology "does not fit into accepted categories of heresy because it accepts all the existing language but gives it new meaning." In March, Ratzinger sent a delegation from his Inquisitorial Office to Bogotá, Colombia, to push for a condemnation of liberation theology from CELAM, the conference of bishops of Latin America. But on March 16, two weeks before he died, the venerable German theologian Karl Rahner, in what was probably his final public act, wrote a letter of support of liberation theology to Cardinal Landazuri of Lima. In it he said: "The theology of liberation that he [Gustavo Gutierrez] represents is entirely orthodox. A condemnation of Gustavo Gutierrez would have, it is my full conviction, very negative consequences for the climate that is the condition in which a theology that is at the service of evangelization may endure. Today there are diverse schools and it has always been thus . . . It would be deplorable if this legitimate pluralism were to be restricted by administrative means." This letter, when shared with other bishops, helped to head off a censure of liberation theology. Ratzinger had lost that round.

On May 15, 1984, Ratzinger went after Leonardo Boff of Brazil and his writings on liberation theology, which he claimed constituted a "pitiless, radical assault" on the church (meaning the hierarchy) because it emphasized the "church of the people" (the phrase invoked from Vatican II emphasized the "people of God" understanding of church as opposed to mere hierarchical understanding). In late August, Ratzinger attacked anew with an "Instruction on Certain Aspects of the Theology of Liberation." In it he warned that "new miseries and new types of slavery" would come

Leonardo Boff

about because of liberation theology and declared that "this system is a perversion of the Christian message as God entrusted it to His church."

One liberation theologian, Uraguayan Jesuit Juan Luis Segundo, responded that Ratzinger was in effect denying the teaching of Vatican II that God's grace is universal and we are to partner with others in social liberation. Ecclesiology was at stake, not Marxism, he observed.

Also in September, Ratzinger met with Peruvian bishops who gathered in Rome. His agenda was to get them to condemn Gutierrez, but instead they issued support, and in a document on November 26 they expressed appreciation for the "spiritual deepening" that liberation theology brought regarding the truth of social sin, the reality of class struggle, and the need for greater distributive justice. It boasted that liberation theology was a movement "born on our soil"—which could not have sat well with Ratzinger, who, as we have seen, believed it to come out of his own Germany.

In 1987 a group called the Conference of American Armies came together to discuss liberation theology. Its members included representatives of the armies of fifteen Western nations, including the United States and El Salvador. It condemned liberation theology and accused its leaders of being hardcore Marxists who support "the objectives of the Communist revolution." On the list of so-called hardcore Marxists was Jesuit Father Ignacio Ellacuria, who would later be one of six Jesuits murdered at the University of Central America in 1989 along with their housekeeper.

In 1988 the Vatican carved up the diocese of São Paulo, Brazil, where one of Boff's biggest supporters, Cardinal Arns, was in charge. (Arns was a national hero for having stood up almost alone against the military junta that ran Brazil for fourteen years, but his courage and witness against the military regime did not matter to the Vatican.) The bishops appointed to head the four new dioceses were not supporters of liberation theology and Arns was left to oversee the wealthy central part of São Paulo. "The move was a signal that supporters of liberation theology, even at the highest level, were not immune from Vatican pressure."

In September, Ratzinger did an unusual thing: He silenced a bishop, Bishop Pedro Casaldáliga of the diocese of São Felix, located in the Amazon forest. We will discuss this holy and courageous man later in this book and the "sins" that Ratzinger condemned him for.

There are many naïve journalists who like to praise Ratzinger as a "great theologian." Ratzinger, in my opinion, surrendered all rights to be called a theologian when he took on the job of chief inquisitor and attacked his confreres mercilessly, driven by his own ambitions and most probably intellectual envy as well. Ratzinger killed theologians and theology itself. Was Torquemada a theologian? He was a policeman, just like Ratzinger, who will not be remembered as a theologian but an antitheologian.

Allen talks of the "demolition of liberation theology" carried on by Ratzinger, and he also speaks of the "mean streak" that Ratzinger displayed by attacking Gutierrez and Casaldáliga for supporting their friend Miguel D'Escoto's hunger strike. I believe that wherever there is bullying both aggression and shame are in evidence, issues that are endemic to a sick masculinity. Shame is about exclusion, and it may be that Ratzinger felt shame early in his life, excluded as he was from sports with his fellow seminarians and possibly again when he was growing up in Germany after the war, a country beset by its own guilt and shame among other nations. He who is shamed will shame (and exclude) others—often unconsciously and therefore hyperaggressively. As we saw above, bullies seek out their own private club to belong to, to feel at home at, to feel included by, and in doing so exclude others. Ratzinger seems very at home in his sectarian clubs, whether the CDF or Communion and Liberation, as we will see below. This dark dance of shame and aggression and bullying may go a long way to explain the behavior of the curial minds of the past two papacies. Felt excluded by Vatican II, they took "their church" back with vengeance and declared a pox on all the "outsiders." They get their revenge.

While about half of the world's one billion Catholics live in Latin America and the world's two largest Catholic countries, Brazil and Mexico, are there, the attacks on liberation theology have killed any attempt at Gospel values supported by the church. John Allen puts it this way: "Bringing the gospel into contact with society ought to be like dropping a live electrical cord into a pond; every corner of it should feel the jolt. That Latin American Catholicism has not had such an effect in the 1990s is, to a large extent, Joseph Ratzinger's responsibility."

Ratzinger's Chosen Enemies

✠

The Spanish Inquisition, at first limited to Spain itself, was exported to Spanish colonies in the New World—to Mexico and Chile in particular. The Roman Inquisition was for the most part restricted to the Vatican States or what we know today as Italy. But Cardinal Ratzinger's inquisition, partly because of modern communications whereby unknown accusers can contact Rome in record time by fax and by e-mail, is truly a global inquisition. No continent save Antarctica has been exempt from the attacks of heresy hunters from Ratzinger's office, many of whom have been elevated to bishop, archbishop, and cardinal positions during his long tenure in office. More than ninety-one theologians, from six continents, have been hounded, condemned, ridiculed, often spat upon, and deprived of their livelihoods.

Homage and thanks are due these theologians and activists for their courage and their dedication in trying to serve in our time—not shame, not separation from the community, not condemnations, attacks, and constant distractions from their demanding work. One theologian has commented how it is almost "laughable" how much time he has wasted having to defend his teaching on petty matters such as masturbation or the right to wear condoms in an age of AIDS when serious matters such as war and peace and poverty and survival are everywhere. But, as was pointed out earlier, this may be part of the strategy at work to detour theologians from their real work by siccing the wild attacks of right-wing fanatics upon them. Such attacks have shortened lives, rendered theologians penniless (an ex–French Dominican brother of mine was last seen driving a taxicab in Paris as a means of livelihood), and literally put them on the streets.

Following are brief stories of just a few of those persons attacked, silenced, sidelined, or driven out of their work as theologians and often their lives, livelihoods, and communities as priests or religious. They come from different countries as will be noted since today's Inquisition is global, not regional. After listening to the stories, the courage, and the teachings of these victims, I put to you, the reader, the following question: Who will history remember as trying to live out the way of Jesus—Cardinal Ratzinger, with all his ecclesial powers at his disposal, or Father Bernard Haring? Cardinal Ratzinger or Father Leonardo Boff? Cardinal Ratzinger or Sister Jane? Let history decide. Let the reader decide.

CHAPTER 3

THE INQUISITOR'S ENEMIES: HARING AND BOFF

✠

Father Bernard Haring

FATHER BERNARD HARING WAS A MEMBER of the Redemptorist order. He has been called "the greatest moral theologian of the twentieth century," and for many that is hardly an exaggeration. As a young priest he was drafted into the German army in 1940 and ordered to do medical service in France.

In May 1941, his division was deployed to Poland near the Russian border, and while there he began to hold Bible classes for Catholic and Protestant soldiers and Polish citizens. For this he was brutally interrogated by the Nazis. He worked with some German soldiers to help free Russian prisoners of war and some Jews. He was made a prisoner by the Russians but was freed by a group of Poles, who made him their pastor.

What did he learn from all this? "The diabolical actions of German Christian soldiers during the war in the name of obedience forever affected Haring's thinking as a moral theologian. He was determined that the core concept in his moral theology course would not be obedience but responsibility, the courage to be responsible, which is true obedience."

Father Haring taught more than three thousand students of theology, among them the American theologian Father Charles Curran, also silenced by the Vatican. It has been said that "no one had done more to move Catholic moral teachings from rigid legalism toward groundedness in compassion and love" than Father Haring. He was the author of eighty books translated into numerous languages and more than one thousand scholarly articles. All of his work was an effort to comment on today's moral issues in light of the teachings of the Gospels. Though quiet spoken and serene in demeanor, he was clear and courageous in his positions.

When the birth control encyclical of Pope Paul VI hit the world like a bombshell in 1968, Haring was on a lecture tour in the United States. He issued the following statement, which was published on the front page of the *New York Times* and reprinted worldwide: "Whoever can be convinced that the absolute forbidding of artificial means of birth control as stated by *Humanae vitae* is the correct interpretation of divine law must earnestly endeavor to live according to this conviction. Whoever, however, after serious reflection and prayer is convinced that in his or her case such a prohibition could not be the will of God should in inner peace follow his/her conscience and not thereby feel her/himself to be a second-class Catholic."

Six weeks before he died at age 86, he demonstrated "pride and joy" at having been among the very first to sign the German *Kirchenvolksbegehren*, a document calling for democracy in the church and women's ordination, among other things. The retired bishop of Innsbruck, Reinhold Stecher, spoke affectionately of Haring. "Both Stecher and Haring are passionately opposed to blind obedience to authority because they experienced the dark side of unthinking submission to power during the Nazi era," Dr. Ingrid Shafer, a biographer of Haring, explains. Lessons from Nazism were learned by Haring. Not by Ratzinger.

Haring warned theologians working in the upper echelons of ecclesial administration when he wrote:

Theologians, especially those who exercise the official Magisterium, along with their immediate collaborators, constantly must watch over the purity of their motives: all for the greater honor of God and for the salvation of men and women. They can sin gravely and defame theology through cowardice as well as through arrogance. They can distort the approach to truth for themselves and others by striving for offices and positions or titles of honor, which was so radically forbidden by the Lord. Such sins can be institutionalized, indeed all sins carry within themselves the tendency to incarnate themselves in history. A theologian or group of theologians becomes inauthentic when rather than suffer for the truth, they allow themselves to be frightened and choose to bury the talents of creative freedom and creative loyalty in favor of "safe" repetition of old formulas.

One can see in these remarks Haring taking direct aim at Ratzinger and his cohorts in the CDF. The issue of "striving for offices and positions of honor" must have hit quite close to home in Ratzinger's case. Mincing no words, Haring challenges theologians and so-called theologians to throw off cowardice as well as exaggerated calls to obedience because both produce a "useless and inauthentic" person.

In November 1988, Pope John Paul II addressed the Congress of Moralists (organized by the Opus Dei), and Haring was shocked by what he heard. The pope's "rigid interpretation of *Humanae vitae* and sexual morality in general" disturbed him deeply along with the very "text and tone of the papal address" with its "severe interpretation." Said Haring: "I no longer recognized the Karol Wojtyla whom I knew and respected. Like many others, I was shocked and at first speechless. Numerous telephone calls, letters, meetings with religion teachers, priests and pastoral assistants have aroused me out of my silence."

What are some of the "dangerous" teachings of Haring that Ratzinger and others wanted burned like the Nazis of old burned books and like the Inquisition of old put on the notorious Index of Forbidden Books (an index that was itself disowned and forbidden by the Second Vatican Council but reemerged in the form of condemnations by Ratzinger's inquisition)?

We might summarize Haring's theology with the following sentence from his own pen: "We stand not under naked legalism, but rather under the rule of grace. This must be felt in all of our pastoral work." Unfortunately, powers that be in the Vatican were not in agreement. Haring holds up the role of conscience and the courage to live it when he writes, "Despite a certain trend towards conservatism in parts of the church and society, I am convinced that we have moved into a new era that will be determined by people who live by their own conscience and are particularly qualified to act as discerning members of community and society . . .

the era in which almost everyone was content to be born and to live as a member of a certain church or 'organized religion' is over. The people who will shape the future of believers of all religions are those who have the courage to make their own choice, whatever pain may be involved, and to do so with personal responsibility."

He calls for a responsibility marked by "liberty, fidelity and creativity" that will usher in this new era of morality. And he calls for "the rethinking of a number of doctrines, traditions, teachings and practices, and to distinguishing the deposit of faith from ideologies, taboos and other obscuring factors." And he separates moral theology from moralizing because moral theology "is not concerned first with decision-making or with discrete acts. Its basic task and purpose is to gain the right vision, to assess the main perspectives, and to present those truths and values which should bear upon decisions to be made before God." This is why he begins his book with what constitutes the Biblical vision and perspective.

Haring recognizes the "summit" of the teaching in the Hebrew Bible to be "the history of the prophets" who "unmask the atheism of ritualism and of all forms of religion that do not bear fruit in love, justice, mercy." He takes a lesson from the history of the priests in Israel, which history he calls "a great tragedy." The priestly class "misleads and seduces Israel to make religion a symbol of its own power. This will always happen where the priestly class seeks status, symbols and power (cf. Ex 32:1–30)." The priestly class must be cleansed by the prophets for "where priests think and act as members of a privileged caste, they are alienated; they have no God-experience, no wisdom and no discernment. Through their ritualism and legalism they become a source of alienation to the entire people. Their lack of fidelity and of creative liberty is unmasked by the prophets and by their own unwillingness to listen to the prophets."

In the New Testament, Haring finds the "basic virtues or character of the disciples of Christ" to be "ongoing thanksgiving for what the Lord has done." And this doing has to do with liberation. "It was not obedience to an external law but to his (Jesus') mission to make manifest the liberating power of love for the Father and trust in him (cf. Phil 2:5–11). For Christian morality this means, 'Let your bearing towards one another arise out of your life in Christ Jesus' (Phil 2:5)." Ever critical of legalism, Haring observes that "it is not a good sign if Christians are scrupulous about the very words of many laws, yet fail to show fidelity to the great law of compassion and mercy proclaimed by Jesus Christ in life and death. 'Be compassionate as your Father is compassionate' (Lk 6:36)."

Haring challenges the church "to be and become an ever better embodiment of the freedom and fidelity for which Christ has set us free . . . The Church must never appear as a slave woman whose children are under bondage. She is the freeborn woman, the spouse of Christ who is the Liberator, Freedom Incarnate." He very much acknowledges the failure of the church in history and in the present. "We appreciate everything in the Church that is faithful to this calling, and we suffer whenever we see her falling short. However, if we say 'church', we must look first at ourselves and judge whether we are making an embodied contribution to the church's progress in her vocation to be the free and embodied response to Christ, the Liberator." In saying we must first look at ourselves he is invoking the teaching of the Second Vatican Council that the church is not primarily hierarchy but it is the "people."

Haring calls for repentance on the part of the church for her many misdeeds. "The effects of distorted authority structures, and unfaithfulness of officeholders and members, have created within the church many embodiments of unfreedom and false understandings of both freedom and law. All too often, in her liturgy, her canon law, her inflated administration and defensive, intolerant attitude towards others, she has evidenced that 'Christians have not always been tolerant and freedom-minded, often committing dreadful atrocities, and have often canonized forms of society that were anything but free.'" It is part of freedom to bring these truths to consciousness.

For Haring, "the church ought to be a community of liberated people committed to the liberation of all, in response to the longing of all creation to share in the liberty of the children of God. She ought to be a sacrament of the history of liberation, celebrating in liturgy and life God's liberating love, remembering all the events in which she truly responded to her vocation, and remember also, in repentance and humility, the many instances when she has fallen short."

He calls on the church to "contribute to the whole society by building up model communities" and he embraces the works of St. Benedict and St. Basil as examples of that contribution. "What really distinguishes a community from a merely utilitarian organization is the level of liberty, fidelity and creative co-responsibility." And he distinguishes this from "massification, where the driving force is 'psychic contagion.' For the process of infection, no spiritual creativity is required." One senses his disgust at the experience of Hitler's pseudo-sense of community in this naming of "massification." One can see that Haring would be ill at home with some of the "communities" that Ratzinger so allied himself with.

Shortly before he died Haring was interviewed by Italian journalist Gianni Licheri.

> *Question: Looking back now, how do you see your experience with the Church and your work in and for the Church? Which predominates: The positive or the negative?*
>
> Haring: Were I to identify the Church with the tradition from the Roman Inquisition to the Doctrinal Congregation as I have experienced both with others and also for myself, I would say that the balance for me is rather negative. I can understand why people who fix their view only on this institution leave the church out of disillusionment. However, such a fixation contradicts our faith.
>
> I see the Church embodied and presented in exemplar Christian families as I have experienced it in my parents' house and in many other places. There the Church is tangible. In Russia during the Stalin period I experienced the Church in families and in neighborhood circles who had held on to their faith and their lively trust in God throughout a long period without priests. Reason enough for joy!
>
> I experienced the Church time and again in the saints through the reading of their lives which bore such a strong witness. Still more I have known the Church in encounters with the small unpretentious believers of our time as well as with imposing prophetic figures . . .
>
> Time and again in Africa I gratefully experienced what a living liturgy can be, a joy in God and a joy in community. The numerous catechists and their families whom I met in many countries in Africa impressed me deeply. They remind me of the reports in the Acts of the Apostles of the first generation of deacons. Here is a new form of 'cleric' without clericalism.
>
> I experienced Church in the base communities of Africa, the Philippines and Brazil. It is the 'church from below,' the humble, saving-historical Church the all-embracing 'People of God' Church which gives hope for the future.

Question: What would you now view as the most significant things for your vocation which you took away with you from this absurd war [meaning the Second World War]?

Haring: The experiences of the war, the intimate experience of senseless killing and dying, the personal witnessing of the brutalizing of many, have made me into a sworn enemy of war. I find it absolutely laughable and at the same time frustrating that at my age I still have to pour out so much energy on questions like flexibility or inflexibility concerning the forbidding of contraception and in the struggle against sexual rigorism. I am most deeply convinced that my main calling is and must be that of an untiring peace apostle for the elimination of war, for a world culture that is free of violence, for a radical love that will not allow us to become enemies, for a 'transformation of armament' to a nonviolent defense. That is the most important thing that has been written onto my conscience as a result of my war experiences.

Question: Did you know about the death camps of National Socialism when you returned from the East?

Haring: I learned to be ashamed of myself as a Christian, that even Christians and Church authorities had in many ways been guilty of anti-Semitism.

From the knowledge of the death camps it was also clear to me how important and at the same time how difficult reconciliation and healing of such deep historically guilt-laden wounds would be. But precisely for these reasons a love that overcomes enmity, a reconciliation as well as nonviolence must be a special fundamental goal of Catholic moral theology.

Question: In your book War Memoirs, you reflected on your war experiences and wrote a kind of narrative theology. What significance did these experiences have for your development as a theologian?

Haring: I learned to live with risk. This was often very necessary for me later when I became more and more known as a theologian. I learned to overcome fear. Fear has always been a stimulus for me to stand up courageously in the Church for my convictions.

. . . I learned to trust in divine Providence again manifoldly mediated through good people. My return from the East was possible only through an entire chain of extraordinary acts of human goodness. Thus I experienced together the goodness of human beings and the working of Divine Providence. That was decisive for my vocation as a moral theologian.

Unfortunately I also experienced the most absurd obedience by Christians—God have mercy—toward a criminal regime. And that too radically affected my thinking and acting as a moral theologian. After the war I returned to moral theology with the firm decision to reach it so that its core concept would not be obedience but responsibility, the courage to be responsible. I believe I have remained true to this decision—of course not to the damage of genuine obedience that is, to an obedience that is responsible and joined to openness and a critical sense.

Question: I know from other theologians of the council majority that you came into conflict with the Holy Office, later known as the Doctrinal Congregation. How did this happen?
Haring: You have sensed how difficult it is for me to speak publicly about things which have long been secret and which touch me in an inmost way . . . I believe that we have arrived at the point where it can no longer be disputed that we are in a pathological situation.

Is a certain triumphalism, a covering up and silencing of the humiliating conditions in the Church not a greater scandal, indeed a scandal in the moral sense, that an objective stating of the sobering truth?

Fully aware that we ourselves must always remain on the path of an ongoing conversion if we are to call for the reform of the Church, I see, however, how inauthentic the preaching of conversion on the individual level can be if one will not also participate in the constant reform of the Church and its structures. This concerns indeed nothing less than being true to the Gospel, to the credibility for our witness and of the entire proclamation.

Question: How have you shared the suffering that other men experienced from the Holy Office?
Haring: Before the Council everyone who was struck by the lightning of the Holy Office, of Indexing or condemnation was treated as a leper in his surroundings. He was simply excluded and branded . . .

But after the council the Congregation for the Doctrine of the Faith was on the warpath again looking for heretics and it undertook a doctrinal trial against Father Haring based on his book on medical ethics. They even attacked him for two years when he had serious throat cancer. He finally wrote them a letter pointing out that he had been interrogated by the Nazis in World War II on four occasions ("twice it was a case of life and death"), but that the accusations of the Doctrinal Congregation were "extremely humiliating and untrue," yet derive from the highest organ of church leadership. "I would rather stand once again before a court of war of Hitler," he declared.

Father Leonardo Boff

Father Leonardo Boff was a Franciscan friar from Brazil who studied with Ratzinger when he was pursuing his doctoral studies in Germany. Boff taught for many years at a seminary in Petropolis, Brazil. On May 9, 1985, he was silenced by Ratzinger and was forced to step down as editor of *Revista Eclesiastica Brasileria,* the most influential theological journal in Brazil, and to cease teaching or writing. Boff was, however, supported by three cardinals and ten bishops of Brazil and a whole community of liberation theologians from Latin America who were not unaware that his silencing was a silencing of the entire movement that was so alive and charged with reinventing the Church at the base community level. Ultimately Boff left his order and sought an official laicization.

Harvard Protestant theologian Harvey Cox, who deemed Boff's silencing worthy of a serious study in his book *The Silencing of Leonardo Boff: The Vatican and the Future of World Christianity,* identifies three basic issues at stake in Ratzinger's attacks on his former student:

The spectacular rise of liberation theology and the fierce opposition it has engendered. (Remember that this opposition has come not only from extreme right-wing Catholic groups but also from the United States government and CIA under President Reagan.)

The emergence of "Third World Christianity" and the consequent "de-Europeanization" of theology. (At issue therefore are cultural, racial and historic issues that a truly "catholic" church must consider. To be "catholic" cannot mean to become Roman, can it?)

The composure of currently dominant religious institutions in the face of energetic new grassroots spiritual movements.

All this and more was at stake in the very public silencing of Boff by Ratzinger and Pope John Paul II. Nor were these stakes lost on those affected, be they champions for justice and rights for the poor especially in Third World countries, or those clinging onto their privileged ecclesial or civil status among the wealthy in Third World countries or those wielding power in so-called First World countries.

Liberation theology, contrary to the myths propagated by the CIA and the State Department under Reagan and by the right wing in Latin America, who had everything to lose by its success, was above all *a* theology. It was a way of interpreting the message of the Gospels, the words of Jesus, and the history of prophetic thought from the prophets of Israel to the prophets of today. Says Penny Lernoux, a North American journalist who lived in Latin America for twenty years, "Liberation theology was the herald of a larger movement of the excluded—women, non-whites, the poor—onto the stage of history."

It was also a way of critiquing the Catholic Church from the inside. Penny Lernoux, writing from South America, comments: "In contrast to the cardinal's [Ratzinger's] hierarchical Christendom, the symbol of authority in the church of the poor was service, not power . . . But Ratzinger's church tried to substitute for it, by claiming all the truth for itself because truth was power. Boff was not brought to trial by Ratzinger for any Marxist heresy, anymore than the real cause of Galileo's inquisition had been his scientific teachings. They were persecuted because they were political agitators against papal omniscience." Liberation theology was a threat to the ecclesiastical status quo. It based itself on the principles of Vatican II but it also applied these principles to the concrete and dire circumstances of Latin America in the struggle for justice and equality.

Liberation theology grew up as a response to a critical situation. "By 1973 the church was at war with the state in many parts of Latin America. The more priests and nuns were persecuted, the angrier became the bishops, who also suffered repression because of their outspoken criticism. By the end of the 1970s, when more than 850 priests and nuns had been martyred, the minority of bishops who had been committed to upholding the needs of the poor had become the majority." One would think that the Vatican would be sensitive to the 850 martyrs who had given their lives for Gospel values. But instead, Ratzinger attacked the effort at bringing justice in the name of Christ to a continent that for so long had bled the blood of conquest and exploitation, first at the hands of the Europeans and more recently at the hands of North America.

Yet, as Lernoux observes, Ratzinger "knew nothing about Latin America. With his Eurocentric view of the world, Ratzinger was incapable of grasping the originality of Latin American theology as a specific response to a social location . . . [Liberation theology] was no academic exercise but an awakening that came from actually living with the poor—being exposed to the hunger, smells, noises, and sickness that constitute the daily struggle for survival in an overcrowded Third World slum."

The first book on liberation theology, A Theology of Liberation: History, Politics, Salvation, was published by Peruvian theologian Gustavo Gutierrez in 1971. The basis of Gutierrez's "analysis of liberation was not Marxist revolution but the Exodus and Christ's Good News to the poor of freedom from oppression. Therein lay its originality, for in the framework of Catholic Latin America the God of the Exodus and the Christ of the poor were much more radical than the unintelligible dialectics of Marxist intellectuals. Gutierrez also reinterpreted classic doctrines of sin to include the sins of societies as, for example U.S. behavior toward Latin America and that of the Peruvian oligarchy toward the country's peasants."

When Ratzinger attacked Gutierrez and the Peruvian church's support of him in 1983 and 1984 he "came across as a supercilious German who thought he could tell the 'colonies' how to behave." In the face of Ratzinger's theological fuming, one bishop remarked that the Latin American churches had other, more pressing issues to deal with such as "millions of starving people." Cardinal Landazuri of Lima flew to Rome to confront Ratzinger and first met with the pope. "He emerged all smiles from the meeting, which should have been a warning to Ratzinger . . . Ratzinger was therefore left to fend for himself and lost every round to Landazuri."

Ratzinger wrote an "Instruction" to try to kill base communities in Peru but lost the battle. "The bishops expressed appreciation for the work of 'those who practice liberation theology,' noting that it had been the means to a new commitment to the poor, a resurgence of religious vocations, and a spiritual deepening. They also reiterated a call for 'the right application of distributive justice and the establishment of institutions and structures that truly incarnate it.' Goodwill was not enough to change unjust structures, they said, because the poor needed to be united and organized to active bargaining power." Gutierrez said that "a church born of the blood of martyrs cannot be held back by a document." It is in this context that Ratzinger lost the first battle.

Lernoux believes that Ratzinger "consistently suffered defeat" because he believed himself culturally superior. "His arguments against liberation theology were easily challenged by the Latin Americans because they knew what it meant to live an option for the poor, whereas Ratzinger thought poor Latin Americans stupid and easily misled."

Uruguayan Jesuit Juan Luis Segundo argued, "The cardinal had set everyone off on a phantom chase after Marxist theologians when in reality the real issue was Vatican II. At the heart of Ratzinger's argument was the old demand for a separation of the religious from the secular, the church from the world, that had been rejected by the Second Vatican Council . . . Ratzinger's theory denied a crucial point—that structures inflicted far greater misery on generations of human beings than individual acts of sinfulness. The worst type of sin, in fact the only "mortal sin" which has enslaved man for the great part of his history is the institutionalized sin' wrote African liberation theologian Jaurenti Magesa. Under the institution, vice appears to be, or is actually turned into, virtue. Apathy toward evil is thus engendered.'" Rome was primarily concerned about the loss of power—the change from an ecclesiastical hierarchy to a more democratic institution in which the people revered and obeyed their pastors because of their courage, humility, and vision, not because it was foreordained by Rome.

In 1986, Ratzinger produced a second "Instruction on Christian Freedom and Liberation." It emphasized the "spiritual" values of poverty and the bestowing of charity. It did *not* emphasize justice. Ratzinger, in truly non-biblical fashion, loves to separate love from justice.

The phantom chase culminated in a well-publicized invitation to Boff to come to the Vatican for an encounter with Ratzinger. By putting Boff on trial, Ratzinger was in fact accusing "the Third World's most powerful church of heresy." Opus Dei sympathizer and archbishop of Brasilia Jose Freire Falcao was on the consultative board of the Congregation for the Doctrine of the Faith and was vehemently anti-Boff.

Cox asks the question: Why does the Vatican find Latin American liberation theology so very threatening? I would answer, first, because the Vatican finds all new movements of life in the church, and all theologies that support them, threatening. Anything and anyone they cannot control—be it women, gays and lesbians, scientists, the "modern age," parents choosing to use birth control, lovers trying not to get AIDS or venereal diseases—all these threaten the current Vatican. But in many ways the threat from liberation theology came first.

The Vatican under Ratzinger and John Paul II was clearly interested almost exclusively in ultraconservative movements like the Legion of Christ, Opus Dei, and Communion and Liberation, as we will see in the next section. And they wanted to promote obedience and the orthodox law and order that goes with it, not creativity and courage and the search for new answers to pressing questions. They sought alliances with dictators such as Pinochet in Chile and Marcos in the Philippines. In 1968 (that critical moment for Ratzinger's "conversion"), in Medellin, Colombia, the Latin American bishops proclaimed that the church stand for a "preferential option for the poor." This flaunts the extreme-right movements so favored by Rome that are "preferential options for the rich." Liberation theology is committed to this same preference in favor of the poor as it attempts to listen to the stories of the poor and to celebrate them in their base communities while linking these stories to those of the teachings of Jesus in the Gospels.

While CIA propaganda spread the notion that liberation theology is Marxism reincarnated, that is not so. Marx was Jewish and he was writing from the perspective of the Jewish prophets when he protested in the nineteenth century against industrial capitalism, which was exploiting workers, youth, and environment alike. His contemporary Charles Dickens was writing about similar issues. Cox maintains that liberation theology "is in no sense a liberal or modernist theological deviation. Rather, it is a *method*, an effort to look at the life and message of Jesus through the eyes of those who have normally been excluded or ignored." The emphasis on the poor who gather in base communities to discuss the application of gospel values to their lives is a threat to the status quo both secular and religious.

I recall being at a gathering in the rain forest of Brazil in 1990 during the forced "sabbatical" I took when silenced by the Vatican for fourteen months. The bishop had gathered about 150 church workers who were assisting indigenous tribes in their struggle against landowners and corporate powers who were trying to tear down the rain forest for their profiteering. One evening there was a simple Mass held in an auditorium in which each person was invited to light a candle and pronounce the names of three persons they knew who had been tortured and killed for defending the rain forest and its indigenous peoples. Everyone there went up and pronounced three names. Afterward a participant said to me: "The hard part was limiting it to three. I could have named ten people without even trying." That is the courage, that is the dedication and commitment to justice to which liberation theology and its base communities gave witness.

Cox identifies the largest threat to the Vatican from Boff and liberation theology to be a "grassroots religious energy boiling up from a bottom and the edges." A non-European Christianity and the faith of the oppressed and colonized and exploited—that is the not-so-hidden agenda that scares Ratzinger and company so much.

Boff has published more than forty books; the following have been translated into English: *Church, Charism and Power: Liberation Theology and the Institutional Church* (1986); *Ecclesiogenesis: The Base Communities Reinvent the Church* (1986); *Jesus Christ Liberator: A Critical Christology for Our Time* (1978); *Liberation Theology: From Dialogue to Confrontation* (1986); *The Maternal Face of God* (1987); *Passion of Christ—Passion of the World* (1987); and *St. Francis: A Model for Human Liberation* (1982).

Cardinal Paulo Evaristo Arns, a Franciscan, was a graduate of the Sorbonne who speaks seven languages fluently and is admired as a fighter who dared to stand up to the military dictatorship in Brazil for years. He holds a special place in Brazilian hearts for his fearless opposition to the twenty-one-year military regime that ended in 1985. Arns received so many death threats during the dictatorship that he lost count. He supported Boff 100 percent. One influential Brazilian church leader commented on Boff's trial: "Rome is jealous of the vibrancy of our church, dislikes our theology because it is not European, and is fearful of our numbers. This is a conflict over power, period."

Three Brazilian cardinals, including the president of the four-hundred-member Brazilian bishops' conference, offered their support and expressed a willingness to be present during Boff's "colloquy" with Ratzinger. None were allowed to accompany him into Ratzinger's chamber, however. This itself was an ominous sign of things to come from Ratzinger and his pope since it was a slap in the face to bishops' synods everywhere—a dismantling of the authority given bishops' groups around the world and a sign that henceforth more and more decision making was to come exclusively from Rome. All this was contrary to the spirit and teaching of Vatican II.

About his trial in the Vatican before his former professor Ratzinger, Boff had this to report according to Harvey Cox:

He had gone, he said, expecting to meet far more fairness and openness than he actually found. The "colloquy" to which Ratzinger had invited him turned out instead to be a full-scale interrogation, an ecclesial trial followed by a verdict and, a few weeks later, by a sentence. Like many a previous visitor to Rome, Boff told his colleagues he had come to feel, sadly, there was something distinctly warped, maybe even evil, about such a colossal concentration of ecclesial power . . . Leonardo's visit to the Eternal City had only strengthened his opposition to the ways the Catholic Church presently organizes and exercises its sacral power.

In 1985 Boff was silenced. A few months later, and after a meeting of the Curia, the Brazilian bishops, and the pope, the silence was lifted.

When I visited Boff during my enforced fourteen-month "sabbatical," Boff told me that I should never accept an invitation to go to the Vatican to a so-called "colloquy." It is all "predetermined," he said. "Don't waste your time or your health . . . Simply refuse to go." We also agreed that neither of us, in the name of being human beings with voices and conscience, would ever go silent a second time.

Let us look now at some of Boff's teachings. These teachings have been missed or minimized in the Catholic consciousness since his dismissal. We should remember that when a Catholic theologian is silenced or expelled or otherwise marginalized, it means that *all* of his or her writings are tainted and considered suspect, somehow out of the mainstream of Catholic thought. This is a very important point to make: Like the burning of books under Hitler or the Index of Forbidden Books that was supposedly done away with at Vatican II, the marginalization of Catholic thinkers means simply that Catholic consciousness is deprived of what are often its most significant thinkers and ideas. The thinker becomes radioactive—his or her books are removed from parish libraries and Catholic bookstores. Furthermore, the extreme right wing, which is rabid in Catholic circles and feels itself empowered from above (which it is), keeps the Internet busy connecting to one another and with powerful conservative forces in Rome to play the role of thought police—even when they know no more theology than their childhood catechism. They will pounce on every fresh idea (and many old ones) to cut down any thinker the Vatican has put under a cloud by its condemnations.

Boff's book *Way of the Cross—Way of Justice*, published in English in 1980, is a series of meditations on the stations of the cross, which is a traditional Catholic practice that Boff very much updates for our times. The "way of the cross" focuses on the historical Jesus and what he went through, but the "way of justice" focuses on the Christ of faith "who continues his passion today in his brothers and sisters who are being condemned, tortured and killed for the cause of justice." In another book Boff also takes up a familiar Christian prayer—the Our Father—and reconstructs it for our time. In his book *The Lord's Prayer: The Prayer of Integral Liberation* (1983), Boff refutes those who wanted a "spiritual" liberation divorced from the real world of poverty and hunger. Prayer is both "toward God" and "toward us," and we cannot separate the two.

Following are some excerpts from Father Leonardo Boff's writings that have no doubt been diminished by suspicion with which the Vatican has painted him.

From Saint Francis: A Model for Human Liberation

The greatness of Saint Francis consisted in seeing the poor with the eyes of the poor, allowing him, thusly, to discover the values of the poor. The primitive church, until the fourth century, with the advent of the age of Constantine (313 A.D.), was made up largely of the poor. The content of Jesus' message, promising first the Kingdom and salvation to the poor, calling them blessed (Lk 6:20) and the Father's privileged ones (Mt 11:25–26), reached out to meet the religious and social demands of the poor, thus favoring the spread of rising Christianity. The following words of Paul are historical truth: "Brothers, remember that God has called you in spite of the fact that few of you are wise according to human standards, or that few of you are powerful or members of important families . . . God has chosen those whom the world considers fools, despised and unimportant in this world" (1 Cor 1:26–29). . . . Christianity did not introduce social transformations nor was it in a position to do so; but it deeply humanized human relationships, dignifying the poor and placing them on a level of equality and respect among other people. . . .

In the early church (see Acts 2:42–46; 4:32–37) while the majority were poor, and the church was presented openly as a community of the poor, the collective poverty was tempered by solidarity, mutual compassion, and charitable assistance.

Anyone who is not poor may become so through solidarity, and more, thorough identification with the poor. One feels full of compassion and gentleness for the inhuman situation that afflicts the poor and decides, through love, to live together with them participating in the hopes and bitterness. This solidarity is born of a sacred anger and expresses a protest: this poverty, which is impoverishing and dehumanizing, should not be; the poor are generally scorned and abandoned; almost no one is concerned for them, except God . . . This was the way of Jesus. He, who "was rich, became poor for us," with the aim of overcoming the differences between persons, some in affliction and others in consolation that there "might be equality" (cf 2 Cor 8:9–13). He lived poorly, as all who live by their work, because he was a carpenter (Lk 6:3), and he was always poor, living from alms, as any itinerant preacher; he had a common purse with his disciples, and even came to the aid of other poor ones (cf Jn 13:29). In his Passion and the cross he knew the extreme forms of poverty.

The gospel seriousness of Francis is surrounded by lightheartedness and enchantment because it is profoundly imbued with joy, refinement, courtesy, and humor. There is in him an invincible confidence in humanity and in the merciful goodness of the Father. As a result, he exorcises all fears and threats. His faith does not alienate him from the world; nor does it lead him into a pure valley of tears . . .

From Faith on the Edge: Religion and Marginalized Existence

Liberation always comes at a price. Death and resurrection are to be accepted with evangelical joviality and serenity. Sacrifices, threats, even martyrdoms inspire no fear. Hardship of any sort is accepted as part of following Jesus. Our communities have a powerful sense of the cross. They look on it as a necessary step along the word to victory. When justice triumphs, when the people win their struggle and life is worth living, they experience resurrection. Historical liberation is a share in Jesus' resurrection . . . it is the power of the presence of the Spirit at the heart of history.

The biblical God is revealed as a Parent of infinite goodness. The right to call Yahweh our Parent is not won through human effort. The name of parent expresses the very reality of God as creative source of all things. God sustains and preserves all things with power and love, like a mother or a father . . . When we say, with Jesus, "Abba"—"daddy"—we express a conviction that is the fruit of Jesus' own experience: that this all-pervading, all-sustaining Mystery is not a terrifying reality but rather the One who waits and watches for us at home, where our journey will end. Far from threatening us with terrible deeds, this Father and Mother of ours is the only being in the universe who accepts us with absolute, and absolutely personal, love.

From Ecclesiogenesis: The Base Communities Reinvent the Church

The primitive church, in its essential apostolic character, created functions in response to needs or adapted a style already prevailing, as the synagogal concept was adapted in the college of presbyters. Whether or not to maintain past structures was unimportant. To render the risen One and his Spirit present to the world, to make his liberating message of grace, pardon and unrestricted love heard, to facilitate human beings' response to these calls—they were the primary concerns. To preserve tradition means to do as the first Christians did. They were attentive to the Spirit, to the word of the historical and risen Jesus, and the pressures of each situation. They created when they thought they should create, they preserved when they thought they should preserve, and in all things they kept uppermost in mind the triumph of the gospel and the conversion of human beings . . . Ever old and ever new, the church has never lost its identity. Christ used all available mediations to render himself present, to reach human beings and save them. The church's way ought not to be different.

Today, as we perceive the possibility of a reinvention of the church, reflections like these present themselves and are astonishingly liberating.

Theology's task is not exhausted in the exposition and explication of the official teaching of the church. Theology also has the mission of seeking out adequate answers to new and urgent problems, using the recourse of the depositum fidei. This "deposit" does not flow exclusively in channels of official doctrine. Nor is it a stagnant cistern. It can run along new paths that, without denying official doctrine, show the real wealth of the Christian "sacrament," the Christian mystery, especially in cases of pressing need. The "deposit of faith" is a spring of living waters—water that flows. This is the service for which one looks to theology. It should extract from its store of treasure, not just the old, but the new as well (cf. Mt. 13:52).

It is not enough to point to the possibility of women's ordination to the priesthood. To what sort of priesthood are women to be ordained? Today's concrete priesthood in the Catholic Church bears the brand of male celibacy, and that brand is deeply ingrained . . . Women neither can nor should simply replace male priests. They should articulate their priesthood in their own way.

From Church, Charism and Power

[T]he institution of the Church is absolutized in such a way that it tends to substitute itself for Jesus Christ, or to understand itself as his equal. Instead of serving as the sacrament of salvation, it makes itself independent self-complacent, oppressively imposing itself on others . . . Dogma is one thing and dogmatism quite another, law versus legalism, tradition versus traditionalism, authority versus authoritarianism. Christianity was reduced in its pathological Catholic understanding, to a simple doctrine of salvation: it became more important to know the truths 'required for salvation' than to be converted to a praxis of following Jesus Christ. . . .

The institutional church, faced with the extremely totalitarian ideology of Nazism, was incapable of separating its ideals and its evangelical message from its interest in survival. The German bishops . . . made clear its position that 'the Catholic religion was no more opposed to the Nazi form of government than to any other' even though it was widely known that genocide was an integral part of the National Socialist doctrine. The church as institution did not act prophetically if there was any danger of its being eliminated in a particular region. It preferred to survive, though it had to know of the grave violations of human rights such as the extermination of millions of Jews and thousands of Polish intellectuals.

There is a great difference between the church of the first three centuries and the later church which rose to power. The primitive church was prophetic; it joyfully suffered torture and courageously gave its life through martyrdom. It did not care about survival because it believed in the Lord's promise that guaranteed it would not fail. Success or failure, survival or extinction was not a problem for the Church; it was a problem for God. The bishops were at the forefront convincing their brothers and sisters to die for the Lord. The later church was opportunistic. . . .

The church [is] almost neurotically preoccupied with itself and, as such, lacking a real interest in the major problems facing humanity.

Jesus did not preach the church but rather the Kingdom of God. He preached a total and global transformation of the old world that, through divine intervention, would become the new world, where sin, sickness, hatred, and all the alienating forces that affect both human life and the entire cosmos are defeated . . . If the Kingdom preached by Christ had been realized, there would be no need for the Church. . . .

The founders of the church kept in mind that it was not so important to look to the past and repeat what Christ said and did, but to look to the present and allow themselves to be inspired by the Holy Spirit and the risen Christ, making decisions that would best lend themselves to salvation and to the passing on of Christ's project . . . Neither Paul nor John fell into a doctrinal fixation, alleging that such and such words were actually spoken by the word of life but rather, with a basic fidelity to the spirit of Christ and his message, they translated those words into concepts and expressions that their hearers could understand, accept and thus be converted to faith. . . .

It is difficult to read Boff's writings and to consider his life and his devotion to the poor—he would often celebrate Mass in the *favelos* or slum areas of Brazil—and not sense the profound injustice in his treatment and the profound loss of his leadership and priestly service to the church and beyond. Since he was forced out of the priesthood and the Franciscan order, Boff has worked as an active member of a Christian base community in Brazil. There are more than 100,000 of these grassroots communities in Brazil.

Today, Boff is freer to speak his mind, and he reports that the Catholic Church in Brazil is becoming increasingly irrelevant to the poor. The people he is working with are committed to social justice not so much because they are Christians but because they are profoundly human. Since the origin of liberation theology thirty years ago in Latin America, he sees the world as having changed considerably. Today the problem is less marginalization of the poor than complete exclusion. The issue now is survival, and basic issues of work, health, food, and shelter preoccupy liberation theology. He has also developed his thinking around issues of ecology: "The earth has arrived at the limits of its sustainability. Our task is not to create sustainable development, but a sustainable society—human beings and nature together." As for the church, "the pope's approach to the world is feudalistic. He wants a church of the rich for the poor, but not with the poor."

CHAPTER 4

THE INQUISITOR'S ENEMIES: CASALDÁLIGA, JAVOROVA, AND CALLAN

✝

Bishop Pedro Casaldáliga

I N 1971 A POET LOCATED DEEP IN THE Amazon jungle etched the following lines in Portuguese with a pocket knife on the back of a wild banana leaf:

We are the people of the nation.
We are the people of God.
We want a place on earth.
We already have one in heaven.

He called his poem "Cry from the Soul," and today these lines constitute a national hymn in Brazil and a rallying cry for 10 million landless and peasant farmers.

The poet's name was Pedro Casaldáliga, a bishop in the Amazon jungle. His diocese of São Felix (technically called a prelature) is the rain forest itself, with millions of poverty-stricken workers and with many indigenous rain forest Indians fighting the efforts of mining companies bent on extracting riches from the forest no matter what the cost to the rain forest and future generations. Like many Brazilian bishops of the late twentieth century, Pedro Casaldáliga stood up to the unholy alliance of military dictatorship and international corporations.

I met Dom Pedro and spent a week with him and his companions in his home, sleeping in his bed, which he generously offered me, the year I was silenced by Ratzinger. Dom Pedro is a soft-spoken man, small and grounded, with piercing blue eyes and a beautiful smile. He is the last one you would imagine would make enemies easily. Penny Lernoux, North American journalist and expert on Latin America, describes Bishop

Casaldáliga this way: "A short wisp of a man with the courage of a martyr, Dom Pedro is typical of the fighting bishops of Brazil," whom she recognizes as "leaders of the world's largest Catholic Church and in many ways its most progressive." Dom Pedro calls the Brazilian church "a church of the catacombs," because during the thirteen years in which the military regime reigned (supported by American gunboats stationed outside the major port cities), the church was persecuted relentlessly. The Brazilian church  to its credit stood up to the military in many ways, and it also led the post–Vatican II church in pioneering experiments in new forms of worship and communication, community base groups, lay-directed Masses "in realizing the goal of Pope John XXIII and Vatican Council II to create a more responsive, democratic church, a true 'community of God'. . . the Brazilian church is the church of tomorrow."

The truth about Bishop Casaldáliga is that he supports strongly the indigenous peoples of the rain forest and, of course, in doing so alienates those powerful forces bent on raping the rain forest for their personal and corporate profit. He had imagination, as I witnessed when I saw him attend a gathering in which he wore not the traditional miter of a bishop but a quiver of arrows on his back representing the people with whom he lived and worked. He is also a poet and a genuine mystic as well as a prophet—as are many in his diocese. Over his bed was a charcoal drawing of himself made by a priest of São Felix while in prison. He was tortured to death in that prison. He had many artifacts that he kept in a box that came from sisters, lay workers, and other priests who were tortured and imprisoned because of their support of the poor. In the backyard of the home where he and other church leaders lived was their "chapel"—outdoors and around a tree is where the group gathered to pray and worship. The bishop and the residents of his house—a priest, some sisters, and some lay workers—were themselves imprisoned for a while under the military regime of Brazil.

These are the kind of heroes who saw Casaldáliga as their leader, a holy and courageous man silenced by the Vatican. Why? Cardinal Ratzinger ordered him not to speak publicly, write, or leave his diocese without explicit permission ("diocese arrest"?) after an interrogation in Rome conducted by Joseph Ratzinger and Cardinal Bernardin Gantin, then the prefect of the Congregation for Bishops. The complaints against him were five: (1) He refused to come to Rome on required *ad limina* visits, which a bishop is required to make every five years to the Holy See. He told me that it cost a lot of money that his poverty-stricken diocese could not justify, and besides no one in Rome listened to what he had to say about his people anyway. (2) His favorable writings on liberation theology. (3) His travel to Nicaragua to support his friend Miguel D'Escoto's hunger strike. (4) He helped create a Mass that was centered on Indian and black culture in Brazil. (He proudly shared with me a recording of the Mass, and it moved me deeply and probably had some influence on the future Techno Cosmic Masses that I would develop later as an Episcopalian.) (5) He referred to Archbishop Oscar Romero as a "martyr." He refused to sign a statement saying he would back down from all these activities, and he was silenced three months later.

Many priests and church workers had been killed in Brazil by the military government. One priest who protested against the destruction of a health clinic built by the peasants was jailed and sentenced to ten years in prison for "inciting the people to revolt." In October 1976 Father João Bosco Penido Burnier and Bishop Casaldáliga went to a local police station in the jungle town of Ribeirao Bonito in the southern part of Amazonas State to protest the torture of two peasant women, one of whom was forced to kneel for hours on bottle caps while pins were stuck in her breasts and beneath her fingernails. A policeman struck Father Burnier in the face, then shot him. He died on the spot. Casaldáliga was at his side during the entire ordeal. The villagers were so incensed by Burnier's murder that on the day of his funeral they tore the police station apart stone by stone. A cross was erected in front of the ruins to mark the spot where "the police killed Father João Bosco, who was defending freedom." This is the kind of world Dom Pedro lived in and ministered to.

Another priest, Father Rodolfo Lunkenbein, was assassinated in July 1976 by the henchmen of a large landowner because he had attempted to protect the land rights of the Bororos Indians. In 1900 there were approximately 1 million Indians living in Brazil. By 1980 that number had dwindled to 110,000. Lunkenbein had protested to government authorities on nineteen different occasions about the ranchers' campaign against the Indians, and it was public knowledge in the Bororos region that the landowners had been gunning for him since 1974. "Rodolfo knew he was going to die," said one of his friends. These are the battles that Bishop Dom Pedro is fighting. This is his parish and his diocese.

Other problems abound throughout Brazil. In many cities, "abandoned children are considered eyesores to be removed from downtown streets, usually by police trucks which round up the unlucky youths and transport them to another state, where they are left with a warning never to return. Brazil's 3.5 million abandoned children are not seen as a social ill but as statistics to be eliminated." Such roundups are normal procedure. When the bishops spoke out dramatically about such policies, one bishop was seized from his car, stripped naked, and painted in red paint; his car was seized and blown up in front of the place in Rio de Janeiro where bishops gather. This happened at the hands of a right-wing group with ties to the military dictatorship.

The response of the bishops as a whole to this act was to lash out at the government and demand the return of democracy and rule of law. In response to these attacks, Brazil's bishops issued a thunder-and-brimstone letter in November 1976, in which they stated that no amount of persecution will silence them or sway them from their mission to protect the poor and the oppressed. Furthermore, said the bishops, the church no longer is willing to accept a situation "in which the people only receive the crumbs from the table of the rich but is demanding a fair distribution of (the nation's) wealth. 'Why is it that only a few people can eat well while the majority go to bed hungry?' the bishops asked. 'Why is it that some people, including foreigners, are able to amass millions of acres of land for cattle and the export of meat when our poor people are not even allowed to continue cultivating the tiny piece of land on which they were born and grew up?' 'Why is it that only a few people have the power of decision?'"

They continued: "The organized forces of evil do not want to share anything with the poor and the humble who constitute the majority of the (Brazilian) people. Only the great and powerful have rights. The humble are allowed to possess only that which is strictly necessary to survive in order to continue serving the powerful. To mistreat these poor people is to mistreat Christ." Because the church dared to stand up and protest against these "organized forces of evil," more than one hundred priests and sisters were imprisoned, expelled, or murdered, and threats and physical violence against bishops were rampant. The regime censored or shut down church media, including newspapers and radio stations. But the church was too powerful to just disappear under the military. It is said that "the more persecution the church suffers, the more it becomes 'a church of the prisons,' the greater its political and moral influence in Brazil."

Bishop Casaldáliga was threatened with expulsion by the military rulers in 1975, but the government backed down when world opinion got news of the threat and raised an outcry. One of the best-known churchmen of Latin America, Archbishop Miguel Fenelon Câmara of Teresina, was sure that he would have been murdered had it not been that he was nominated for a Nobel Peace Prize and thus had some protection thanks to the world press. Câmara's very special seminary has been dismantled by Ratzinger.

At least a dozen bishops in northern Brazil walked around with a price on their head. Reprisals have been taken against priests, nuns, lay leaders, and peasants. The bishops, more public and more protected, have chosen "to put ourselves at the front of the firing line in order to shield the rest," said one of them.

Lernoux comments that Bishop Casaldáliga stood "at the head of the line" of these courageous church leaders since he "has exasperated the large landowners and military authorities in the Amazon region of Sao Felix by organizing peasant cooperatives, schools and health units and by giving the landless *posseiros* moral support." Dom Pedro encourages people to unite and to know their legal rights. "He also is a thorn in the federal government's side because, in addition to writing enormously popular verses, he keeps publishing these documents about the *latifundia* of Volkswagen, Rio Tinto Zinc, Swift Meat Packing Company, and other multi-nationals that have received tax write-offs to develop cattle ranches in the Amazon."

But in 1988, the Vatican, in a very unusual action, silenced the courageous Bishop Casaldáliga. Having met in Rome with Cardinal Ratzinger three months previously, Dom Pedro refused to sign a document that would restrict his work by forbidding him to put political meaning into processions and limit his written and spoken words so that he could not mention liberation theology. The unsigned document also forbade him to celebrate Mass or preach in other countries without approval of local bishops. According to the *New York Times*, this was the "first time a Brazilian bishop had faced disciplinary action" from Rome. From the military, yes. But not from Rome. The document was leaked to Brazilian television even though the Curia in Rome and the papal nuncio in Brasilia had refused to comment on it publicly. Said Dom Pedro: "I can't sign this document. It has lost credibility and respectability by being leaked and it does not respect the time that I need in order to reply. As far as I'm concerned, we're back to square one."

Upon his silencing he commented, "My attitude is a reflection of the view of the church in many regions of the world. I have criticized the curia over the way bishops are chosen, over the minimal space given to women, over its distrust of liberation theology and bishops' conferences, over its excessive centralism. This does not mean a break with Rome. Within the family of the church and through dialogue, we need to open up more space."

In spring 1997 Bishop Casaldáliga wrote about the fears in the church today and of the search for a new way of "Being Church." He writes:

> It is important to state that we are not talking about "another Church, but another way of Being Church." . . . It is possible and necessary to be the Church of Jesus, but in a different way. Throughout history, the Church of Jesus has taken on different forms and there have always been different ways of being church within it . . . There is insecurity and fear, but on the other hand there are also demands which are growing more explicit and even collective, and becoming experiences of liberation. There has never been so much diversity in the Church of Jesus as today, particularly in terms of the laity. This is true not only in Latin America, but also in Europe. The base communities are an alternative experience of Being Church compared to the traditional parish model, for example.

Dom Pedro lists some fears that exist in the church today, and in doing so I think it can be said he is listing the legacy of Cardinal Ratzinger and his contemporary Inquisition. Among these fears spawned by the Vatican is a "fear of the modern secular world that has pushed the church out of the public sphere, relegating it to the private sphere." Dom Pedro sees a fear of "ecumenical dialogue" as well as interreligious dialogue. He sees the church as a "landlocked port" because there is so great a fear of episcopal collegiality.

"Centralism exists in the Church and we need to recognize it." There is fear of the laity and especially there is "fear of women, which is one of the greatest fears . . . If women can and should be equal to men in society, why not in the Church?" There is also a deep fear of theologians: "there have been many books written by theologians that have not been published and will not be published because they might be censored. I personally know of several cases." There is fear of "liturgical changes" (he was himself censored for helping to create an intercultural version of the Mass that welcomed the black Brazilian experience of poetry, music, and dance) and a "fear of reviewing things like the ordained ministry, optional celibacy, lay ministries, to say nothing about women's ordination." And, of course, so close to his own heart, the fear of "base communities" and of Latin American liberation theology.

He tells the story how during a visit to Central America Pope John Paul II was asked if liberation theology was over now that the Berlin Wall had fallen. The pope replied that liberation theology was no longer a problem. Dom Pedro says, "I believe, with due respect, that it never was a problem. For us, it was of great importance, a relevant solution and it continues to be." And not just Latin American liberation theology but that of Asia and Africa also, he hastens to add.

Dom Pedro cites the document "We Are the Church," which emanated from Austria and was signed by millions in Europe, including a number of bishops. Says Pedro Casaldáliga: "It calls on the church to adopt a message that is happier, full of hope and even tenderness, instead of its message of control, restriction, and threats." He sees this as an assertion of lay rights and ideas in the church and believes that "the process can only accelerate. The church will become increasingly less hierarchical. There will continue to be a hierarchy, but it will be *less* hierarchical. The laity will have greater protagonism. We will be more communitarian." The "spirit of community" is what is key—not democracy so much as "a fraternal community with the full participation of all people, each person with his or her service or ministry but with total participation."

Above all, he insists that "we need to categorically affirm that we are 'church' just as much as anyone else, including the pope. We are more or less church if we are more or less followers of Jesus . . . This awareness of Being Church should fill us with gratitude, responsibility and freedom of spirit which should enable us to live it with greater awareness, freedom and reality." He recognizes the church as both "chaste and a prostitute," citing an early Christian saying. And he celebrates church reformers who "through time have been good for the Church because they shook it and reminded it that it had to change with the times." He believes it is important to criticize the church and "recognize the nonsense it has created, creates and will create." And he suggests asking for forgiveness "for our crimes: slavery, the crusades, the conquest of America." A good act of penance is a "good way of recovering credibility," he proposes. He recommends that we cease talking about "church as institution" and instead "talk about ourselves and others and that each of us assumes his or her responsibility" since we participate in a "priesthood common to all the faithful."

When we die, he says, we will never have to talk about religion or church again. Only about the kingdom of God. So we should start practicing here below. He cautions: "Do not be scared. I have changed my God and I will always be changing my God. Thank God for that." A new ecclesiology will present us with a church that is "more communitarian, serving, more dialogue based, inserted in history and in reality with the poor, thirsty, concerned and hopeful as the Council asked us to be in *Gaudium et spes*." He resists a call to a "parallel church in the pejorative sense of the word. We must be church and this depends on us."

These are the words of a very courageous and sensitive man.

After Pope John Paul II visited Nicaragua in 1983 and a shouting match broke out during his homily from Catholics upset with his denunciations of base communities, there was widespread upset among Catholics there. Dom Pedro visited and was asked to give his views. He said: "You want me to talk with you about the pope . . . The manner and style that the pope has lived and acted throughout history, the way he lives and acts today, that is open to discussion. Peter is one thing and Vatican something else . . . You people don't like the Vatican; I don't like it either, as it is. That in no way lessens our faith. We have the right and the duty to want the church to be—and to make it—ever more authentic and a better example. You are also 'the' church.

"Obeying the pope and the bishops doesn't mean keeping your mouth shut in their presence, like little children who have no responsibility, and simply accepting everything they say or do. In the church we should be adults. We are all church: holy and sinful, 'the chaste prostitute,' as one of the ancient saintly fathers of the church put it. Vatican Council II has providentially rediscovered that the church is the People of God, gathered in Christ. A people journeying toward full liberation."

Bishop Casaldáliga prays that "prophecy and theology will defeat the devil," and he challenges a kind of ecclesial disobedience when he comments that the church is involved in a "kind of aggression, which I cannot fathom." He challenges the church to wake up. "If a great part of the church in old and beloved Europe doesn't want to go to the border-line—because they're tired, because they're contented, because they've forgotten there are other worlds, because they've lost that enthusiasm of the child and of the Christian for creativity . . . at least the church is on the border line here in Latin America, in the Third World . . ." He reminds his listeners that "a higher law—the gospel itself—and exceptional circumstances . . . justify an exception to canon law. In fact, such exceptions have been made hundreds of times in the past and also today in the Catholic Church with far less justifications."

Dom Pedro ended his trip to Central America with a pilgrimage to Oscar Romero's grave in El Salvador, Romero being the archbishop who stood up to the military death squads and to the Vatican, who regularly called him in to scold him for supporting the poor peasants and not yielding to the military. He was murdered by the military while saying Mass in a public place. One of the reasons Ratzinger gave for silencing Dom Pedro is that he called Romero a "saint." (In traditional Catholic theology, a martyr is considered a saint.) Dom Pedro knelt at Romero's grave and he composed a poem that ends this way:

> You knew how to drink
> the double chalice
> of altar and people
> with a single hand anointed to serve.
> Saint Romero of the Americas, our pastor and martyr
> No one
> will silence
> your final sermon!

Ludmila Javorova

In 1996 a priest with twenty-five years of experience in the priesthood was called into a bishop's office in Brno, Czechoslovakia, and told that Rome demanded that that priest not practice the Catholic priesthood any longer. Indeed, the priest was informed that one's priestly ordination a quarter century before was "invalid." What was Rome objecting to? What was Cardinal Ratzinger objecting to?

The priest in question was Ludmila Javorova. Ludmila was a woman. She had been ordained secretly in 1971 by a bishop in the underground church of Czechoslovakia during the fierce Soviet occupation of that largely Catholic country—when many bishops, priests, and others were jailed, tortured, or killed. Now she was formally forbidden to talk about the fact of her priesthood of twenty-five years. As she says, "A prohibition was issued, and no consideration was given to what would happen next. There was no concern for the person." A young new curate fresh from training in Rome came on board in her parish and made it his special task to persecute her. Back in 1983 she had written Pope John Paul II a secret letter informing him of her ordination but never heard a word in return. This word from her bishop, that she desist all work as a priest and that she hide the fact of her priesthood, was the first response she had heard from Rome.

The same man who had ordained Ludmila, Bishop Felix Maria Davidek, had ordained sixty-seven other priests (six of them women) and had consecrated sixteen bishops secretly in the underground church from 1967 to 1987. By all objective criteria, Davidek was a hero of immense courage and intellectual strength in the violent struggle of communism versus Catholicism in Soviet-occupied Czechoslovakia. How did he come to the conclusion that it was appropriate to ordain women in the Catholic Church? Let us briefly consider his story.

Felix Maria Davidek was ordained a priest shortly after World War II ended, on July 29, 1945, in Brno by Bishop Stanislav Zela, the auxiliary bishop of Olomouc. His first Mass was celebrated in the Chrlice section of his hometown of Brno, and in attendance was a thirteen-year-old girl mesmerized by it all and in awe. Felix had been born on January 12, 1921, was very talented at piano and science, and read voraciously. He surprised his rather unpious parents when he told them as a teenager of his desire to enter the priesthood. The Nazis invaded and occupied his country in 1939, and he enrolled as a theology student from 1940 to 1942, all the time planning with others to found a Catholic university in Moravia in the future. He had a special relationship of intellectual sharing with Ludmila's father, at whose home he would frequently visit for late-night discussions on philosophy and theology. He kept up his interest in medicine as well as his theological studies. His spirit and imagination were not easily tamed. Ludmila says: "Felix was truly not typical—a free spirit, spontaneous, unpredictable, with a charismatic zest for life."

Felix Davidek continued his medical studies and graduated from medical school in 1947. He worked both as a physician and as a chaplain. In 1948, he also received a doctoral degree in psychology. The same year, he began to pursue his long-held dream of establishing a Catholic university. It was called the Catholic Atheneum, and existed from 1948 to 1950—when Felix was apprehended by the secret police.

The spirit of postwar celebration was short-lived in Czechoslovakia, where war-weary citizens were to trade the horrors of Nazi occupation and World War II for the horrors of Soviet occupation. In 1946 the Communists won the election. In 1949 Pope Pius XII issued a proclamation stating that any Roman Catholic who supported communism would be excommunicated. The government, now Communist, retaliated by taking control of all seminaries, theology faculties, and schools and established the Peace Committee of Catholic Clergy to divide the church from within. Religious orders were banned and their members sent to labor settlements. Bishops were jailed or put under house arrest. A majority of priests were sent to army camps, where they were consigned to hard labor. Many of the clergy were murdered.

What was Felix's response to this persecution? He started an underground seminary, then was arrested in 1950 and put into a maximum security prison, one of the harshest facilities in the country. He escaped out a bathroom window at the police station and eluded state security during six months of hiding. He stayed in touch surreptitiously with his faculty at the Atheneum and was planning an escape from the country. But a Communist infiltrator gave them away and he was caught again. He was sentenced to twenty-four years in prison plus the loss of all his assets and his civil rights. He also had to pay a fine. Police went to the parish house and confiscated everything, including all his books.

Felix was then dispatched to Mirov, the dreaded medieval prison about 150 kilometers north of Brno. There he spent most of the time in solitary confinement—yet he still managed to survive. Held in an underground cell with no windows, with one meal a day consisting of a slice of bread and something hot that tasted like water, he made it a point to walk around the cell twelve hours a day. He slept on a plank bed, a single sheet his only defense against the frigid winters. "He earned those accommodations by verbally resisting unjust guards, by coming to the defense of others, and by absolving prisoners during walks. Whenever he was out of solitary, he would do something to tweak the system, and the cycle would begin again. He organized a university, even there among the prisoners." He challenged other educated prisoners to teach other inmates, often by walking with another prisoner back and forth in the yard.

Felix also wrote poems in prison on snippets of paper. "These clandestine activities—the lecturing, writing, possession of contraband, such as pencils and pieces of paper—were all strictly forbidden, which helps to explain how he was able to accumulate so much solitary time. A number of his infractions came from his practices as a priest, a doctor, a concerned human being. Ministering to others was not permitted. He took the risk and paid for it with confinement for months on end. Davidek was incorrigible because of his unfailing spirit and a compassionate heart." Contrary to all rules, he secretly celebrated Mass using raisins soaked in water as wine and a coffee spoon instead of a cup or chalice. The men who were incarcerated with him—bishops, priests, professors, and ordinary people—"never forgot all that Davidek did to help lift their spirits."

At the prison there were separate quarters for women, and he tried to minister to them through the walls. But it is there that it dawned on him that if women were priests they could minister to each other.

In February 1964, having served half his sentence, he was released from prison (the times were changing). He had spent fourteen years in jail. On returning home, he looked up his old friends, including Ludmila, and he took her on as a pupil in philosophy. He also had students studying secretly for the priesthood under him. He was on probation for ten more years—if caught he would go to prison again, maybe for life. He knew he was under constant surveillance and taught others how to deal with it. Ludmila, in turn, kept her work secret even from her parents so they would not get in trouble.

Felix taught current politics and world news and his philosophy "especially stressed creativity. To Davidek, it was vitally important to cultivate an ability to discern new forms of life in any given time." He defended evolution and Teilhard de Chardin, who was under suspicion still in many Catholic quarters. The Communist regime was still very vigilant, so they went underground and gathered students secretly to do school at night. They all got very little sleep because they went to work during the daytime. The students dared not take notes or write things down at first.

They were preparing students for ordination, but no bishop would ordain out of fear of the regime. "No one was willing to ordain for us. They felt it was too risky." Some had waited twenty years to be ordained. Eventually, Pope Paul VI allowed for a secret ordination of Jan Blaha as bishop in Germany in October 1967. The next day Bishop Blaha consecrated Felix Davidek a bishop. Felix was to be the presiding (though secret) bishop of Brno. They evaded the secret police by ordaining people in Ludmila's brother's home, in Davidek's house, and other secret locations. The newly ordained swore not to tell any one, not even their parents, because of the need for secrecy. They formed small, clandestine communities. In 1968 Davidek ordained twenty-one new priests. Thus an ever widening circle of small communities emerged.

When the Soviet army invaded in 1968, Davidek got the message that bishops and priests would be arrested and deported to the Soviet Union. Presuming he would be among that number, he consecrated other bishops but under the condition they would minister as bishops only if they were arrested or deported. By the end of 1970, he had ordained about forty priests. He also collaborated with the Greek Catholic church in ordaining married priests. He ordained Ludmila's younger brother Josef Jovorova, who had been married for seven years and had two children, in February 1969.

Unlike many priests, Felix was at home with women and did not look down on them. Says Ludmila: "He was spontaneous with women, which was very atypical." Felix made Ludmila his vicar general, since she was already doing the work throughout Moravia and Bohemia. It made a statement about women in the ministry. He was aware of this and saw it as part of his educating of the clergy. Bishop Davidek made many pastoral visits to sisters living in religious communities. Many of them had been imprisoned and had no access to priests. Davidek said: "Society needs the service of women as a special instrument of the sanctification of humanity." In 1970 he gave a lecture on how and why women historically had been excluded from the priesthood. "He felt there was no dogmatic basis for continuing such a practice, particularly when the signs of the times revealed such a pressing need for women in ministry. He criticized the 'Neolithic thinking' that was so degrading to women, and made it clear that this outmoded tradition left the whole church deprived."

Davidek always tried to work with the church council, and he called a council to discuss women's ordination. Felix explained that, sacramentally, there was no problem. Canon law, however, was a problem, but "life takes precedence over a codex. I am willing to take the risk. The sign of the times comes from God and we are obliged to deal with it . . . The people need the ordination of women. They are literally waiting for it, and the church should not prevent it. If we have returned to the life-giving springs of early Christianity in everything else, then so shall it be in this." Two bishops sided with Felix while four stood against him and tried to disrupt the proceedings. Both Ludmila and Felix were exhausted by the ordeal. Ludmila comments: "The unanticipated betrayal by four of his bishops who were colleagues and friends, and the divided vote on ordaining women, had cut him to the core." He had not anticipated such fierce resistance.

What most drove Felix Davidek, in addition to his study of the early church, was the pastoral need—a need he had seen up close and personal in his fourteen years in prison and also in visiting women's religious communities. Eventually, he made the decision to act based very much on the uncertainty of the times. He felt he might soon be arrested. He said it was "a matter of conscience" and that "if we wait for a man to approve this, it will never happen, so we must go ahead without it." "Why have you chosen me?" Ludmila asked. He replied: "It is natural. It is one minute to twelve." The issue of women priests was urgent and could no longer be ignored. He promised to inform the pope himself. On December 28, around 10 p.m., Ludmila Javorova went to Felix's home, where the bishop ordained Ludmila a priest in the middle of the night following exactly the Rite of Ordination according to the Roman Pontifical.

A total of seven women were ordained as priests in Czechoslovakia, but only Ludmila remained a priest because there was so little support for this "secret within the secret church." Ludmila's ministries were in hospitals and to individuals, all of it by necessity underground. Not even her parents knew of her ordination. Davidek wanted to inform the pope personally of his ordination of women, but he was prevented from leaving the country by the government. Javorova saw the handwriting on the wall, as Davidek's health began to fail him, and so she made the gesture after informing Felix. She wrote a simple letter to Pope John Paul II that said: "Holy Father, I have received priestly ordination under these circumstances . . . and now I am announcing it to you." She brought the letter to Cardinal Frantisek Tomasek, the archbishop in Prague, so that he would hand-deliver it to the pope. She admitted to the cardinal that she was ordained. The cardinal never told her he had delivered it. Instead, she heard rumors that she was excommunicated but that the pope had then rescinded the excommunication.

In fall 1989, Communism fell. Czechoslovakia was liberated. The pope came to Czechoslovakia in April 1990 and again in 1992. All the bishops around the world go to Rome every five years for their *ad limina* visit with the pontiff, so the Czech bishops now did so for the first time in forty years. There was great excitement now that the underground church could come aboveground.

A surprising thing happened instead. Those clergy who collaborated with the Communists were "quickly reconciled." At the same time Rome withheld official recognition of the underground priests waiting for proof of validity of ordinations, but this was hard if not impossible since a strict code of secrecy and no written documents had prevailed during the time of persecution. "Suddenly, in Rome's eyes, what had been considered legitimate under the forces of communism was now perceived as a parallel priesthood and a problem to be solved."

In 1992 Cardinal Joseph Ratzinger, as prefect of CDF, signed a Vatican pastoral letter demanding an ordination *sub conditione* for all underground priests. "The priests themselves have never doubted the validation of their ordination. This is a problem only with Rome," comments Ludmila Javorova. About fifty priests submitted to this reordination. Married priests also had to be reordained in the rite of the Greek Catholic Church. Twenty-two of them complied. But a number of priests, both celibate and married, refused. "They resent the implication that their years of priestly ministry under difficult and dangerous conditions and their own personal integrity are now being called into question . . . At the center of the controversy concerning valid ordinations and consecrations was and still is Bishop Felix Maria Davidek."

Today Ludmila summarizes the role of Bishop Davidek this way: "He suffered so much for ordaining me. It was a completely new thing, uncommon, without precedent. I do not resent anything he has done with regard to my ordination, for there was no other way he could have gone about it. He is my intercessor now, and not only mine, but intercessor for all women who have the priestly charism."

Ludmila Javorova herself grew up during awful times of World War II. First came German invasions and then Russian invasions of her country. Food was scarce; death was everywhere. Her oldest brother was killed by a bomb explosion when just a teenager. Her education was aborted and her desire to join a convent was frustrated by the realities of war. She worked tirelessly, selflessly, and courageously nonstop to assist Felix, first as a priest upon his release from prison and then as a bishop, as he worked on the front lines of a dangerous situation of a secret church within a spied-upon church.

She worked a regular job during the day so as not to draw suspicions from authorities and gave herself to church work at night. She received an excellent education from Felix and helped pass it on to many who would become priests and bishops, endangering her life on a daily basis to do so. One wonders how she survived physically with so little sleep and so much stress. Everything had to be handled underground, by secret communications. All of this she organized and executed successfully. She helped Felix keep together the church in her persecuted country.

Her reward for all this loving sacrifice? How did the church acknowledge her generosity? By telling her that her twenty-five years as a priest were "invalid," and that she should never talk about it. She comments: "I have been a priest [now] for 30 years and nobody can erase that. They cannot say it did not exist . . . What happened to me occurred during an exceptional time in history and in a particular place. In the history of salvation, God accepts things at certain times that are not permitted at other times. God permitted my ordination."

She continues: "It was so unexpected. I did not anticipate being ordained. Accepted it as God's gift . . . I didn't aspire to power, I didn't do it to compete, I just wanted to serve. I wanted only to make the life of others lighter. I believe that the essence of the Gospel is to make the yoke lighter for people and I wanted to help." Ludmila Javorova makes the point that "Christ made no distinction between women and men. If a woman is able to communicate or to bring these moments closer to people, why should she be prevented from doing so?"

She asks the questions: "Should we just leave the future of women's ordination to one half of humankind? Should we leave the decision to men? Then I think it will never happen. These two halves, men and women, have to meet somewhere on this. Only by coming together, by understanding each other, can we take the next step forward."

Ludmila bears witness to the fact that, in her own words, "the charism for priesthood for women does exist. It [her story] also introduces the question of whether the Spirit of God in ministerial service is being systematically extinguished through juridical decision-making."

The juridical decision maker was Cardinal Ratzinger, now Pope Benedict. It is a wonder to contemplate how, instead of awarding Ludmila and the deceased Bishop Davidek the praise of a grateful church for their bravery and creativity amid persecution and danger, he has subjected their names and personhood to denouncement of all their work. How strange it is to see this same Ratzinger associate women's ordination with "radical feminism," as he does whenever the subject is raised. Had he ever met with Ludmila Javorova? Is there anything about her story that suggests she did it as a "radical feminist"? Or that Bishop Davidek did it out of "radical feminism"? They did it to serve a persecuted church. They both read the authentic signs of our times and that sexism and patriarchy has no place in an organization supposedly operating in the name of Jesus the Liberator. Someday history will reward them with the praise they deserve.

Father Jim Callan

In Rochester, New York, there was once a very alive Roman Catholic community named Corpus Christi Parish. Its leader was Father Jim Callan, who was appointed parish administrator in 1977. One of his first acts was to hire Sister Margie Henninger to go out into the streets to discover neighborhood needs. Based on this assessment, their first collective decision was to found a drop-in center and outreach program that developed into a health center serving thousands of uninsured people in need of health care.

The next year the parish began a 10 percent tithe of the weekend collection for the poor and a regular ministry of parishioners visiting inmates in the local Monroe County Jail and Attica State Prison. In 1979, they collected money for Sister Isabel Lumpy in Port-au-Prince, Haiti, and they have been supporting a ministry in Haiti every since. In 1980 they opened a supper program for the homeless working out of the church kitchen. That year they also opened a childcare center for the working poor and established Rogers House, a home for male ex-offenders.

In 1982, they opened a winter shelter for the homeless in the church basement. Two years later a sanctuary opened for undocumented Salvadoran refugees in collaboration with the Downtown United Presbyterian Church and other faith communities. Parishioners traveled to El Salvador to connect with two sister cities there.

In 1986, the parish opened Dimitri Recovery House for men in recovery. The next year they opened Isaiah House, a home for the dying and a restaurant with the explicit purpose of employing people coming out of prison. One year later the parish raised its tithing percentage from 10 percent to 12 percent to serve the poor. In 1990 they established Mary's House, a home for women with AIDS, which the Diocese of Rochester oversaw. In 1991 they opened Matthew's Closet to sell "gently used clothes" and give away clothes to the poor. The next year the Mission Possible Youth Retreats began for parish teens to participate in a week of outreach. In 1994, retreats were sponsored in Chiapas, Mexico, and in 1995, a trip to Borgne, Haiti, resulted in setting up a health clinic, a grain mill, water purification projects, and education initiatives. In 1998, they set up Pearl House to house female ex-offenders.

This was the ministry of Corpus Christi Catholic Church under the pastoral guidance of Father Jim Callan and other leaders and parishioners of the church. Bishop Matthew Clark of Rochester, a progressive and forward-thinking man, supported them strongly. Other innovations that made these ministries possible included the divesting of stocks, bonds, and bingo games—all accomplished in 1978. Also that year the first of sixteen houses were donated to the church and more than one hundred cars were donated to staff members and its paid employees. In 1988 parishioners provided zero-interest loans of $100,000 to fund interior church renovations, and in 1991, services were conducted to denounce the Gulf War and pray for the people.

It is difficult to see the activities of this church and not recognize the spirit of the Gospels and of Jesus' teaching in all of them. All around Rochester people responded enthusiastically, with thousands of people attending Mass and hundreds of people volunteering in many capacities. Indeed, by 1998, more than seventy paid employees worked in the parish, supporting its various ministries.

But not everyone was impressed. The far right-wing Catholics in New York, members of Catholics United for the Faith (CUFF) and CREDO, hated Bishop Clark "with a fury," as one local observer noted, and would denounce him and the parish in constant letters to Rome. Making his once-every-five-years *ad limina* visit to Rome in 1997, Clark was "read the riot act" and was told he either had to close down the church or he would be replaced. On August 13, 1998, Bishop Matthew Clark, on orders from Rome, removed Father Jim Callan as administrator after twenty-two years at Corpus Christi Church. Reluctantly, he chose to reassign Callan to a much less visible parish in Elmira, New York, and Rome then appointed a priest who fired everyone connected with Corpus Christi and their extensive and impressive social ministry.

Parishoners protested Callan's removal. A few days after he returned to Rochester to celebrate Mass on December 1 with the community, who were then meeting at a different church, Father Jim was suspended from the priesthood. Six staff members were abruptly fired on December 14, including the director of the prison ministry, the director of Dimitri Recovery House, the family minister, the adult education director, the hospitality minister, and volunteer staff residents at the prison ministry for women ex-offenders. The following night the community raised more than $30,000 to support the fired staff.

Father Callan and his right-hand person, Mary Ramerman, founded a new parish "in the Catholic tradition" and called it Spiritus Christi (with an echo of the former Corpus Christi). The new church was born on Christmas Eve 1998, and 1,300 people gathered at Salem United Church of Christ for its conception. All of these had been part of the Corpus Christi church.

On January 30, 1999, five hundred people gathered at a visioning day for the new community. Mary Ramerman became the pastoral administrator of the new parish. They rehired the former staff of Corpus Christi and rented space from Salem United Church of Christ. Fathers Jim Callan and Enrique Cadena, also from the previous parish, were to be leaders as well. More than 1,100 people attended the first weekend Masses on February 13 and 14, 1999. Ten days later, the diocese declared that the members of the new community had excommunicated themselves. The parish voted to adopt a statement of identity: "We are a Christ-centered Catholic community reaching beyond the boundaries of the institutional church to be inclusive of all."

By September 1999, Spiritus Christi was a "full-service" church offering religious education, funerals, baptisms, weddings, unions, weekend Masses, and daily Masses. Same-sex unions were held also in the church.

The commitment to ministry to the poor was continued. In 2000, volunteer psychiatrists and therapists formed Spiritus Christi Mental Health Center, and today more than fifty volunteer caregivers offer their time to provide mental health care to those without insurance. In 2002 Jennifer House was established to welcome women released from prison and their children. Dozens of volunteers continue to visit area jails and prisons each week. The commitment to the people of Borgne, Haiti, has continued, and a credit union for small business loans was established there as well. The ministry in Chiapas, Mexico, was expanded to include a cooperative coffee business and a credit union. The ecumenical dimension of the church was prominent from the outset. The Downtown United Presbyterian Church in Rochester, the Episcopal Church of the Ascension in Buffalo, and Riverside United Methodist Church in Elmira all celebrate regular services from this tradition.

What were the issues that so upset the Vatican and Cardinal Ratzinger given the amazing ministries and outreach at Corpus Christi Church? What killed Corpus Christi Church? All the issues center on *inclusivity*. There were three issues on which neither the leaders of the parish nor the parishoners would compromise. One of them was the treatment of women. In 1975 girls were invited to serve on the altar, and in 1977 women were invited to preach on Sunday. Beginning in 1983, all liturgies included inclusive language. In 1988, Mary Ramerman and Julie Rinella were invited to lift the cup during the celebration of the Eucharist, and in 1993 the liturgy committee presented Mary Ramerman with an alb and half-stole. In 1993, a gay union was celebrated—not on church premises but in the couple's home. The issues around the role of women, the blessing of gay unions, and inviting anyone who was hungry or thirsty for the Eucharist to take communion (this became a regular practice in 1984) are what provoked the right-wing members of CUFF, the same ones who spit on me when I lectured on Hildegard of Bingen in the Seattle Cathedral and who forwarded documents to Rome that launched the investgations against me. In response to CUFF's howling Rome shut down the church rather than permit such "horror of horrors" as allowing a woman to hold up a cup at the altar.

In the new Spiritus Christi community, all these elements of inclusivity remain in practice, and the issue of ordaining women was taken up and studied for two years. Following the period of study, Mary Ramerman was ordained a priest by Bishop Peter Hickman of the Ecumenical Catholic Church on November 17, 2001, at the Eastman Theater. Nearly three thousand people attended, including representatives from Catholic and interfaith clergy from around the world. In 2003, Denise Donato, who had been ordained a deacon the previous year, was ordained a priest, and the former assistant pastor of Corpus Christi, Enrique Cadena, left his position at Spiritus Christi and became an Episcopal priest in the diocese of Buffalo.

It is difficult not to see gospel values and signs of the Spirit in the energy and vitality and dedication to service of this Christian community. It is equally difficult to imagine why Cardinal Ratzinger and others in Rome would want to kill so life-giving a gathering in the name of cold and rigid ideologies of male exclusivity, obedience, and control.

CHAPTER 5

THE INQUISITOR'S ENEMIES: THE CREATION SPIRITUALITY MOVEMENT

✛

M Y LIFE'S PURPOSE FOR FORTY YEARS has been to bring alive that alternative wisdom tradition in Christianity which is its deep mystical and prophetic side and which, God bless them, biblical scholars are today agreeing is the actual tradition of the historical Jesus. The lineage I discovered while studying with Father M. D. Chenu in Paris he called "Creation Spirituality," as distinct from the "Fall-Redemption" tradition that begins with the idea of original sin and so readily feeds into imperial and ecclesial structures that control by way of guilt and shame. Father Chenu was one of those great theologians of the Second Vatican Council who was redeemed by the council after having been exiled for twelve years, forbidden to write by Pope Pius XII. His particular emphasis was felt in the document known as the Pastoral Constitution on the Church in the Modern World (*Gaudium et spes*), for he was always aware of the prophetic dimension of the church. He was silenced by the Roman pontiff because he had supported the worker priest movement in France, which had followed on World War II and whose purpose was to bring the church more in communication with the blue-collar workers of that country.

I have told my story in some length in my autobiography *Confessions: The Making of a Post-Denominational Priest,* but it very much involved Cardinal Ratzinger, since he was on my case for at least twelve years when he first silenced me for fourteen months, had me removed from being director of the spiritual program I had founded nineteen years previously, and then, with the help of a Judas-like betrayal of myself and thirty-one other faculty members by a Canadian priest who had been my codirector, effectively killed my program at Holy Names College in Oakland, California. (From there I went on to start the University of Creation Spirituality in downtown Oakland, where we had an amazing nine-year run.)

At the time of my silencing I took the occasion to publish a public letter to Cardinal Ratzinger. Though that happened more than twenty years ago, having reread it recently, I think its criticism of the man who is now pope still holds, so I repeat it below, after providing some context related to Creation Spirituality.

First, let me summarize some of my work that so aroused the ire of Ratzinger. It has everything to do with church renewal, for my interest for years was around the spiritual life of Christians.

What do the mystics have to teach us? Is there a mystic in every one of us? If so, why is religion so silent about it? How do you—indeed, can you—teach mysticism? How—if at all—do prayer and mysticism relate to social justice, economic justice, ecological justice, and gender justice? What is prayer really, and how do we know it is authentic? How do we bring vitality to tired and rote-like forms of worship? What does contemporary science have to say about our spiritual lives? How useful is it that we are being gifted with a new cosmology at this very moment in planetary history when so much devastation against the planet—its fishes and waters, its animals and birds, its trees and soil—is happening at the hands of humans?

How can a meaningful spirituality help to reverse the trends of anthropocentrically driven assault on the earth? Who are the great thinkers, activists, and souls of our own Western tradition that can deepen our spiritual consciousness and show us ways to health and deep living? What about the shared wisdom from other spiritual traditions of the world in this time of a shrinking planet and global mixing of cultures and religious traditions? Can you teach spirituality in a European model of education? What do the indigenous people have to teach us about worship, about the sacredness of body and earth? What do neglected women leaders and writers have to teach an excessively male-dominated consciousness? How does authentic spirituality impregnate our work world and bring it to life? What do Jesus and other Christian mystics and saints have to teach us about these matters? And what does the Jewish tradition—which was Jesus' tradition—offer us as well?

These are some basic questions that have driven me over the past forty years and have informed the thirty books I have published and the many lectures and workshops I have sponsored. They also brought about a pedagogy that I developed in 1976, wherein I taught and gathered other teachers around me to teach master's degree students and then doctoral students in the ways of Creation Spirituality. It has been a great privilege to be able to resurrect the greatest mystic of the West, Meister Eckhart, as well as Hildegard of Bingen, and to reevaluate the contribution of St. Thomas Aquinas and provide a hermeneutic for rereading our spiritual tradition through the fresh and biblical eyes of the four paths of Creation Spirituality instead of the tired three paths of purgation, illumination, and unity. The four paths are the *Via Positiva* (joy and delight and awe), the *Via Negativa* (silence, letting go, letting be, and suffering), the *Via Creativa* (creativity), and the *Via Transformativa* (justice-making and compassion and celebration).

Our goal, based on my book *The Reinvention of Work,* was to bring an authentic spirituality to our professions as well as to reinvent education itself. The students and faculty we attracted for twenty-nine years were exceptional in both mind and spirit. One of our graduates is Sister Dorothy Stang, who died a martyr in the Amazon, where she was defending the peasants against rapacious land owners. Her murderers have just recently been apprehended and tried. On graduating from our University of Creation Spirituality she wrote us monthly, telling us how much our program and teachings supported her decision to stay even among death threats.

I think also of Bernard Amandi, an engineer who taught for twenty-seven years at the University of Colorado and who came to us "burned out," ready to quit both engineering and academia. After two weeks in our program he came to me and said, "I have my soul back." What did he do? He went back to Colorado and started Engineers Without Borders, which today has more than ten thousand members eager to bring solar-generated irrigation systems and other engineering miracles to Haiti, the Amazon, Africa, and Southeast Asia. Another graduate, Gina Halprin, launched a very successful program in interfaith ministry and healing, and other graduates have published numerous books, served as deans at various universities, created new kinds of ministries to prisoners, and provided interfaith leadership, alternative rituals, and much more. Many, many stories of our graduates can be celebrated as well.

My educational program began at Mundelein College in Chicago, and after seven strong years there we moved it to Holy Names College (HNC) in Oakland, California. When Cardinal Ratzinger pressured us to close the institute and forced me to go silent for more than a year, this put severe pressure on certain conservative members of the board of trustees. The president, a sister of the Holy Names Order with a doctorate in sociology, had strongly supported us for ten years of battles with Ratzinger, as did my Dominican Order for most of those years. (The Dutch Dominicans, to their credit, supported me strongly to the very end.) But the president of HNC retired, and new college personnel plus the wearing down of my provincial all conspired to give me a final ultimatum from Rome: Either quit Oakland and your program or leave the order. In all conscience I could not quit. But neither did I volunteer to get off the bus without a fight. Eventually, Ratzinger had his way, and he, with the help of an ex-student I had hired to be codirector of the program, dismissed me on the grounds that I had disobeyed my Dominican superiors.

On my exiting Holy Names College, the school's dean gave my faculty of thirty-four persons a choice to stay with the hijacked program or come with me [for I had decided to start the University of Creation Spirituality (UCS) in downtown Oakland]. Thirty-one of the faculty chose to come with me to UCS, and we had nine rich and productive years there, years that included students such as Sister Dorothy, Bernard Amandi, and many more, and faculty that included Jewish scholars, scientists, artists of many stripes, Buddhists, Hindus, Christians, goddess worshippers, Native Americans, and more. It was a true praxis in deep ecumenism, and it invigorated both faculty and students alike.

Following is the public letter I wrote to Cardinal Ratzinger after he silenced me. It was immediately picked up by the *National Catholic Reporter*, which ran it in its entirety on the front page. The editor later told me that no article in its entire history had received so much response— and such positive response. Affirmative comments came from European and Latin American theologians as well.

August 8, 1988
Feast of St. Dominic

Cardinal Joseph Ratzinger
Congregation of the Doctrine of the Faith
Vatican City

Dear Brother Ratzinger,

For the past four years the Congregation of the Doctrine of the Faith (formerly known as the "Holy Office of the Inquisition") has been questioning the theological orthodoxy of my work. During this period your concerns have been parlayed through my Masters Generals and through my provincials. At your request a team of competent American Dominican theologians were appointed by my provincial to examine my work and in particular, three of my books: *Original Blessing: A Primer in Creation Spirituality; Whee! We, Wee All the Way Home: Toward a Sensual, Prophetic Spirituality;* and *On Becoming a Musical, Mystical Bear: Spirituality American Style.* That formal process, conducted over an eighteen-month period, resulted in a document that exonerated me of any theological heresy, saying in its conclusion that "there should be no condemnation of Father Fox's work" and commending me for my "hard work and creativity." The three Dominicans on that board, all with PhD's in theology, were eminently qualified for this task, and two of them were named Masters of Sacred Theology, the highest honor awarded by the Dominican Order.

In spite of this, your Congregation has continued to insist that my work is unorthodox. Your request that my provincial hold a new trial was turned down by him, yet you persist in demanding that I be silenced and that my work at the Institute in Culture and Creation Spirituality "be terminated," as you put it in your most recent correspondence. Since the Institute is located in a liberal arts college that has been serving a diverse and ecumenical audience from all over the world for the eleven years of its vital existence, your interference in its affairs is a matter of grave concern and could have serious public repercussions. Interference in the tradition of academic freedom in liberal arts colleges is not taken lightly in our country. It is not the Vatican that accredits the school where ICCS is situated but the state of California and WASC, the Western Association of Schools and Colleges, a public accrediting institution.

I have not only had the full and consistent support of the Dominican Order, but you know as well that the Bishop of the diocese in which I work supports me as does the administration of Holy Names College, an institution of higher education that has been serving the church and society in Oakland for 120 years.

Throughout these years of investigation, I have complied with every request of my provincials and Master Generals and I have remained silent about this affair, as I was asked to do. I believe, however, that the issues we treat at ICCS regarding the spiritual crises of our time—issues of the survival of Mother Earth, of the despair of our youth, of the inadequacy of Western worship, of the loss of our mystical tradition, of justice toward women, native peoples, and all of God's creatures, of the emergence of a living cosmology from the new physics of our time—all these are of such immense moral and spiritual concern that the time for my silence about this investigation has ended. "Obedience" means "to listen" (from the Latin *obedire*). My obedience must be to the suffering of Mother Earth and all her creatures; the four-legged ones, the winged and finned ones, and the tree people of our planet and not to the two-legged ones alone.

I am therefore writing this pastoral letter to you and to the People of God, to whom I have dedicated my work as a theologian, in order to discuss the issues at stake. I write you as a brother human being and a brother Christian. I hope that the ear of your heart is opened to hear. It is evident from reading your letters over the years that your concerns are not theological so much as political and pastoral. Beneath all your communications there lie issues of the heart that are not being addressed. I hope to treat them here. My fellow American theologian, Leonardo Boff, addresses some of these issues in his book, *Church, Charism and Power*, when he writes about pathologies in a church that teaches without learning first. Other theologians have contributed their significant reflections on the issues of freedom of theological inquiry within the church. One thinks of Juan Luis Segundo's *Theology and the Church: A Response to Cardinal Ratzinger and a Warning to the Whole Church*; of Hans Kung's and Leonard Swidler's *The Church in Anguish: Has the Vatican Betrayed Vatican II?* to which many distinguished theologians contributed including Bernard Haring, Charles Curran, Leonardo Boff, Rosemary Ruether, and David Tracy; and of Harvey Cox's *The Silencing of Leonardo Boff: The Vatican and the Future of World Christianity*.

With this letter and the issues it raises I take my place beside my brother and sister theologians who have been under attack for their efforts to incarnate the Good News in a post-European cultural situation. I find—and believe others will find as I make our correspondence public—your "objections" to my writing so theologically thin that I have concluded that the issues between us must be pastoral rather than theological.

An example of the weakness of your critique of my work can be found in the document that lists your "major concerns about my principle [sic] work," *Original Blessing*, which you label "dangerous and deviant." You object to my calling God "Mother" and "Child." Let me cite Pope John Paul I—whose life as pope was sadly cut short after one month—who said in a formal statement that "God is both Mother and Father but God is more than Mother and Father." My work has demonstrated that the great Creation mystics of the Middle Ages such as Hildegard of Bingen, Francis of Assisi, Mechtild of Magdeburg, Meister Eckhart, and Julian of Norwich call God "Mother." They also talk about God as "playmate" and as "child," thus celebrating the child or *puer* in all of us. The scriptures, too, talk about God as Mother on several occasions (see Is 49, for example).

This same document claims that I "deny the existence of original sin and the doctrine of the Church in its regard." As my provincial pointed out in his letter to the Master General of April 26, 1988, this statement is totally untrue. I do not deny the doctrine of Original Sin (in fact, I define original sin as "dualism"), but I decry the influence of this doctrine and its use as a starting point in religion. Sin is anthropocentric—a human invention. God's creation, on the other hand, has been an original blessing for [13.7] billion years and continues to be so for those who have eyes to see and ears to hear the awesome cosmic story of our holy origins.

You erroneously state that I deny the validity of infant baptism and give the page number (page 51) where I supposedly do this. I challenge anyone who can read English to find on that page or any other page in *Original Blessing* a denial of infant baptism.

What do I conclude from this misreading of my book? I must keep in mind, of course, that English is not your native tongue and difficulties in reading my books are perhaps understandable. But the real issue is not your inability to read carefully; it is your determination to read with a closed mind. Your Congregation has been similarly closed-minded in dealing with other non-European theologies; for example, when it made a caricature of Latin America and Liberation Theology and then denounced it, silencing Father Boff in the process.

Your Congregation prides itself on being party to the "magisterium," that is, the teaching function of the church. Yet if I have learned anything in seventeen years of teaching it is this: The only true teacher is a constant learner—one who is seeking truth wherever one can find it. Two years ago a Black preacher, who is pastor of the most vibrant Black church in Oakland, held up my book *Original Blessing* before an audience and said, "My folks need this more than they need jobs. Why? Because slavery took away our pride." I listen to him; and then I read your report calling the same book "dangerous and deviant." I must conclude that your Congregation has not done either its intellectual homework *or* its inner work. I detect a kind of intellectual sloth in those who condemn without studying, and a spiritual sloth in those who accuse without feeling the oppression of others that is addressed in my and other works of liberation theology.

What Is Creation Spirituality?

What is Creation Spirituality? It is the oldest tradition of the Bible. The Yahwist or J source of the Hebrew Bible is creation-centered, as are the prophets and the wisdom literature. Even the Genesis story as we have it begins not with human sin but with the goodness of creation. John's Gospel begins, "In the beginning was the **word**," not, "In the beginning was human sin."

Creation Spirituality is thus non-anthropocentric; it begins with the amazing news of the gift of the universe over fourteen billion years to us, a creation story now being retold by science that elicits wonder and awe at our being here on this amazing planet with so many generous creatures who give their very lives for us. Creation Spirituality is not found only in the Bible, however; it is the tradition of native people of America, Africa, Asia, and Europe. It is still very much alive among the native peoples of the Americas, as well as Blacks and Asians in our culture. It is the tradition of the great mystical awakening in Western Christianity that began in the twelfth century and that gave us Hildegard of

Bingen, Francis of Assisi, Thomas Aquinas, Mechtild of Magdeburg, Dante, Meister Eckhart, Julian of Norwich, and Nicolas of Cusa, among others. It is the tradition of scientists and of artists, women as well as men. Creation Spirituality celebrates the wisdom of women's experience of spirituality. Justice is the cornerstone of the spirituality. As Meister Eckhart said, "the person who understands what I say about justice understands everything I have to say."

This tradition speaks deeply to persons all over the world today because Mother Earth is so wounded; the young are in such despair; worship is so one-dimensionally anthropocentric; the human soul is so cosmically lonely; our patriarchal institutions are so arrogant; the artist is secularized and therefore cut off from spirituality; good work is so scarce; women and minorities are so oppressed.

Creation Spirituality is in many respects a liberation theology for so-called "First World" peoples because it comes from the deep and ancient traditions of the most oppressed peoples, the native or primal peoples of the world, and from women's experience. Creation Spirituality liberates peoples and structures from consumerism and materialism, dualism and patriarchy, colonialism, anthropocentrism and arrogance, boredom, homophobia, adultism, and the trivializing of our lives. Creation Spirituality liberates us from the bondage of Newtonian mechanism and from one-dimensional education that haunts the "First World." Creation Spirituality liberates because it moves us from head to body where heart and passion (the source of compassion) will be found. In reawakening the divine child, the mystic within and around us, Creation Spirituality leads persons from self-consciousness to unself-consciousness, and this capacity to let go and to play is vital to the liberation of so-called First World peoples over the most pressing moral issues of our time.

Three Pastoral Issues

There are three pastoral issues I wish to address in this letter which are, in my opinion, of great significance for the future of the church and of civilization.

Is the Catholic Church a Dysfunctional Family?

During my four years of waiting and watching while the Dominican Order, my bishop, students and others communicated with each other about my work, I have attempted to observe and analyze what was going on. Over the twenty-one years of my ministry as a priest, I have listened to the wounded ones in our church—women, married couples, divorced people, homosexual people, priests and former priests, sisters, and the young. More recently, I also hear deep dissatisfaction from cardinals about your concessions to Marcel Lefevre and Vatican support of Opus Dei; I hear bishops telling jokes about the Vatican and begging that the pope not come to their diocese lest it, too, be thrown into insurmountable debt; I hear leaders of religious orders telling me that your Congregation has "nothing but third-rate theologians in it," etc., etc. Yet no one tells **you** these things. Everyone refuses to confront the person who most needs to hear the truth.

Recently, in the brilliant work being done on addiction in persons and in organizations by such scholars as Dr. Anne Wilson Schaef, I have found a category and a language for the phenomena I have been observing. This behavior is identical to that which goes on in a dysfunctional family, where the alcoholic father, for example, is always appeased and placated in hopes that he will not become violent yet another time. Those who do the appeasing are called "co-dependents." Their silence sucks them into that very sickness that has so overtaken their violent father. Yet silence and denial prolong and intensify the suffering of everyone in the family. Indeed, as Schaef puts it, addicts need "the collusion of co-dependents to maintain their closed addictive system."

Regarding my own situation as a priest, a theologian, and an educator within the church, some people have cautioned me to continue playing the game; to remain silent and hope that Cardinal Ratzinger will be appeased some day; to be as patient and long-suffering as John of the Cross when he was beaten by his brothers; or as Teresa of Avila, whose *Autobiography* was forbidden publication during her lifetime by the Inquisition of **her** day; or as Teilhard de Chardin, whose work was largely unpublished until after his death.

I believe there is a time for patience and a time for impatience; a time for obedience and a time for disobedience—or a deeper obedience than that exacted by human laws and institutions. There is a time for continuity and a time for discontinuity. Ours are times—because of the unprecedented crises of Mother Earth, of our youth, of the spiritual vacuity of institutional Christianity in Europe, of the boredom that most worship instills in persons—for holy impatience, disobedience, and discontinuity. The Soviet poet Yevtushenko wrote recently to his people that not all blame in recent Soviet history can be laid at the feet of the ruling clique. The people "allowed the clique to do whatever it wanted. Permitting crimes is a form of participating in them, and historically, we are used to permitting them. It is time to stop blaming everything on the bureaucracy. If we put up with it, then we deserve it." I believe that it is also time that Catholic theologians, ministers, and laity speak out about the injustices occurring within the Catholic Church. Servile patience is a sin.

My conscience urges me to speak out, to break my silence. My brother Thomas Aquinas teaches that it is a sin to go against one's conscience. What will happen to theology in the future if today's theologians simply remain silent in order to appease the Inquisitor of our day? Or in order to keep their jobs or safe guard their pristine reputations in a church that may, in fact, be quite unwell? I believe that for years I have been protecting you from the consequences of your behavior by remaining silent. To continue to do so would be sinful, for your behavior is becoming increasingly scandalous with greater and greater repercussions for the future of our church.

Addictive systems, such as the Catholic church has increasingly become since the open-filled and inspiring days of Vatican II and of leaders like John Paul I, can crumble if either party steps out of the disease process. By this letter I consciously step out of that process and wish to tell the people what is really happening in our church. "To deny or ignore what is going on is to become part of the disease," note Dr. Anne Wilson Schaef and Diane Fassel.

Basing my analysis on the Addictive Organization, I see ten parallels within the Roman Catholic Church today that convince me that our church is indeed a dysfunctional family, a dysfunctional organization.

1. Addictive leaders have the power to bring an organization to the brink of destruction. I believe that is happening in the church today. The Vatican had a deficit of $63 million this year and $54 million last year. Its best priests and sisters are leaving, have left, or simply ignore the folly ensuing from it. The Vatican ignores the advice of its most pastoral bishops and leaders of religious orders. Instead it listens to theologically illiterate fanatics who behave like religious thugs, using violent tactics, spitting on scholars, and making libelous accusations. Instead of consulting sound publications the Vatican reads rabid, ultraconservative newspapers totally lacking journalistic credibility. It is these groups who have initiated your attacks against me and against the many other theologians and religious victims of your regime, such as Archbishop Hunthausen, Hans Kung, Leonardo Boff, and more.

2. The Vatican's obsession with sex is a worldwide scandal, which demonstrates a serious psychic imbalance. In Ireland this is referred to as the "pelvic morality" of the Catholic Church. Repression and obsession go together. Misogyny in the church grows daily as the hierarchy accepts married clergy from the Anglican Church so long as they are abandoning their tradition over the issue of women's ordination. Now we have married clergy—not Catholics but ex-Anglicans—who could not accept ordained women. Obsession with sex is characteristic of the dysfunctional personality.

3. Illusions of grandiosity are a kind of "fix" for the addictive personality (p. 124). The grandiosity of "star mentality" the media lends the present-day papacy is short-lived and full of pitfalls. And the heightened sense of power that members of a modern-day Inquisition feel who share vicariously in the illusion of power is another kind of "fix."

4. Part of this illusion of grandiosity is an "illusion of control"— games that the Vatican plays that are nothing more than control games. For example, appointing bishops whose only gift is their blind obedience to Vatican edicts. Appointing "ruthless managers"

is a sign of an addictive organization according to Schaef. Appointing Opus Dei bishops in Latin America is another example of this trend in the Vatican. The desire to control is ultimately the desire to "try to be God." The Vatican—like any organization—is not God, cannot be God, and will ultimately fail in its attempts to be God. It is a "morally bankrupt organization," Schaef teaches, that finds it necessary to control and to "try to be God" instead of entering into interaction with its members and the wider society. Instead of trying to control ICCS and the amazing response to Creation Spirituality and *Original Blessing*, why doesn't the Vatican ask WHY such immense interest has been aroused in our model of education, in our reclamation of the medieval mystics, and in our attempts at constructing a living cosmology? "Control is the prime characteristic of the addictive organization," Schaef warns.

5. A dysfunctional organization communicates only indirectly (p. 139). A system of triangulation exists wherein there are no direct communications with the victims, but only indirect ones. There is talk about the victim but never with the victim. This approach has been used by your Congregation regarding me for over four years. Secretiveness is a part of the dysfunctional system. And there is "little or no straight talk."

6. A loss of memory is common in addictive persons and organizations (p. 145). Not only has the Vatican lost the memory of the spirit and work of the Second Vatican Council (just one example of this is the failure to practice collegiality between bishops and pope), it has also lost most of the memory of its own mystical roots, the memory of the Cosmic Christ, the memory of a living cosmology in belief and in praxis. **These are exactly the contributions of ICCS—we are "going back" to a time in Western Church history when cosmology was alive and the Cosmic Christ was a living spiritual archetype and when education was about one's place in the universe.** One of your criticisms of my work is that I reject Plotinus' and Proclus' identification of the spiritual journey in the three paths of Purgation, Illumination, and Union. You seem to have forgotten what is best within our own tradition. Plotinus and Proclus were neither Jewish nor Christian and their spiritual

categories were not inspired by the Scriptures. It would be well if the Vatican would **come back with us into the Scriptures** where the spiritual journey is indeed presented in the four paths of *Positiva* (delight and awe), *Negativa* (darkness), *Creativa* (creativity), and *Transformativa* (justice and compassion).

Forgetfulness means that we are frequently unable to learn from past mistakes. The Vatican erred in the sixteenth century in missing the point of Luther's effort to reform the church. Why do you insist on repeating the same error in the twentieth? Creation Spirituality offers an opportunity for renewal to the churches in our critical times. Has the Vatican so quickly forgotten its embarrassment in the Seattle archdiocese in its attempt to depose the saintly peace bishop Raymond Hunthausen? Why is the hierarchy of the church so threatened by creativity that it continually seeks to abort genuine efforts at renewal?

7. The magisterium is failing to grasp its own spiritual heritage and to teach it. Bureaucracy and control and making television personalities of popes is not what the church is meant to be about. As Schaef puts it, "Addictive organizations get into their most serious trouble when they forget to keep the primacy of their mission before them." What is the mission of the church? To preach the Good News, to show people the way **out of sin,** to excite the Spirit of God within humankind and to offer that Spirit as a creative gift to the cultures of our world. Creation Spirituality has been contributing to the fulfillment of this great mission. "Organizations can keep their mission in focus if they can remember their history and can tell it," as Schaef puts it. ICCS is rekindling the memory of Western mysticism. Indeed, we are rediscovering ways to elicit the mystic and prophet from every person as well as to bring together mystical wisdom from all the world's traditions.

What is the alternative to what we are doing? The church's failure to share the great wisdom of our Western mystical tradition constitutes a grave sin of omission which results in patriarchal cynicism and the loss of hope. It feeds the kind of collective hysteria that arouses the christofascists of our day, those who, in the name of Christ or Jesus, terrorize us. Carl

Jung writes, "Loss of roots and lack of tradition neuroticize the masses and prepare them for collective hysteria . . . [which] leads to an abolition of liberty and terrorization."

8. A dysfunctional family or organization refuses to engage in self-evaluation and self-criticism. In its arrogance it sees all its problems as coming from the outside—as if Protestants, liberation theologians, women, homosexual people, theologians of Creation Spirituality, and the press were the source of the church's problems. Such an organization "is willing to face anything but itself."

9. A dysfunctional organization practices isolation. This "allows it to persist in seeing its reality as the only reality" when it stays "out of touch with . . . those it serves, and with the society at large." The amazing success of ICCS began with no endowments and at small Catholic colleges that were traditionally women's colleges, derives from the fact that we are reaching a very deep need in persons' lives today. So much so that people actually sell their homes and travel thousands of miles to study with us. Instead of resenting this work, the Vatican should be learning from it—if it were in touch with the people it was meant to serve. People desire today—as they did in the twelfth century Renaissance—to learn what science is saying about the universe and how this awesome creation story relates to our religious heritage; they desire ritual that awakens, that truly heals and transforms instead of bores them; in their prayer and ritual, they desire to learn from the ancient and earth-centered ways of the native peoples of America, Africa, Asia, and Europe; they want to be empowered by getting in touch with their creativity through art as meditation, which is the most basic form of mystical practice there is. They want to relate their mysticism to the struggle for justice. They want to reground art in spirituality. They seek to recover the mystic child—the Cosmic Christ in themselves and in society: This is why ICCS has such a diverse faculty and why we have so much to teach the churches and synagogues of our day.

10. The dysfunctional organization wants to kill the future. A canon lawyer familiar with Vatican politics told me that what is really at stake between your office and me is that the

Vatican knows I am right, that the only future for the church is spirituality and the Vatican's bureaucratic games are not the future. Nevertheless because your office so resents the future it desires to kill it. To kill the future constitutes the ultimate act of adultism for it renders the young without hope. Artist-philosopher M. C. Richards writes that "the sin against the Holy Spirit is the sin against new life, against self-emergence, against the holy fecund innerness of each person." I fear that a Eurocentric Vatican will leave behind an ecclesial wasteland when it kills the creativity of the churches in the Americas and elsewhere. Today, the power of the Spirit is moving beyond a European context. Recently, I met a German Jesuit priest who has been a missionary in an African country for twenty-three years. He told me that he no longer reads German or French theology, but "Liberation Theology from Latin America and Creation Spirituality from North America." He said these are the theologies to which non-European Christians will increasingly look for direction and inspiration.

Without a vision for the future—with no eschatology—ministers in the church are burning out. Schaef points out that addictive behavior leaves "employees with a sense of moral exhaustion and deterioration." This is very sad, for as Schaef points out, "people are a company's greatest asset. When organizations refuse to recover, they run the risk of losing their best people" (p. 209). An organization that continues to function addictively "can expect to 'bottom out' just like any addict." The Roman Catholic Church is undergoing this bottoming out at this time in history, I am convinced.

Notice that Schaef's language is about recovering. A dysfunctional family is not evil but sick. Yet through this sickness much evil can happen and is happening in the Roman Catholic Church of our time. Like Saint Hildegard of Bingen, Creation Spirituality calls the church to repentance and wellness. In her day, Hildegard wrote the pope the following warning: "O man you who sit on the papal throne, you despise God when you don't hurl from yourself the evil but, even worse, embrace it and kiss it by silently tolerating corrupt men. The whole Earth is in confusion . . . and you, O Rome, are like one in the throes of death . . . For you don't love the King's daughter, justice" (*Hildegard of Bingen's Book of Divine Works with Letters and Songs*, p. 275).

Is the Catholic Church Reverting to Fascism in Our Time?

Fascism arises from the control of creativity and the desire to play God. Creativity requires trial and error, success and failure. A dysfunctional family often requires persons to seek a kind of perfectionism or ideological purity. The result is what American philosopher Susan Sontag defines as fascism: "institutionalized violence." Is the Catholic Church involved in institutionalized violence? So often we hear the defensive remark from Rome that "the church is not a democracy." It would be difficult to argue otherwise. Maybe it should be, however, because democracy is much closer to Jesus' understanding of authority, of his example of servanthood, and of the celebration of the charisms of all persons, of which Paul writes, than is fascism. Surely, Jesus did not intend a fascist institution, did he? Surely, Jesus did not have in mind that the Christian Church would represent the last of the European monarchies. The time for the church to emulate European monarchies is past, in spite of your repeated calls for a "restoration."

What are some signs of creeping fascism in our church? First is your method of dealing with diverse opinions by attempting to silence persons and abort meaningful dialogue. In a healthy and inspirited organization one would expect discussion and dialogue, not the violent suppression of ideas and differences of opinion, not the denial of opportunities for defense or due process of any kind. Your treatment of scholars is not unlike the burning of books in fascist regimes. To silence a thinker is to arouse anti-intellectualism and to promote rabid ideological behavior.

A second sign of fascism in our church is judgmentalism, which is a typical characteristic of the addictive personality and system. There is a big difference between disagreeing with someone and condemning someone—between saying, "I don't like that" and "You are bad." But addictive organizations never make the distinction. "Judgmentalism requires separating from and judging the other, and is nonparticipatory." All the correspondence from your office about me smacks of a mean-spiritedness that suggests that you have utterly lost this distinction.

A third sign of fascism is scapegoating. The venom shown in the documents from your office toward Starhawk, a member of our faculty, begs for some kind of explanation, especially since she teaches only two elective units out of a total of ninety. This woman, who holds masters degrees and is on several graduate faculties in the San Francisco area, has published three scholarly books. Yet she is treated as an object of rancor by you. Is it because she is a feminist? Is it because she is Jewish? Is it because she is trying to recover the Wicca tradition of spirituality, a tradition close to the earth and to the wisdom of the cultures of peasant women, that you are so threatened by what she represents? I find the rancor toward witches to be unbelievable—as if Christians, in killing anywhere from three hundred thousand to three million through the centuries, have not had enough of witch hunts. But you, in the year 1988, seem intent on reinstating them instead of learning from the mistakes of the past.

When the Second Vatican Council formally declared in its Declaration on Non-Christian Religions that it is "foreign to the mind of Christ to discriminate or harass persons because of their religion," it did not make an exception of the native European religion of Wicca. When it acknowledges that "from ancient times down to the present there has existed among diverse peoples a certain perception of that hidden power which hovers over the course of things," it does not make an exception of the Wicca tradition. To seek out scapegoats is an "obscene practice" with "the most sinister social implications," notes psychiatrist Anthony Stevens.

A fourth example of fascism in our church today is the launching of Opus Dei, a secret society of Catholics begun in fascist Spain and spreading broadly over the world today with the special approbation of the Vatican. Today, since the Jesuits of Latin America have rediscovered the social justice imperative of the Gospel, the oligarchies of that land no longer send their children to Jesuit schools but to newly-opened schools run by Opus Dei members.

A fifth way in which our church functions in a fascistic way is in choosing to reward authoritarian personalities. Dr. Anthony Stevens has written about the kind of personality that goes with fascism and in doing so, I believe, offers insight about your work against women, homosexual people, Liberation Theology, Creation Spirituality, and academic freedom. He writes that "The authoritarian character is thus the individual basis of a collective fascism, where the social and political structure is dominated by an order imposed by a single masculine authority. Fascism is the ultimate expression of father-dominance." Perhaps this is why your congregation cannot read straight or see straight or remember the past when I write of "God as Mother." Because fascism—father dominance—has no place for a Motherly God in it.

The authoritarian character is "essentially sadomasochistic." Such a person "admires authority and tends to submit to it, but at the same time he wants to be an authority himself and have others submit to him." These personalities distinguish only two kinds of persons—the strong and the weak. As Stevens puts it, "he worships the former; for the latter he has nothing but contempt. Power fascinates him with all the luminosity of a naked archetype." Such persons become predatory at the first sign of weakness. Yet, just "as all sadists have a masochistic side, so the authoritarian has a need to respect an authority greater than himself. He not only likes to constrain the freedom of those whom he controls but also enjoys the sense of submitting himself to a leader, God, or Fate. As a soldier this kind of man is a martinet to his subordinates but, at the same time, finds deep satisfaction in submitting himself with unquestioning obedience to his superiors. As a monk he will be dictatorial with the lay brethren but totally submissive to the Abbot and the Rule of the Order." Sexuality and aggression, Stevens points out, are unresolved conflicts in such a domineering and fascist personality.

In all honesty, I feel that Stevens' analysis is much more to the point in explaining the aggression and hostility of your attacks on American theologians than are the theological debates. If "the Fuhrer is always right," which is what the authoritarian personality needs to believe, then healthy theological debates will always take a back seat to games of political power.

It concerns me deeply that today's Catholic Church seems to reward authoritarian personalities who are clearly ill, violent, sexually obsessed, and unable to remember the past. I lived and worked for thirteen years in Cardinal Cody's archdiocese and even before the scandals that enveloped him near the end of his life I was asking myself, "How is it possible that a man of this little morality and spirituality could 'make it to the top' in the Catholic Church?" I have learned about the Mothers of the Disappeared in Argentina. I read that, of the eighty-three bishops in Argentina during those hard times of sadistic and fascistic military rulers and torturers of their children, only three bishops spoke out on their behalf. Others were busy giving communion to the military who were torturing the young people.

Last year I taught a class called "Renewing Christian Worship." I believe in the power and importance of worship and therefore I believe in teaching classes to renew it. Creation Spirituality is helping to give people the tools for the renewal of worship. Several hundred persons came to each of our Cosmic Masses. That ought to make our church leaders rejoice and ask: What is going on that was so attractive to people of all ages and backgrounds? So few young adults the world over are interested in worshipping in prayer forms that lack a living cosmology and are therefore boring and tired and increasingly meaningless. (I have been told that only seven percent of the Catholics in your homeland currently attend Mass on Sunday—a pastoral concern, I would propose.)

At one of our Cosmic Masses last fall a group of angry, violent protesters arrived. They tore down our signs and put up their own saying "Cosmic Mess" with hex signs painted on them. Fortunately, we had the assistance of three Native American persons who understood nonviolent techniques and they were able to hold the protesters at bay when they tried to physically storm their way into the building where we were praying. We invited those who were willing to pray with us to do so. Many of them stayed outside and shouted the rosary at us in a hateful tone during the entire liturgy. Several of those who did come in were, in fact, converted by our prayer and thanked our leaders afterward for "a beautiful experience." Following the celebration numerous persons who had come to pray reported that they felt "great reverence" from the Mass; others that they "felt healed," and others reported that they felt a connection between their bodies and their faith "for the first time in their lives." (The theme of the Mass was Thanksgiving for our Bodies.) In short, what many experienced was a beautiful and moving Mass. The Native Americans who were present told me how scandalized they were by the attitudes and actions of the protesters. These Native Americans, not being Christian, have never known persons who would disrupt another group at worship.

It is these same violent protesters who wrote you about our Cosmic Mass. As is your practice, you gave them full credibility and judged me based on their reports without soliciting the viewpoints of others. I am puzzled by the fact that you would take the word of reactionary groups—persons who are untrained theologically and have never given a day of work to church life other than to shout obscenities at theologians with whom they disagree—over the word of bishops, ministers, provincials, Master Generals, and boards of theologians. The only explanation I can come up with has to do with the rise of fascism in the church today.

The Roman Catholic Church today, dysfunctional family that it is, is involved in institutionalized violence. I believe that as the consciousness of people throughout the church is raised, especially in the Americas, the resistance to this trend will intensify.

The alternative to fascism in our church is Jesus' teaching of justice and compassion. "Be you compassionate" (Lk 6:36). Compassion is about our ability to be interdependent, to be equal at the level of being and beauty from God, and interacting through and with one another. As Meister Eckhart puts it, "Love will never be anywhere except where equality and unity are," and "Compassion means justice." Jesus teaches that authority—which comes from the word *author* or *creative one*—is not to be the kind that lords it over others. Part of creativity is to welcome diversity. It is sad to see the Roman Catholic Church, after the explicit efforts of Vatican II to combat abuse, become increasingly tainted by this worldly and sinful abuse of authority. The organization of our church needs a complete overhaul so that beauty and justice might become requirements for leadership once again. It is patent hypocrisy for the church to call for justice in society when it is itself so mired in injustice. The structure as it now stands allows no way to depose the unworthy, the sick, the megalomaniac. This lack of accountability constitutes a serious lacuna in our ecclesiology. It is not unlikely that lessons might be learned in this regard from the impatience of Americans with the so-called "divine rights" of European monarchies.

I believe that intrinsic to all fascism is a heresy which denies the Trinity. Authoritarianism becomes such a total cosmology in the fascist way of seeing the world that God the Creator is denied—that is, creation loses its locus as a place of the sacred, a temple of the Cosmic Christ. In addition, the teachings of Jesus are ignored, and the work of the Spirit—"who blows where it wills"—is aborted.

My Commitment to New Paradigm Education

Twenty-nine years ago the leaders of my Dominican province invited me to go to Europe to study for a doctorate in spirituality. After consulting the monk Thomas Merton, I chose to go to the Institut Catholique in Paris. It was there that the Creation tradition was first named for me by my Dominican brother and mentor, the renowned church historian M. D. Chenu. (So you can see I did not "invent" the Creation spiritual tradition as one of your documents credits me with doing.) Having come of age in America in the sixties, during the civil rights struggles and Vietnam protests, the most pressing issue that I brought to my studies was the following: What is the relationship—if any—between mysticism and social justice? All my writings and work since then have been in some way an attempt to answer this question in theory and in practice.

Upon receiving my degree three years later, I returned to America and taught at Aquinas Institute and at Barat College. It was at Barat, a women's college, that I listened to the stories of women. I learned of their struggles in our culture and my own feminism was born. A nation-wide poll conducted by the National Conference of Diocesan Directors of Religious Education chose me to conduct a study on "Spirituality and Religious Education." I wrote a series of articles critiquing the current efforts at spiritual education in America and offering a blueprint of what a healthy program might look like.

I studied all the programs then operating in this country and found them lacking vis-à-vis feminism, art, social justice, and the eliciting of mystical wisdom in their students. Too much of the typical program was "still a head trip" as a student in one of the healthier programs told me.

Two years later, in 1977, I started the Institute in Culture and Creation Spirituality at a college in Chicago, Illinois. Six years later we moved the program to Oakland, California. ICCS is dedicated to discovering the new cosmology of our time. Cosmology I understand as the coming together of our creation story (we have a new one today from contemporary science), of mysticism (we have a rich tradition of mysticism in the Bible and in the church that has often gone untapped), and of art (the artist must awaken us through music, dance, dreams, massage, native rituals and current rituals to the mystic and the prophet and the artist in all of us so that we pass on the cosmology).

In designing this program eleven years ago, I realized that spirituality could not be effectively taught in a Kantian or Cartesian model of education. ICCS is as much a renewal of education as it is a renewal of our spiritual roots. Our model of education is deliberately right and left brained, that is, it is both conceptual and experiential. It includes lectures and seminars, reading and papers. But it also includes a great deal of "art as meditation": practices ranging from painting and dance and clay and massage to Tai Chi and Aikido and dream work and improvisation. This is its power: we teach people to pray in an adult way that is also a childlike way. We help persons to make the connections between our Western mystical heritage and that of other cultures. The whole goal of the four paths of Creation Spirituality is to become more compassionate, as Jesus teaches. Compassion is about celebration and justice-making. This we teach—and we do a good job of it.

There are innumerable stories of healing and conversion and empowerment that could be told by the nine thousand people who have attended our program or workshops over the years. I would love to tell you of the beauty of these people, the calling they feel to commit themselves to this ancient tradition, to come to the defense of Mother Earth, and to excite our youth with wonder and awe once again. I suggest that you listen to just one of these persons rather than dozens of the sad, violent persons who have written you about us. Read the many letters that tell me how people are returning to Christianity because the paths of Creation Spirituality have been named for them.

Our faculty is unique and diverse. Scientists teach with us, helping us to revision our cosmic story. This is not unlike Thomas Aquinas, who went to Aristotle (a "pagan scientist") to get a similar influx of cosmological truth; we have many artists who lead us in art-as-meditation and body-prayer experiences. We have a Biblical scholar, social justice activists, psychotherapists, and community organizers. Included in the curriculum is a course on "The Wisdom of Native Spiritualities" team-taught by a Native American spiritual teacher (who also leads us in rituals like the Indian sweat lodge); an African spiritual teacher who teaches African dance; and a scholar in the Wicca tradition who is so deeply committed to nonviolent resistance to nuclear weapons that she has spent many days in prison in defense of justice and peace. Others on our faculty have also made such sacrifices for you and me and Mother Earth. All of us on the faculty are feminists to some degree or another. Our students and faculty come from a great variety of religious and spiritual traditions and from all continents of the world.

When Europeans set themselves up as experts on spirituality in other cultures and then condemn it as you do Liberation Theology in Latin America and Creation Spirituality in North America it does not sit well with us. We remember that the last time this was tried a veritable holocaust resulted vis-à-vis the native people of our land. When European Christians landed in America there were eighty million persons here and fifty years later there were ten million. When are you, instead of judging us, going to choose to learn from us? The church desperately needs the ancient wisdom this continent has to offer.

Our work at ICCS has contributed to the reclamation of our rich mystical heritage by translating the writings of the great creation mystics so that they can be read and understood once again.

I have published a translation of thirty-six of Meister Eckhart's sermons with a commentary after each one. We have now published six books by Hildegard of Bingen or about her, plus meditation books by Mechtild of Magdeburg, Nicolas of Cusa, Dante, and Julian of Norwich. We have also made available tapes of Hildegard's music and slides of her mandala paintings.

Recently a mature man, a Jungian analyst in his sixties, who also holds degrees in theology, told me simply, "The Institute in Culture and Creation Spirituality is at the cutting edge of spirituality and education in the world. There is no way that you can allow the Vatican to close it down." I thought this an interesting comment since psychologists are generally non-directive and the passion with which he spoke was so real.

Are you irate at the wisdom and the play, the deep ecumenism and the love of the spirit, the empowerment and the feminism that is happening at ICCS? (Psychologist James Hillman points out that the negative senex—the older person who has lost touch with his or her *puer* or mystic child—projects folly onto others and therefore has no wisdom and no hope for the future.) Instead of trying to kill this joy, why don't you join us? Why not take a year off and step down from your isolated and privileged life at the Vatican to do circle dances with women and men, some in their twenties, some in their seventies, who come from all over the world in search of an authentic spirituality? Alice Miller has worked in Germany over twenty years with victims of Nazis who were wounded by their parents. She believes that it is never too late for a conversion experience. She writes: "The human soul is virtually indestructible, and its ability to rise from the ashes remains as long as the body draws breath." If you could but open your heart, I believe that you could understand and celebrate Creation Spirituality. As Meister Eckhart tells us, "Compassion begins at home with one's own soul and body."

On May 9, 1988, my Master General, as a result of the pressure you exerted on him, imposed on me a period of silence. I am being silenced without any due process, without any direct communication between us whatsoever, in contradiction to the conclusions of the team of Dominican theologians who examined my work, and in flagrant disregard of the wishes of the leaders of my province and Order and the hundreds of persons to whom I have ministered by way of writing, teaching and lecturing over the past eighteen years.

Being silenced places me in very special company. One thinks of my brother Leonardo Boff in Brazil, of my sisters who are silenced by not being allowed to preach the Good News, of the *anawim* whose gifts are not celebrated in churches, of the non-two-legged ones who, while having so much to say, are effectively silenced by a deaf church which is an anthropocentric one. The poor have always been silenced by the excessively powerful. Silencing me will not destroy Creation Spirituality any more than silencing Leonardo Boff destroyed Liberation Theology. The truths of the Four Paths of Creation Spirituality resonate too deeply with persons' experiences to be silenced. Creation Spirituality articulates too clearly "the great underground river" (Eckhart's phrase) of truth found in all mystical traditions of the world—from Goddess to Buddhist to Native American—to be silenced. Creation Spirituality is too familiar a path for those who know the wisdom literature of the Bible to "go away." As Meister Eckhart said, "The path of which I speak is beautiful and pleasant and joyful and familiar." Such good news can never be silenced. You can never silence the hundreds of thousands of persons who have studied Creation Spirituality, are living it, and teaching and preaching it every day.

For my part, I would rather be silent than deaf. For faith "comes from hearing," as Paul says—from listening to the signs of our times and those in pain in our times. I pray that this letter might move you to listen and not just condemn. If it does, you will come to realize that Creation Spirituality is not an enemy of a healthy church but one of the signs of the power of the Spirit in our time. A church that chooses to remain deaf is no longer healthy. It may even be already dead.

As a sign of my continued good faith, I will comply with the wishes of my Master General and, as of December 15, 1988, I will cease "teaching, lecturing and preaching."

Wishing you compassion, I remain your brother,

Matthew Fox, O.P.

In this section we have touched on just seven persons and movements or communities that Cardinal Ratzinger aborted (yes, he who is so completely against abortion!) and denounced. There are more than eighty-five more. Allow me to name just a few. Consider Hans Kung, a Swiss theologian who, with Ratzinger, was the youngest peritus at Vatican II and who made ecclesiology his specialty and actually invited Ratzinger to join the faculty at Tubingen. Consider the late Father Edward Schillebeeckx, a Dutch Dominican who so nobly rewrote the theology of sacraments and gave birth to solid books, one on Jesus and another on Christ. Consider the founder of liberation theology, Gustavo Gutierrez, who was hounded by his Opus Dei bishop so severely that he recently joined the French Dominicans to survive. Consider Jon Sobrino, the Jesuit theologian from El Salvador who was a key theologian to saintly Archbishop Oscar Romero and whom Ratzinger had condemned in his eighties just the past year. Consider Anthony de Mello, an Indian Jesuit and spiritual storyteller who was condemned eleven years after he died. Consider Sister Jean Grimmack, whose ministry has been for thirty years with gay and lesbian Catholics in the United States, who had to leave her order and join another to find refuge from her "heresies." Consider Father Paul Collins in Australia, who established a radio ministry to bring thinking people and the Catholic tradition alive and who has, after constant harassment, left the priesthood. Consider Father Charles Curran, who studied moral theology under Bernard Haring, was banished from his teaching post at the Catholic University of America, and is in exile at Southern Methodist University for the "sin" of asking questions about birth control. Consider Archbishop Hunthausen of Seattle, who had the courage and conscience to refuse to resist the militarism of country and refused to pay his income taxes and who was subjected to fierce attacks by CUFF and by CDF. Consider Ivonne Gebara of Brazil, who held two doctoral degrees and who dared to teach feminist theology and ecology; she was silenced for two years and told to go to Europe to study theology all over again. Consider Father Andre Guindon, who taught at St. Paul University in Ottawa and whose book *The Sexual Creators*, which proposes that sexual intercourse should be viewed as an ingredient of human intimacy and not merely a function of reproduction, was called to Rome six times to defend himself before the CDF; while packing to go the sixth time he died of a heart attack.

Consider the millions of individuals in base communities or in the Creation Spirituality movement or in alive churches like that in Rochester who have had their source of spiritual nourishment cut off by the watch-dogs of so-called orthodoxy. Consider good priests who could not in good conscience be enforcers of Vatican policies on birth control or the exclusion of women. Consider these theologians, many of whom lost their livelihoods, their reputations, and their vocations to serve their communities, effectively aborted.

My experience has been that the most certain test of spirituality is courage. So many of these people are deeply courageous people, truly spiritual people. I have rarely seen evidence of courage on the part of people sitting in bureaucracies and condemning others. A bully is not a paragon of courage.

In the Appendix to this book I have established a theological "wailing wall," a monument of memory to the thinkers and activists who tried to serve their church but were emasculated by the violence of Cardinal Ratzinger and his wrecking crew. It would be good to ritualize the memory of these good (not perfect) souls just as we do at the wall of the Vietnam Memorial in Washington. We must not forget the sacrifices of all those whose lives have been damaged, especially the young, because Ratzinger's CDF was so afraid of the future. When one considers the beauty and sacrifice of so many martyrs in South America alone over the past decades, one is perplexed by Rome's lack of praise. Perhaps there is a hint of what is at stake in the observation by St. Thomas Aquinas seven centuries ago when he wrote: "A tyrant is more afraid of good people than of bad people." There is something about Ratzinger that fears good people.

The great fourteenth-century Dominican mystic Meister Eckhart poses a very important question when he asks, "Who is a good person? A good person praises good people." I have always found this to be a very practical spiritual test. It is not unlike Jesus' observation that "by their fruits you will know them." The fruit of the labors of these theologians and activists speaks for itself. Those who are unable to praise them—and in fact choose to make war against them—render judgment on themselves.

RATZINGER'S ALLIES:
WITH FRIENDS LIKE THESE, WHO NEEDS ENEMIES?

✝

You can tell a lot about a person by the company he keeps and by the people he praises. Publicly Pope Benedict XVI has kept the company with and praised Opus Dei, Communion and Liberation, and the now discredited Legion of Christ, among other far-right-wing groups. He and the previous pope gave Opus Dei (a lay organization dominated by clerics) a near carte blanche that allowed them to operate in dioceses around the world without any interference whatsoever from bishops or others. And since actions speak louder than words—and this is especially the case in a person as glib at words as Ratzinger is—his associations with Opus Dei, the Legion of Christ, and Communion and Liberation will tell us much about what is behind his own words.

Joseph Ratzinger and his mentor, Pope John Paul II, made attacking theologians and movements a priority as we have seen—especially liberation theology and Creation Spirituality and the movements they spawned (base communities with the former, and educational reforms with the latter).

In this section we explore what they did not make a priority: a response to the grave crimes of pedophile priests. Here we find who and what movements Ratzinger and the pope supported.

All these allies share the following points in common: an extreme right-wing political agenda, a fierce theological ideology that is not about studying and interpreting the legacy but essentially about obedience to the pope as the sole teacher and enforcer in the church, and a good deal of financial and sexually scandalous activity that puts a lie to the claim of goodness and righteousness.

Said Jesus, "By their fruits you will know them." The fruits of these individuals and groups supported by Pope John Paul II and Cardinal Joseph Ratzinger are anything but healthy. One bishop, Bishop Morelli in Rio de Janeiro, called them "neurotics for orthodoxy." Indeed, while the priestly pedophile crisis festered for decades with feeble action from the Congregation for Doctrine of the Faith, the head of CDF was instead attacking theologians relentlessly and building up rigid lay movements. Each of these movements was led by a person of questionable character: Escriva in Opus Dei, Maciel in the Legion of Christ, and Cardinal Law in the United States. The latter two in particular were part of the simmering pedophile scandal.

Part of the strategy of Ratzinger and John Paul II for thirty years has been to replace the historic movements of the Jesuit order and the Dominican order and others with so-called "lay" societies that put papal obedience and rigid ideology before intelligent theology and gospel praxis. Furthermore, the papacies that held them up for emulation and privilege also put 95 percent of their moral eggs in the basket of sexuality. Issues such as birth control, masturbation, homosexuality, abortion, and sex outside of marriage became the singular litmus tests for orthodoxy. Even within this narrow and frankly sick preoccupation with all things sexual, these movements flunked their own tests by a mile. The hypocrisy of it all is currently coming to light on a daily basis.

What each of these groups and their leaders have in common is a love of authoritarianism and a fierce resistance to the missing feminine dimension in religion. Their allies are invariably politically and financially and fanatically right wing. Dictatorships are preferred to democracy. Ratzinger Two shares in those commitments. Indeed, he is their champion every chance he can get. Witness how, in the midst of current revelations of sexual coverup and silence, Ratzinger still chooses to appoint a bishop who is an Opus Dei member as the new archbishop (soon to be cardinal) of Los Angeles, the largest diocese in the United States. Here Ratzinger's true agenda is revealed.

CHAPTER 6

OPUS DEI

✠

A FEW YEARS AGO WHEN I WAS ON A lecture tour in Germany, a German journalist invited me to have tea in downtown Frankfurt. As we were talking, he motioned to the window overlooking the busy street in downtown Frankfurt and said, "See all those new skyscrapers going up all around us? Every one of those skyscrapers is a financial institution. The center of European finance is moving today from Switzerland to Germany because of the Euro and the EU. And," he pointedly said, "at the top of each of those skyscrapers is Opus Dei."

I was severely struck by this lesson. For years I had wondered why this secret organization was so important to Cardinal Ratzinger and the previous pope—why they bent all the rules of canonization to rush the founder into sainthood in record time and with no authentic debate (testimony from long-time members of Opus Dei was not even sought, and if offered was rejected by the usual saint-makers contrary to the rules of canonization). For years rumors have circulated that Opus Dei members have been appointed to the American Supreme Court by Republican administrations as well as their serving as heads of the FBI and CIA. Since Opus Dei is as secretive as it is, the truth has been difficult to affirm or deny. We do know for certain that the greatest traitor in American history, Robert Hanssen, about whom the film *Breach* was made, was a long-time CIA principal who gave away state secrets that resulted in the killing of more American spies and contacts than anyone in history. Hanssen was a devout Opus Dei member. We also know that Opus Dei loves to target professional power people, as a recent correspondence from Ireland describes: "The secret organization Opus Dei has targeted the socially powerful in Irish society, and many public servants would be slow to protest against a group when such dissention may result in covert professional censure."

Many persons are slightly familiar with Opus Dei through the best-selling novel by Dan Brown (and the movie that followed) titled *The*

Da Vinci Code, which presents the organization in a sinister light and does not hide its penchant for strange spiritual practices such as self-flagellation. The Opus Dei ideology also came through strongly in Mel Gibson's sadistic portrayal of Jesus in his strongly anti-Semitic movie, *The Passion of the Christ*. Gibson employed both Opus Dei and Legion of Christ priests to advise him on this movie. Andrew Greeley, a respected sociologist and best-selling novelist as well as a Catholic priest, calls Opus Dei a "devious, antidemocratic, reactionary, semi-fascist institution desperately hungry for absolute power in the church. It ought to be forced either to come out into the open or be suppressed."

Cardinal Ratzinger and Pope John Paul II pushed relentlessly for special privileges for Opus Dei in the Catholic Church, including an unprecedentedly swift canonization of its founder, now known as St. Josemaria Escriva de Balaguer.

Opus Dei is a highly secretive organization that as of 2005 boasted about 85,000 members in eighty-seven countries. It has three times the number of members than do the Jesuits. It finds itself in very high places both within the Catholic Church and in the secular world.

Michael Walsh, a former Jesuit who is currently librarian at Heythrop College, University of London, as well as author of *The Triumph of the Meek: Why Early Christianity Succeeded* and editor of *Butler's Lives of the Saints*, has written an extensive study of Opus Dei drawn from many interviews with members of the organization, as well as previously unavailable documents including its very well guarded Constitutions.

Under Pope John Paul II, the group became "for all practical purposes, an autonomous entity." The spokesman for the United States Conference of Catholic Bishops, Russell Shaw, like the spokesperson for Pope John Paul II, Dr. Joaquin Navarro-Valls, was a member of Opus Dei.

Walsh found it "sinister" that he was not allowed to speak directly with Opus Dei members without their first getting permission from higher-ups within the organization. Secrecy or "discretion" is paramount. "A member will admit to belonging, but will not say who else belongs." There are three classes: full members or "numeraries" (about 30 percent);

"oblates" who live outside Opus Dei residences but share similar commitments (20 percent); and "supernumeraries," who are still governed by the Constitutions of Opus Dei (50 percent). Walsh found the society, which on first glance seems to have a healthy emphasis—that of laypeople at work in their professions—to be, on further investigation, "priest-dominated, narrow in outlook, and ultraconservative."

In its origins, Opus Dei was part of the National Catholicism movement in Spain following the Civil War. "Its fundamental tenet was the identification of being Spaniard with being a Catholic. Love of country was to be associated with a rejection of all heterodoxy, Protestant or Jewish, liberal or socialist. Religious faith and political identity were as one: they were integral"—thus they were known as *integristes*, as were similar right-wing movements in France and elsewhere. In this same spirit, the late Pope Pius XII sent Generalissimo Francisco Franco a telegram congratulating him on his victory in the Spanish Civil War, calling it a "Catholic victory." Students became "the preferred objective" and Opus Dei "operates secretly among university students."

Founder Escriva decided that clericalism should trump laity in his "lay" organization and he wrote this up as Maxim 61: "When a lay person sets himself up as a master in moral matters mistakes are frequently made: lay people can only be disciples." From after the Second World War to 1950, Opus had established centers in Spain, Italy, Portugal, England, France, Ireland, Mexico, the United States, and Chile. Those who joined as numeraries were expected to take traditional vows of poverty, chastity, and obedience—and from this point of view the Opus Dei command structure is like other Catholic religious orders. "What was odd was Escriva's insistence that Opus Dei was not a religious order at all, but a lay organization. At that level it did not make sense. Nor did it make sense when the male and female branches are compared. Escriva was unable to take women seriously and equal to the male members of his institute."

Hierarchy played a big part of the Opus mentality. There were three classes of members and "movement up these grades depended on the whim of Escriva and his consulters." Other religious orders were disbanding the rigid hierarchies, for example, of lay brothers and clerics, while Escriva was imposing them. From 1951 to 1964 Opus Dei established itself in additional countries, including Colombia, Venezuela, Germany, Peru, Guatemala, Ecuador, Uruguay, Brazil, Austria, Japan, Australia, and the Philippines. Its University of Navarra in Pamplona, Spain, though private, received public funding for many years. Its two best-known departments are business studies and journalism—two areas that Opus especially yearns to influence.

In its special desire to recruit young candidates, Opus Dei sets up university halls of residence both for men and for women such as Netherhall House in Hampstead (one of the more expensive areas of London), Greygarth in Manchester, and Grandpont in Oxford. In the diocese of La Rioja in Spain the rector of the seminary complained that the Opus Dei members within and outside the seminary were waging a kind of war and heresy-hunting crusade that was dividing the seminary and the diocese itself, and that this situation was happening elsewhere in Spain as well. All this came about after Pope John Paul II (and Ratzinger) gave Opus Dei the status of "personal prelature." This status means that local bishops cannot control or oversee Opus Dei; only the pope has such full and final authority. Walsh comments: "It is difficult not to think of Opus as a church within the church, which is exactly what the Spanish bishops were afraid of when they lobbied Rome unsuccessfully against granting Opus the status it now, quite clearly, enjoys."

When Escriva died on June 26, 1975, his successor, Father Alvaro del Portillo (ordained a bishop and prelate of Opus Dei in 1982), offered this observation as part of his funeral homily: "In addition to having God our Father who is in heaven we have our own Father who is in heaven, and from there he concerns himself with all his children." This language became something of a slogan to the Opus Dei members culminating in his canonization.

Escriva, as president of Opus Dei, preferred before all titles that of "Father." And he preferred his members to be children in relation to himself, as he writes in his Maxim 457: "Who are you to pass judgment on the decisions of a superior? Don't you see that he is better fitted to judge than you? He has more experience; he has more capable, impartial and trustworthy advisers; and, above all, he has more grace." As Walsh comments, "Father knows best."

Further, Escriva praises victimhood, calling it beautiful (Maxim 175), and he calls for intransigence, coercion, and shamelessness (Maxim 387). Masochistic practices of wearing a *cilice* for two hours a day and taking the discipline at least once a week are prescribed in the Constitutions. Such practices might begin with a member who was only fifteen years old and who heard the stories of how Escriva would spatter his blood on the walls of the bathroom in his zeal to perform such rites. I know a Chilean whose parents were Opus Dei who tells me that as children the family would gather to pray the rosary and he was forced to kneel on bottle caps throughout the ordeal. His knees were bloodied on a regular basis. Part of the Opus Dei "spiritual practice" ideology is to create suffering.

Nor did Escriva have a good opinion about the rest of the church. In fact, he seems to define his movement in opposition to others in the church. He wrote: "As I have not ceased to warn you, the evil comes from within [the church] and from very high up. There is an authentic rottenness, and at times it seems as if the Mystical Body of Christ were a corpse in decomposition, that it stinks . . . Ask forgivingness, my children, for these contemptible actions which are made possible in the Church and from above corrupting souls almost from infancy." Confession to an Opus Dei priest was insisted upon so rigorously that Walsh recognizes it as "a major form of social control. Its use by members is restricted in practice to priests who are themselves members, and it is used to inspire feelings of guilt because of failure to live up to the highest ideals and thereby damaging the whole institution." Sounds like a sect to me.

A Jesuit priest and clinical psychologist who studied the *Cronica*, a private journal circulated within Opus Dei, expressed "alarm" about its deliberate theological confusion of God as "our Father" and Escriva as "our Father." He called the way Opus Dei deals with prayer and young people a "highly manipulative approach." The common maxim in Opus Dei, that "filial fear is the gateway to live" may "sum up the whole Opus approach," but "it's got nothing to do with the Gospel." Might the filial fear apply to a member of Opus Dei toward the founder who is also "Father"? There is a striking distrust of conscience in the teachings of Opus which in fact promote an "ideology of submission." Obedience of heart and mind frees members, we are told, from a "sterile and false independence . . . that leaves a man in darkness when it abandons him to his own judgment." Yet conscience is—as Thomas Aquinas taught seven hundred years ago—about one's own judgment. That is why it is so honored.

While claiming that it is solely interested in the work of "souls," Opus Dei aligns itself with political powers wherever they may be. As early as 1951, Opus members were working in Francisco Franco's cabinet. Opus Dei made rapid advances in the Franco government under Admiral Luis Carrero Blanco, an Opus Dei sympathizer who, as premier, virtually ran the country. Until Carrero's assassination in 1973, Opus Dei leaders were arguably the strongest conservative political influence in Spain. Two cabinet members were Opus Dei, and the director of Spain's biggest bank and the director of another large bank were also. The Opus Dei group at one time controlled four ministries as well as numerous lesser government posts. Walsh points out that "there is no argument that, from the mid-1960s to the early 1970s, General Franco chose a number of his government ministers from the ranks of Opus members. Most commentators would regard the number of Opus ministers at any one time as surprisingly large."

Professor and priest Raimundo Panikkar (who died on August 10, 2010, during the writing of this book), was a member of Opus Dei in his early days. Panikkar believed that Opus Dei set out to see if they could take charge of the Spanish state—and almost succeeded. One Opus Dei member published the following observation in the Madrid daily *ABC*: "Freedom of conscience leads to loss of faith. Freedom of speech to demagogy, mental confusion and pornography. Freedom of association to anarchy, and to the rejection of totalitarianism." Franco thrived on the support that Opus gave him as a Catholic organization.

Archbishop (later Cardinal) Pietro Palazzini in 1972 was secretary of the Roman Curia in 1972 and an Opus Dei supporter who denounced the Spanish bishops when they began to distance themselves from Franco and his policies of oppression. A very contentious issue took place in the Spanish church when faked documents were inserted in the press to take issue with the Asamblea or gathering of Spanish bishops and clergy representatives in September 1971. (Two members of Opus Dei, including its future head, had authored the faked documents.) When the bishops made a concerted effort to begin distancing the church from the Franco regime, this did not sit well with Opus Dei. Walsh draws lessons from this sordid affair: "The affair of the Roman documents reveals the degree to which Opus has been prepared to manipulate the media in pursuit of what it sees to be either its own good, or the good of the Church—though for Opus members the distinction is an unreal one . . . In such a context it is easy to understand why Opus appears to put such a premium on the media, controlling magazine television companies, schools of journalism." In many countries Opus members publish extensively in local newspapers. American Archbishop John Foley, the former president of the Pontifical Council for Social Communication (i.e., the mass media), is a strong

Opus Dei sympathizer. Opus Dei has inserted itself more and more into the American media as well.

Opus Dei came into full flower and favor when John Paul II became pope. Opus Dei, which had courted the pope since his days as archbishop of Krakow, invited him to speak at various Opus Dei centers in Europe and at their headquarters in Rome. When in Rome for the funeral of John Paul I, he went out of his way to pray at the crypt of Escriva, who had died three years earlier. John Paul II personally ordained Opus Dei priests, and Father Fernando Ocariz, an Opus Dei priest, served as a top adviser to Cardinal Ratzinger's Congregation for the Doctrine of the Faith. More and more Opus Dei priests and sympathizers were appointed bishops in Latin America, Europe, and, more recently, the United States. The future head of the largest American diocese, co-adjutor archbishop Jose Horacio Gomez of Los Angeles, is a priest of Opus Dei, ordained as such at age twenty-six in 1978. Says a Vatican correspondent about the prelature, the pope "likes their activism, their anticommunism, their internal compactness where no plurality of ideas exist."

Two years ago I received correspondence from a theologian who knows the Peruvian church well. He wrote the following:

In Peru Opus Dei bishops are everywhere. All of the major cities are now under their control. There are 13 to 15 of them which is nearly half of the Peruvian episcopacy. It's clear that they've been given a *carte blanche* by Rome to disassemble anything connected with liberation theology and the popular church. The most insidious of them all, because he's simultaneously smart and vicious, is [Cardinal] Juan Luis Cipriani, the archbishop of Lima. When he was the archbishop of Ayacucho in the early 90s he described the human rights efforts of NGO's and people in the church as "bullshit." He was also a buddy of Fujimori [the former president of Peru] who is now in jail for murder and corruption.

The m.o. of Opus in Peru has been to first drive out progressive priests, even those who are essentially centrist. They then go after any church-related groups that work in the area of human rights and social justice. In the indigenous areas of the country, specifically Cusco and Puno, they've shut down anything connected with pastoral work focused on Andean culture.

More recently we had a follow-up phone conversation in which he said an obvious pattern is developing in Latin America, where in Peru now 35 to 40 percent of the bishops are Opus Dei. "They have a game plan: to control the universities. They are also getting aggressive in the indigenous areas of Peru. Lots of racism is involved. The Opus Dei archbishop of Lima is currently involved in a huge legal fight in Lima to take over control of Catholic University. It is about money as well as ideology, because the university owns a lot of real estate. They expelled the Maryknoll order and shut down social justice centers everywhere. It is going to happen here in the United States as they amass more and more power. Los Angeles is an example. Yes, the CIA is involved. They are lining up their ducks."

Opus Dei was very influential in Augusto Pinochet's Chile. Opus Dei members and sympathizers supported the CIA-backed coup that overthrew Chilean president Salvador Allende, and one of them, Hernan Cubillos, became General Pinochet's foreign minister. He was later identified as an "important" CIA agent by the *Los Angeles Times*. In his book *The Church and Politics in Chile* (1982), Professor Brian Smith, who teaches politics at the Massachusetts Institute of Technology, makes the case that Opus Dei members were among the first chief administrators of the brutal military regime of General Pinochet, which threw over, with the CIA's help, the duly elected government of Salvador Allende and subsequently tortured and killed many citizens (the recently retired president of Chile was one of those tortured by the Pinochet regime). In December 1975, the Latin American newsletter *Noticias Aliadas* published a story that Opus Dei in Chile had begun receiving funds from conservative foundations in the United States as early as 1962 and, with this money from the CIA, had opposed the unions that brought Allende to power.

Penny Lernoux established that "Opus Dei and Fatherland and Liberty [a right-wing terrorist group] worked together in Chile during the Allende years, and General Juan Carlos Ongania, dictator of Argentina from 1966–70 seized power after making a religious retreat sponsored by Opus Dei." One Opus priest wrote a regular column under the name of Ignacio Valente in the Santiago daily *El Mercurio*, a paper sympathetic to Pinochet's government. While other priests protested Pinochet and were tortured for it, this Opus priest remained committed to his writing ministry on behalf of the brutal right-wing government. Under Pinochet over 400 foreign priests were expelled and several indigenous priests were murdered when the dictator said the church was trying to set itself up as "a new political party." He warned: "all those who go around defending human rights and such things would be expelled from the country or imprisoned." He made true on his threats.

In the 1970s the German Catholic aid agency Adveniat gradually replaced the CIA as the helpmate of the military regimes in South America. Adveniat was controlled by bishops sympathetic to Opus Dei, including Cardinal Höffner, archbishop of Cologne and a close friend of Ratzinger's. Höffner attempted in August 1984 to hand two parishes of his Cologne diocese to two Opus Dei priests, but the parishioners protested so vehemently that he had to abandon his strategy. Martin Lee wrote in *Mother Jones* in July 1983 that CIA money went to support an Opus "think-tank," the Chilean Institute for General Studies.

In Bogotá, Colombia, the elite families now send their children to Opus Dei schools, "where they will not be exposed to the new 'theology of liberation' with its concern for the restructuring of society in the interest of greater justice for the poor."

All this makes it a bit hard to swallow the claim Escriva made in *Time* magazine: "Opus Dei has nothing whatever to do with politics. It is absolutely foreign to any political, ideological or cultural tendency or group." Another apologist writes: "Opus Dei is not to the right or to the left or to the center, as the aims of the Association are not political but spiritual." Is this another element Ratzinger admires about Opus Dei, its claimed political neutrality, which is in fact a cover-up for its support of tyrants? Yet its Constitutions say clearly: "Public offices, and especially those which involve management, are the institute's particular means of its apostolate" (para. 202). Walsh comments: "The truth is more complex. Opus spirituality and structures inculcate a view of life which is socially stratified, self-confessedly committed to the bourgeois ideal, highly disciplined and over-respectful of authority." A student of its activities in Latin America comments that "its strong endorsement of a class society can also be used as a rationale by the middle and upper classes to justify their lifestyles, even though they may not be members. And because it serves the purpose of the upper classes, it is able to exert an influence on the political and economic situation."

Currently, instead of the brave churchmen who stood up with the poor and for social justice after Vatican II, Rome has appointed Opus Dei hierarchy all over Latin America: at least three bishops or archbishops in

Argentina, two in Brazil, two in Venezuela, and one each in Colombia, El Salvador, Equador, Paraguay, and Uruguay. In the United States Opus Dei bishops now preside in Newark, Kansas City–Saint Joseph, Brooklyn, and Los Angeles. In Canada Opus Dei operates five houses in Montreal alone, and Canadian bishops and/or cardinals preside in Hamilton, Ottawa, Montreal, Quebec City, Toronto, and Vancouver. Cardinal Marc Ouellette of Quebec City is on his way to join the CDF in Rome.

Opus Dei has been called the "holy mafia" because of its frequent scandals. Banking and financial disgraces abound in the recent Opus Dei history. In May 1985, $250 million was paid in the name of the Vatican to creditors of Banco Ambrosiano, which, by Pope John Paul II's own admission, was undergoing a financial crunch. Walsh hints that Opus Dei may have had much to do with picking up the bill. At the same time the Vatican went to bat for Opus Dei in Spain, seeking exemption from taxes for the society. Walsh presents a strong case that the Vatican Bank, operating through the Banco Ambrosiano, was helping to finance despotic regimes in Latin America that were engaged in the persecution of priests and nuns who worked with the poor and oppressed there. "The Banco Ambrosiano scandal, the rise of Opus and other similarly sectarian organizations within Roman Catholicism, are all evidence of a Church which is today divided against itself."

Lernoux found that Opus Dei apparently had been negotiating with Roberto Calvi, head of Milan's Ambrosiano Bank, to save the Vatican Bank financial losses and embarrassment. Calvi's body, either murdered or a suicide, was found hanging from Blackfriars Bridge in London. His widow said he had been in touch with Cardinal Palazzini, the Opus Dei sympathizer in charge of Escriva's beatification process as prefect of the Congregation for the Causes of Saints, about the rescue operation "presumably to be carried out with the help of Opus Dei members who owned or controlled banks in Spain. The trade-off, according to Vatican observers, was to have been a takeover by Opus Dei members of the Vatican Bank and the Vatican Radio, which had been controlled by the more progressive Jesuits. Letters were found on Calvi from Francesco Pazienza, a Calvi aide with links to Italian and U.S. intelligence, in which Pazienza referred to contacts between Cardinal Palazzini and Calvi."

Among recruitment strategies for Opus is to offer an Opus Dei "club" where youth can find a second home. "Alienation of children from their families go hand-in-hand with the creation of dependency upon Opus."

This tactic is also found among other sects in their eagerness to enlist young followers. Go to the alienated. Many rewards follow, including a pilgrimage to Rome and the Opus Dei headquarters. Young recruits are instructed not to tell their parents about their joining Opus Dei. One mother said of her daughter, who had joined Opus Dei after a recruitment at Lakefield, an Opus Dei catering college in Hempstead, London: "She used to be a marvel of a daughter, and now she has become secretive and introverted." Visits home are severely restricted. Often the children are under eighteen years of age.

People who leave Opus Dei endure severe hardships. One woman who left comments, "When you leave you become a non-person, and no one who is a member is allowed to help you. When a person leaves Opus he or she is on the street, financially, spiritually, psychologically." Raimundo Panikkar, who became a distinguished philosopher and theologian in his own right, says that for Opus Dei members all grace leading to salvation comes through the founder. It is through the grace of the founder that you are what you are. Cut off early in life from their natural family, Opus Dei members come to depend exclusively on their Opus Dei identity. This is very close to other cultic groups, such as the Moonies—only in this instance it comes with the papal seal of approval.

Walsh observes the Opus Dei is the "sworn enemy" of liberation theology, which no doubt endears it to Cardinal Ratzinger. "Opus is the doyen of the neo-conservative movements within the Catholic Church. It is the most powerful, with members in high office in government of Catholic countries round the world [not just Catholic countries—the United States too, as we have seen], and in influential posts in the media and in business."

The right-wing movements in the church are appealing to Rome, Walsh believes, because they are "centralist, and so is the Vatican," which is alarmed by increasing independence of bishop conferences around the world. But also "movements can be mobilized, can be used by the Roman powers that be." Sects are also protest groups against secular society (a big bugaboo for Ratzinger). Sects believe they are right and everyone else is wrong. As one Opus document reads: "We are the remnant of the people of Israel. We are the only ones who, having remained faithful to God, can still save the Church today. Given the state of the Church today, it seems as if it were abandoned by the Holy Spirit. We are the ones who can save the Church by our faithfulness to the Father." Compare this to Ratzinger's comments on the state of the church—they are practically identical.

Walsh observes that "the process of turning [Josemaria] Escriva de Balaguer into a saint had begun long before his death: it was something he connived at." Written before his canonization, these words by Walsh seem prescient: "Given the power, and the wealth of Opus Dei the canonization of its founder seems inevitable . . . Escriva has friends at court." *Newsweek* religion journalist Kenneth Woodward commented that his canonization process proceeded contrary to established procedures. No published writings critical of Escriva were included in the documents given to the judges of his cause. Of the nine judges, two voted against the canonization. The congregation did not investigate Escriva's well-known conflicts with the Jesuits, or reports of his pro-fascist leaning, and Opus Dei's involvements with the Franco government. Amazingly, 40 percent of the testimony came from just two men: Alvaro del Portillo, who died in March 1994, and his assistant, Father Javier Echevarria, who was elected Opus Dei prelate less than a month later. At the beatification process of Escriva, not only was the testimony of the woman who served as his secretary for seven years ignored, so too were observations by Vladimir Felzmann, who claimed that he knew from personal knowledge that Escriva was sympathetic to Hitler, that Escriva had considered joining the Greek Orthodox Church because he was so in opposition to Vatican II, and that he had a severe temper and expressed it on many occasions. Instead, there were attempts made to discredit these hostile witnesses. Monsignor Flavio Capucci declared that protesters against the beatification were ecclesiastical dissidents and are those who give trouble to the church in doctrinal matters also.

Walsh offers his summary of Opus Dei in the following words: "It is, I firmly believe, a basic tenet of Christianity that faith in Jesus Christ should be a liberating force in people's lives, that it should free them to become more themselves, more in charge of their own destinies. Opus with its rules and regulations, its censorship, its control of the minutiae of members' day-to-day living, its class-related structures, its association with elites of wealth and of power, as I have attempted to describe in this book could not claim to be a force for liberation. And to the extent that it fails this test, it is not merely, as a sect, less than Catholic. It is less than Christian."

Who is Escriva, whom Ratzinger and Pope John Paul II so admired and rushed into canonization? One person who knew him well and watched him closely is Maria del Carmen Tapia, who worked for eighteen years inside the organization—seven of those years as his secretary. Maria was born in Spain in 1925 and joined Opus Dei in 1948. She was expelled in 1966 and was subject to a profound persecution before and after her expulsion. She calls the beatification of Escriva (her book was written before his canonization) and its procedural irregularities "scandalous."

Tapia wrote a memoir of her years in Opus Dei. In it she calls Opus Dei members "fanatics" and notes that most members, "particularly the young, have no knowledge of their Founder's bad temper or of Opus Dei's political maneuvering and nepotism in Spain under the Franco era Plan de Desarrollo." Seeing her role as a witness from within the organization, she lists her credentials. She held executive offices in the central government of Opus Dei and worked in the women's branch in Spain and Italy and with the founder. She headed the women's section in Venezuela for more than ten years and had close contacts with Opus Dei women in Colombia, Peru, Chile, Argentina, and Ecuador. She saw it from the inside, not from visits carefully arranged and chaperoned, as so often happened when visitors would come to the Opus Dei centers. Among her charges are that obsessive secrecy rules within the organization and that a "giant puppet show is staged" behind the closed doors of the Opus Dei headquarters in Rome, where superiors "pull the strings to manipulate their members, men and women, all over the world, invoking their legal commitment of obedience." The "formation" of candidates for Opus Dei is more of an "indoctrination."

Money raised for the poor, the homeless, and the unemployed appears not to go to these causes at all but rather to Don Alvaro's name in the Bank for the Works of Religion—though the organization claims to raise money for the poor, she never saw any activities Opus Dei sponsored for the poor, homeless, or unemployed. Opus Dei concentrates its work with "intellectuals from the sciences, banking, and the law; in a word, with the groups who control the money and power in a country. Opus Dei women do apostolate with the wives of influential men."

Opus Dei is very eager to recruit young people (under eighteen years of age) from schools, clubs, centers for extracurricular activities, and university residences, while it also hosts its own schools that recruit children from kindergarten through university age. In the United States they are the Heights School (for boys) in Potomac, Maryland; Oakcrest School (for girls) near Washington, DC; Montrose School (for girls) near Boston; and Willows Academy (for girls) and Northridge Preparatory School (for boys) near Chicago.

In the United States Opus Dei operates residences and centers for young men and women near universities: Petawa Center for women and Leighton Studies Center for men near Marquette University in Milwaukee; another on Follen Street in Cambridge near Harvard; the Woodlawn Residence for men in Chicago; the Chestnut Center at 2580 Chestnut Street in San Francisco; a center near Boston College in Boston; and the Office of the University of Navarra in Berkeley on College Avenue near the University of California. Today there are also centers near Notre Dame University in South Bend, Indiana; in Washington, DC; in Valparaiso, Indiana; and in St. Louis. Superiors at the Notre Dame site coach the students on which theology professors they should and should not enroll to study with.

There is a "constant sexual obsession within Opus Dei," notes Tapia, and informers reside in Opus Dei's female student residences to ensure that "nothing is spontaneous in the ordinary life of an Opus Dei residence of university women." Escriva had an "obsession with security," and in the women's headquarters in Rome, "nobody, absolutely nobody . . . can just open a door and go out."

There is restriction of reading materials and no discussion of world religions. Mail is opened and confiscated. Surveillance of members was common, and microphones were placed in various rooms of residences, which were connected to Escriva's room.

A cultic worship of Father Escriva abounds—constant talk of "the Father has said," "the Father passed through there," "the Father likes," and so on. An atmosphere prevailed that was "like a police state: between the coldness of the superiors, my reclusion, the commandments from on high, and the letter of the spirit instead of the spirit of the letter."

The theological developments of the Second Vatican Council were ignored and disparaged even when it was in session in Rome. Ordinary members are kept in ignorance, and this lack of information "increases the power of the directors, who feel powerful because they know what all the rest do not. Sadly, this sort of practice is familiar to citizens of totalitarian countries."

The most significant area of silence in Opus Dei was that surrounding Monsignor Escriva. From the most trivial to the most important, many details were hushed up. "Many things and many individuals are silenced in Opus Dei. They disappear in silence. Those who left Opus Dei, those who committed suicide or tried to, those who became insane are never mentioned. Even great care is taken not to mention priests who leave

Opus Dei." Many who leave, based on their experience in Opus Dei, regard it "as a sect which has managed to lodge itself within Catholicism."

An anti-intellectualism reigns in Opus Dei. "Opus Dei silences critical minds . . . As soon as someone—who may even be a priest—is outstanding in the field of philosophy or theology Opus Dei will almost certainly end by silencing him. He disappears. Opus Dei hides him. He frequently ends up by leaving the institution or becomes the patient of a psychiatrist . . . There is an 'internal censorship' that reviews articles, books, lectures, or anything that a member wants to publish . . . Outside Opus Dei institutions there are no Opus Dei philosophers or theologians particularly well known and respected for their work at other institutions besides the University of Navarra . . . Philosophers and theologians have no place. This is publicly recognized. I say nothing new but observe a fact."

Tapia was herself held as a prisoner in the headquarters of Opus Dei from November 1965 to March 1966: "I was held completely deprived of any outside contact with the absolute prohibition to go out for any reason or receive or make telephone calls or to write or receive letters. Nor could I go out for the so-called weekly walk or the monthly excursion. I was a prisoner." She was subjected to what she calls "a secret-police interrogation. The most normal things were interpreted as 'war crimes.' What I did not realize then was that these methods of asking about the same thing a thousand times is exactly what is done by the security forces in all repressive regimes. What is intolerable is that in the name of God and the church, Opus Dei would use such an approach to 'obtain information.' After all, the Inquisition was abolished centuries ago. Here, again, the Opus Dei system is identical to that of any sect."

She was forbidden to step out of the building, and when a friend from Venezuela came to see her she was lied to on the phone, being told that Tapia was not in the building. Tapia lost twenty pounds and her hair turned completely white from this ordeal. "They had broken me." Before long the "moment arrived when I doubted my sanity . . . Years later I understood that Opus Dei had brainwashed me; the agents were Marlines Kucking, Mercedes Morado, and, whether directly or indirectly, Monsignor Escriva."

At one particularly harrowing meeting with Escriva, he was in a fit of rage and shouted to priests who were present, "Take that one [referring to a woman named Gladys], lift up her skirt, take down her panties, and whack her on the behind until she talks. MAKE HER TALK!" And turning to Tapia this "saint" said: "You're a wicked woman, sleazy, scum!

That's what you are! Now go! I don't want to see you!" A series of interroga-
tions followed and "advisers" were stationed both inside her room and outside her room who followed her even to the bathroom. "I began to shake
almost constantly as a result of my terror. I was afraid they would take
me to a mental institution as I knew they had done to other members of
the Work." At her final interview with Escriva, he said: "You are a wicked
woman! A lost woman! Mary Magdalene was a sinner but you? You are a
seductress with all your immorality and indecency! You are a seductress! I
know everything . . . You're wicked! Wicked! Indecent! Come on! . . . Hear
me well! WHORE! SOW!"

By subterfuge she was able to sneak a phone call out to an old friend
who was a journalist in Rome, and he arranged her harrowing getaway.
After her escape, Tapia could say to a priest who inquired how she could
still believe in God with all she had been put to, "God has nothing to
do with Opus Dei." At the canonization process of Escriva, Tapia was
forbidden to testify, as were a number of other persons who saw him in
his darker moments. Her book, though it appeared in 1997, was apparently never consulted by those who pushed the canonization through its
very abbreviated though very costly process. The once famous function of
the "devil's advocate" (traditionally employed to raise questions that might
otherwise not be considered about a person's character at the process of
canonization) was eliminated by John Paul II in 1983. "Slander and defamation were used in order that church tribunals reject as untrustworthy
witnesses certain persons able to supply clarifying testimony" in the beatification process of Escriva. Tapia calls the experience of reading the Summary of the Process for the Cause of Beatification of Escriva "painful" and
the pious pronouncements of his holiness a "mirage of sanctity."

Escriva notoriously displayed an unusual penchant for gathering fancy
titles for himself. Walsh calls this "totally unheard-of behavior in any other
saint—at least after his or her conversion. It is a clear occasion of embarrassment to his biographers." In 1968 Escriva petitioned for the title of Marques
de Peralta. He also accepted Spanish decorations such as the Grand Cross
of St. Raymond of Penafort, the Grand Cross of Alfonso X the Wise, and the
Grand Cross of Isabel the Catholic, among others. This despite a line in his
maxims, found in his treatise *Camino*: "Honors, distinctions titles, things of
air, puffs of pride, lies, nothingness" (Number 677).

Tapia does not exempt herself from having fallen for the deceits
of Opus Dei. "I speak about what I know, because to my shame I must

confess that I, too, used the weapon of silence within Opus Dei, accepting and participating in the game of discretion." (Beating of one's body was encouraged so much so that Escriva was reported to have left blood markings on walls of rooms that he occupied, and Tapia testifies that during her stay in Opus "I treated my body with brutality.")

Escriva "did not know how to be alone." He was "rough, brusque, and rude. When he was angry and had someone to reproach, he had no control in his language. His offensive, violent words profoundly wounded persons." While he was "saintly before the multitudes, . . . he was capable of the most terrible insults for the slightest reason. For instance, if a fried egg was not done to his taste, he would abuse the director of the house. If an altar cloth did not hang exactly at the stipulated number of centimeters above the floor he was capable of scolding the director; similarly, he would go into a rage if there was a noise in the kitchen when the pots and pans were scrubbed." Tapia believes that "during the last years of his life, I am convinced that Monsignor Escriva suffered from some psychological disorder since, otherwise, it would be totally inconceivable that a priest, with the aura of a Founder, would say things such as 'If I knew that my parents had not desired me when I was conceived, I would have spit on their tomb.'"

Tapia's book became a best-seller in Spain, Germany, Portugal, and Italy. Some responses to Tapia's book in America, in addition to the deafening silence from Vatican circles intent on beatifying Escriva, included the following comment from the *Boston Globe*: "A fascinating and disturbing book . . . a literary grenade seeking to blow apart Opus Dei's benign and exalted image . . . a picture of an obsessively secretive, manipulative and sexist organization with a virtual cultlike veneration of its founder." If this is so, how could Cardinal Ratzinger be such a strong supporter? Is he also in favor of sexism, manipulation, cultlike attitudes, and obsessive secretiveness? What about its anti-intellectualism? Is he, who prides himself on being a theologian, also in fact anti-intellectual?

The magazine *Conscience* praises Tapia for taking "a long hard look into the heart of darkness behind their [Opus Dei's] familiar descriptions and a far more sinister picture emerges." And *Christian Century* recommends the book for "all who wish to see religion freed from the tyranny of self-proclaimed saints."

Where does Ratzinger stand vis-à-vis the sinister darkness of Opus Dei? Above all, why were Ratzinger and his boss at the time, Pope John Paul II, so enamored of Opus Dei that they would entrust the future of the church to its hands, appointing numerous bishops and cardinals, first in Latin America and ever increasingly in North America, from that organization? Why would they sacrifice all credibility in the canonization process by rushing through the canonization of a Hilter admirer?

If we list all the elements of Opus Dei that have been revealed in this chapter we can put together the following elements that shed light on Cardinal Ratzinger, who has proven such a champion for their cause.

Clericalism
Hierarchy
Money and access to it in high places
Questionable financial dealings
Women as second-class citizens
Women as objects of abuse ("Pull up her skirt")
Extreme right-wing politics including support of Latin
    American dictator torturers such as Pinochet and
    fascists such as Franco and Hitler himself
Anti–Vatican II
Anti–liberation theology
Anti–base communities
Heresy-hunting crusades
"Father knows best"
Do not trust conscience
Obedience first!
Ideology of submission
Ascetic "spirituality" of personal mortification and
    masochism
Anti-intellectualism
Anti-"secularism"
Bias in favor of totalitarianism
Champion of centralized papal power
Anti-ecumenical

In my estimation, these elements of Opus Dei practice and ideology seem to feed and nurture the opinions and positions of Pope Benedict XVI very well. His loyalty to these allies help to shed light on his own priorities and understanding of lay spirituality. His allies become something more: his shock troops, his front guard, on whom Rome can always depend since for them obedience to authority trumps anything called conscience or theology. His and John Paul II's untiring support of Opus Dei also sheds light, I believe, on their equally fierce resistance to letting go of celibacy as a requirement for the Catholic priesthood as an issue of control. It boggles the mind that anyone could call a person who praised Hitler a "saint."

Perhaps the final word around Opus Dei and Escriva should reside with his personal secretary of seven years: "My astonishment is infinite when I hear now that Monsignor Escriva is in the process of beatification." But Escriva is just one ally of the past two popes. There are more to come.

THE LEGION OF CHRIST AND FATHER MACIEL; COMMUNION AND LIBERATION AND CARDINAL LAW

✠

The Legion of Christ and Father Maciel

LIKE FATHER ESCRIVA'S OPUS DEI, Father Marcial Maciel's Legion of Christ was a favorite order of Pope John Paul II and Cardinal Joseph Ratzinger. So enamored of Father Maciel was John Paul II that he invited him on his plane on several occasions when traveling to South America. The two organizations, Opus Dei and the Legionaries, have much in common—indeed the pope saw them in the same light, with Maciel's group boasting of its roots in Mexico and Escriva's in Spain. Both were in bed with aristocratic millionaires, extremely hierarchical, extremely patriarchal, admiring of uber-right causes (Maciel of Pinochet, the Chilean dictator), and run very tightly. In fact Maciel's had a special twist to it: a vow was demanded of its members that they never criticize Maciel or their other superiors and that they report anyone who did. Secrecy trumped everything, and spying was part of the vow. Both were fully committed to papalolatry. Whatever the pope says goes. They made the perfect vanguard for a new and anti–Vatican II religious movement.

As it turns out, there were an extraordinary number of secrets to be kept under wraps. Thanks to some deep investigative reporting by Jason Berry, author of *Vows of Silence*, we have quite a catalog of those secrets at this time. Berry

Father Maciel with Pope John Paul II

calls Maciel "the greatest fundraiser of the modern Roman Catholic church" and a "magnetic figure in recruiting young men to religious life in an era when vocations were plummeting." Both these causes no doubt endeared him to the pope and his chief inquisitor. But what a price was paid! In addition to being a genius at fund-raising (often going after rich widows and well-connected right-wingers, including American Thomas Monaghan, the owner of Domino's Pizza, who later founded Ave Maria University in Florida), Maciel lived several other lives behind the scene. Legionaries called their leader "Nuestro Padre," or "Our Father" and considered him a living saint. Malise Lagarde, who was a member of the Legion for thirteen years, commented after leaving that "members are not allowed to question or think outside group-think. I know that members totally dismiss any discussion of the Legion and Regnum Christi as a cult—I did when I was still part of it—but it sure looks like one once you get out." As in many other cults, the order forbade its members to mix freely with their families.

Maciel founded the Legion of Christ in 1941 and devised a scheme of greasing the palms of many a cardinal in Rome to ensure its success. One Mexican widow of a successful industrialist is said to have donated $50 million to the Legion. In 1958 Maciel managed to build a seminary in Salamanca, Spain, from monies he was given from Josefita Pérez Jiménez, the daughter of a former Venezuelan dictator.

The facts are these. "Maciel was a morphine addict who sexually abused at least 20 Legion seminarians from the 1940s to the '60s." Bishop John McGann of Rockville Centre, New York, was informed of a seminarian who was sexually abused by Maciel from age thirteen to twenty-six. Father Vaca wrote Maciel: "I had arrived at the Legion in my childhood, with no sexual experience of any kind . . . It was you who initiated the aberrant and sacrilegious abuse that night; the abuse that would last for thirteen painful years." Bishop McGann did the right thing and sent a letter by this former Legion priest with complete allegations to the Vatican in 1976, again in 1978, and again in 1989. Nothing was done. Ratzinger did nothing. Ratzinger, it seems, was too busy denouncing theologians the world over than to go after a darling of the pope. Come the 1980s, Maciel set up three families, two in Mexico and a third in Switzerland. In total he appears to have fathered six children by three women and adopted a seventh. His middle son, Raúl, now twenty-nine, tells the story of how his father molested him and his brother from the ages of eight to fourteen.

As teenagers they resisted his advances. Maciel met Raúl's mother in 1977 when she was nineteen years old and working as a domestic servant. Maciel was 57. Raúl sought $26 million from the order to remain silent; he is now suing the order. Maciel supported his girlfriends generously, leaving just one of them homes valued at about €2 million. The two older sons protected Maciel's third son, younger and adopted, by pushing Maciel away and refusing to allow him to be in the room alone with the youngest son. His daughter also was sexually abused by "Our Father." There was even an occasion when Father Maciel brought his children to receive communion from the pope, telling him they were his "nephews."

Meanwhile, the Legion flourished under Pope John Paul II's "Teflon" papacy. Indeed, on January 3, 1991, the pontiff himself ordained sixty Legionaries as priests at St. Peter's Basilica in Rome in the company of seven thousand Regnum Christi members (Regnum Christi being the lay wing of the order), fifteen cardinals, fifty-two bishops, and many millionaire benefactors. The video of this event proved to be a great fund-raiser and recruitment tool for the Legion, which is present in twenty-three countries with 120 seminaries, dozens of elite prep schools, several religious formation houses, and several universities. Today the Legion claims to have eight hundred priests and 2,600 seminarians worldwide, along with 75,000 lay members in Regnum Christi. In 2008, the order's assets were estimated at $25 billion with a $650 million annual budget, according to the *Wall Street Journal*.

The late pope held Maciel up as "an efficacious guide to youth" and did not cease to praise him even after an exposé in the Hartford *Courant* in 1997 laid bare his drug habits and abuse of seminarians.

In 1998, eight ex-Legionaries filed a canon law prosecution against Maciel in Cardinal Ratzinger's CDF tribunal. But Ratzinger did nothing for six years. It was not only Ratzinger who protected him. Maciel was supported by other very powerful Roman Curia figures, such as the secretary of state from 1990 to 2006, Cardinal Angelo Sodano; the prefect of the Congregation for Institutes of Consecrated Life and Societies of Apostolic Life, Cardinal Eduardo Somalo; and Archbishop Stanislaw Dziwisz, the onetime secretary of John Paul II, who was later made cardinal and archbishop of Krakow, in spite of the fact that he allegedly charged people great sums of money to come see the pope pray his private Mass, $50,000 a shot!

In 2004, despite damaging facts about his conduct that were by then quite public, Maciel was honored by John Paul in a Vatican ceremony appointing the Legion to administer an educational and conference center in Jerusalem called the Notre Dame Center.

Cardinal Sodano is now dean of the College of Cardinals in the Benedict XVI pontificate, and Somalo became *camerlengo*, the papal chamberlain in charge of the conclave that elected Benedict XVI. Maciel is said to have gifted both Somalo and Sodano with lots of cash. When the facts came out about seminarian sexual abuse in 1997, Somalo did nothing. Neither did Ratzinger. One ex-Legionary recalled that "Cardinal Sodano was the cheerleader for the Legion. He'd come give a talk at Christmas and they'd give him $10,000." Another priest remembered a gift of $5,000. For nine years the 75,000-member lay auxiliary, Regnum Christi, denounced the seminary victims on their Web site and compared Maciel to Christ for refusing to defend himself and undergoing a "new cross" with "tranquility of conscience." Sodono is the same cardinal who interrupted Easter Mass at St. Peter's in 2010 to praise Pope Benedict XVI and called the pedophile accusations on his watch "petty gossip."

Sodano had forged a special relationship with Maciel in Chile in the 1980s, during the Pinochet dictatorship. Sodano was then papal nuncio and appeared on TV often to support Pinochet even while his regime was torturing priests and nuns and abducting people. Cardinal Silva of Chile at first resisted Maciel's group, known as the "millionaires for Christ," but then approved of their presence in Chile. Later Maciel hired Sodano's nephew, Andrea Sodano, for a project he was constructing in Rome and paid him well over $800,000 for work that the younger Sodano apparently never accomplished. In 2008 Raffaelo Follieri was indicted in New York on fraud and money-laundering charges; Andrea Sodano was vice president of his group. Cardinal Sodano had attended a launch party for Follieri in New York. Follieri is now serving fifty-four months in a federal prison, having pled guilty to fourteen counts of wire fraud, money laundering, and conspiracy.

Maciel's supporters were not just certain members of the Roman Curia, however. Steve McEveety, who produced Mel Gibson's movie *The Passion of the Christ* (and invited Legion priests to advise on the film), supported Maciel, as did former Florida governor Jeb Bush and former senator Rick Santorum of Pennsylvania. Father Richard John Neuhaus, a loud champion of right-wing Catholic causes, wrote that he knew with "moral certainty" that the charges against Maciel were "false and malicious." Former U.S. ambassador to the Vatican Mary Ann Glendon spoke of the "radiant holiness" of Maciel and his "success . . . in advancing the New Evangelization." She taught at Regina Apostolorum Athenaeum, the Legion's university in Rome, and helped plan the order's first university in America, the University of Sacramento. William Bennett, spokesperson for all that is righteous and moral and right-wing, who can be seen regularly on CNN, also praised the Legion of Christ as a "cause for hope in a time of much darkness."

Ratzinger, whose job as prefect of CDF was to investigate charges of priestly abuse, did not act for eight years. Instead of going after Maciel, he hired a canon lawyer to shelter him and demanded "professional secrecy" in doing so. This same priest, Tarcisio Bertone, worked under Ratzinger to shelter Father Maciel by creating "professional secrecy" for clergy and was rewarded for his dutifulness by being named archbishop of Genoa. He was made a cardinal in October 2003 and voted in the papal election that chose Benedict XVI. He currently serves as Vatican secretary of state (it was he who blamed pedophilia on homosexuality). Indeed, when an American journalist, Brian Ross from ABC's 20/20, approached Ratzinger as he was entering his limousine at the Vatican and asked why there was no action against Maciel, Ratzinger hauled off and slapped him. (I saw this exchange on television along with millions of others.)

After he became pope, Ratzinger opened an investigation of Maciel in December 2004 but then shut it down abruptly six months later. Finally, in 2006—ten years after his congregation first learned of Maciel's sordidness via Bishop McGann—Benedict gave Maciel orders to lead a "reserved life of prayer and penance." Though dozens of individual lives had been profoundly damaged by this man's sexual abuse—including his own children—meager punishment was meted out. Indeed, Ratzinger told a Mexican bishop years earlier that it would not be "prudent" to punish someone who had done "so much good for the church." For many years abuse was heaped by the Legionaries and their admirers on Catholic journalists Jason Berry and Gerald Renner for pursing the case.

In 2008, Maciel died in Jacksonville, Florida, at the age of eighty-seven. His daughter and her mother arrived at his bedside, causing quite a scene among Legion members who were present (and some not so present, who hurried to his bedside to shut the case up). Legionaries were told by their leaders that Maciel "ascended to heaven."

Only in 2009 did Ratzinger instigate a serious probe into Maciel's story and appoint five bishops to investigate. Today their investigation is completed and the pope is committed to appointing a special delegate and a commission to study the Legion's constitutions. Says author Jason Berry, Maciel's "life was arguably the darkest chapter in the clergy abuse crisis that continues to plague the church."

This sick man and his sick order and his sick theology were not only tolerated by then Cardinal Ratzinger and Pope John Paul II—it was held up for imitation and trumpeted as the wave of the "New Evangelization." Why? The reasons parallel what we have seen with Opus Dei. Strict obedience to the pope (and anyone who claims to speak in his name) is key, plus access to money (the assets of Legion of Christ are estimated to top $20 billion), the support of dictators and right-wing ideologues, keen opposition to liberation theology and base communities, and a completely antiwomen patriarchal mind-set. These ideologies go very far with Ratzinger's allies, and ideology trumps theology every time.

Communion and Liberation and Cardinal Law

Cardinal Bernard Law came to national attention in the United States as the priest pedophile scandal emerged in all its fury on the front pages of the *Boston Globe* in 2002, while he was archbishop of Boston. Law's name will forever be associated with that sad and ugly episode in American Catholic history—and for good reason. Legal documents show that he oversaw the passing on of pedophile priests from diocese to diocese and from parish to parish in the Boston archdiocese during his eighteen years as archbishop. Just one of those priests, John Geoghan, was accused of having molested 150 youths. Law kept reassigning him, including an eight-year stay in a parish in Weston, where, according to records, he abused at least thirty boys.

Rather than resign when these and other horrors emerged, Law stubbornly stayed on as archbishop for two and a half years, until a petition signed by fifty-eight priests, pressure from lay groups, the cry of the media, and the pursuit of the attorney general of the state of Massachusetts finally forced him to step down. Perhaps his stubbornness is partially explained by his champion, Pope John Paul II, who is reported to have flown into a rage when discussing with key U.S. prelates whom to appoint as archbishop of Boston in 1984. "The pope rose, took off his papal ring, laid it on the table and barked, 'No more weaklings!'" it is reported. On finally stepping down, Law was "rewarded" by being given a fourth-century basilica in Rome to oversee. His salary is $12,000 per month. He was also given a particular honor after Pope John Paul II died when he was asked to lead a special public Mass at St. Peter's. He holds a post in nine Vatican congregations, including one that nominates candidates for bishop worldwide, and as a member of the Congregation for Clergy has a role in handling sexual abuse cases that are sent to Rome.

John Allen of the *National Catholic Reporter* once called Cardinal Law "the poster boy" of the American scandal. Peggy Noonan remarks: "He has also become the poster boy for the church's problems in handling the scandal. And that has to do with its old-boy network, with the continued dominance of those who grew up in the old way." It also has to do with the powerful group Communion and Liberation, which he is in league with and has no doubt had a lot to do with his weighty influence even after the pedophile scandal in his diocese. Many people feel Law should be in jail for his cover-up of such crimes.

In the wake of the Boston scandal, which in turn blew the lid off of many other similar goings-on, Frank Keating, the Catholic former governor of Oklahoma, was named chairman of the American bishops' National Review Board, which was assembled to investigate charges of clerical child sex abuse. Governor Keating later quit his post in disgust and declared: "The American Catholic Church faces a seismic upheaval, and the Catholic lay community is angry and getting angrier. Dioceses are paying huge sums of lay money to settle cases. Recently, the attorney general of Massachusetts—himself a Catholic—writing of the Boston archdiocese, declared that the mistreatment of children there was 'so massive and so prolonged that it borders on the unbelievable.'"

Seven Catholic dioceses have declared bankruptcy because of these scandals: Tucson, Spokane, Portland, Fairbanks, Davenport, Wilmington, and San Diego (though a court voided the latter). Many other dioceses have cut back drastically on their "good works" to the poor. (One priest in charge of Catholic support of the poor in a major American diocese came to see me and cried, saying that because of the pedophile lawsuits and the building of an expensive new cathedral, all workers in his office were let go; he had to rely completely on volunteers. He was seriously considering leaving the church.) So far the scandal has cost the Catholic laity who have contributed to the church some $3 billion to foot the legal bills amassed.

Father Thomas Doyle, an American Dominican priest in good standing and a canon lawyer, most of whose ministry has been as an army chaplain, warned the bishops many years before the news of priestly pedophilia broke about the scandal that they were sitting on. They did little or nothing. (Only in 1993, when lawsuits multiplied, did they institute procedures to address the issue of priestly pedophilia.) Rome did less. Cardinal Ratzinger, whose responsibility it was to pursue such matters as head of CDF, did nothing. Doyle declared, "What we have experienced in our lifetime is a disaster the horror of which is perhaps equaled by the bloodshed of the Inquisition, but which certainly makes the indulgence scam that caused the Reformation pale by comparison. The deadliest symptom is the unbridled addiction to power." The addiction to power seems to permeate the curial bureaucracies of the Vatican. How wonderful it would be if they were all to take a long sabbatical and meditate on this one observation by Carl Jung: "Where love reigns, there is no will to power; and where the will to power is paramount, love is lacking."

An "addiction to power" seems to be a particularly Ratzingerian problem, as illustrated in the following true story. A few years ago I was talking with an American theologian who had studied under Ratzinger when he received his doctorate in theology at a German university. He knew Ratzinger well, and he was so upset by what Ratzinger was doing as chief inquisitor—silencing and expelling theologians right and left—that he made a special trip to Rome to confront him. Ratzinger did meet with him, and they had a serious exchange in German. On exiting the Vatican this former student of Ratzinger's shook his head and said in disgust, "It is all about the pursuit of the purple." In other words, it is all about his addiction to power. This happened before Ratzinger was elected pope.

A few years ago I invited Catholics to write me about how they felt about the goings-on in Ratzinger's church. I received many touching letters from laypeople, priests, sisters, and brothers—more than forty in total. Their grief, their anguish, their loss, and their longing for a better church are extremely moving and inspiring. The vast majority of them asked that their names not be used in order to prevent retaliation or being fired from their jobs. This is what the Catholic Church has become in our time—a place of fear. Mahatma Gandhi has said that "where there is fear, there is no religion."

Cardinal Bernard Law is no ordinary Catholic citizen or Catholic bishop. He was the man who time and time again carried water for the Curia and forces in Rome represented by Cardinal Ratzinger. He was "widely regarded as the pope's man in the United States," reports Penny Lernoux. Law was one of the few American bishops who supported Rome's disciplinary actions against Archbishop Raymond Hunthausen of Seattle, Washington, who had the courage to stand up against the Vietnam War and refused to pay his income taxes in protest. Law went on record in the presidential election of 1984 and denounced the Democratic vice presidential candidate, Geraldine Ferraro, for her stand on abortion. This fed into the Republican myth that the country's bishops opposed the Democratic presidential slate. One bishop actually said, "It's almost been said that if you vote for the Democratic ticket you've committed a serious sin." (More recently, in the 2008 election, several priests have preached the same message about those who voted for Barack Obama, and Rome has not silenced them.)

One bishop said about Cardinal Law that he was "perceived by the bishops as currying favor with Rome, and the bishops don't like it." As a result, Law's efforts in 1986 to get himself elected conference president or vice president and as a delegate to the synod on the laity in Rome in 1987 were all defeated. Eighteen different ballots in all rejected him. Law was a "loner" among the bishops, and he sided with the Reagan administration and opposed his brother bishops by favoring aid to the Contras in their war against the government of Nicaragua. He threw his red hat in with those in Rome who wanted the pope to hold all powers and the bishops none. He was a diehard champion of centralization. "His view of bishops' conferences paralleled that of Cardinal Ratzinger, who believed that they got in the way of Rome's relations with individual prelates. There was only one collegiality, said Law—'a worldwide college of bishops under Rome.'" This position contradicts the teaching of Vatican II.

In 1986, during a graduate ceremony at Boston College, a Catholic Jesuit institution, Cardinal Law wagged his finger at the audience and "lectured the amazed assembly about the need for Catholic universities to avoid the temptations of secularism." Such scolding did not go over with educated Catholics in Boston, but no doubt it appealed to people like Ratzinger in Rome, one of whose favorite themes is the church versus the secular world. Law became to be seen as "the papal enforcer in church communities that have become more democratic through Vatican II's reforms." Because Law, like Ratzinger, dismisses the power held by bishops' conferences, he represents a "reassertion of Roman hegemony over the American church," comments Lernoux. Without the protection of bishops' conferences, it is much easier for Rome to pick off particular bishops one by one and enforce its ideology.

Law set out to establish a $3.5 million think tank called the Pope John Paul II Institute, whose job would include assisting the writing of a new catechism. Law appointed Philip Lawler to work with the institute and to edit the Boston archdiocesan newspaper, the *Pilot*. Who was Philip Lawler? He was the founder of a right-wing Catholic organization called the American Catholic Committee, which opposed the bishops' pastoral on nuclear warfare, among other things. Lawler had been director of studies at the Heritage Foundation, which was set up by New Right strategist Paul Weyrich, a leader in the campaign against Archbishop Hunthausen.

It was actually Cardinal Law who proposed the "universal catechism" at the 1985 synod—"even though the bishops' conference had not asked for it—did not in fact want it." Ratzinger was very taken with the idea, however. Traditionally, the various bishops' groups would create their own catechisms. Having one universal catechism put together by Ratzinger's CDF would be one more nail in the coffin of bishops' conferences. "The catechism project was not popular among American bishops, who saw it as another attempt to assert Roman control over local dioceses." Law adopted the agenda of Cardinal Ratzinger and Pope John Paul—one that put sexual moral issues ahead of any other. "Law is more interested in sexual issues than in war and peace—children are dying daily from abortion, he said, but nobody is dying from nuclear war."

Yet this is the man—the one who plays by the book and who banned lay preachers and insisted that nuns return to their traditional place in the church—who not only sat by idly but was actively involved in the passing on of pedophile priests and the cover-up of these illegal and immoral goings-on, whose diocese was bled of $85 million in a settlement reached with more than five hundred plaintiffs, and never went to jail. He never truly apologized. Instead he was elevated to a new post in Rome, where he now works and lives quite comfortably in the style that Roman cardinals have enjoyed for centuries. Law has friends in high places.

One action that Cardinal Law undertook that helped endear him to his Vatican sponsors was importing Communion and Liberation personnel to his diocese in Boston. Law established the Communion and Liberation movement in Boston, only the second diocese in America to do so

(New York was the first). Up to that time Communion and Liberation was essentially an Italian right-wing movement, "the Italian version of Opus Dei," says Lernoux. But just like Opus Dei and the Legion of Christ, it was destined, with the support of Vatican powers that be, such as Ratzinger, to be imported to other countries like a cancer on the body of Christ. All it needed was sycophant hierarch to jump on board—one who would endear himself to those in influential places. Enter Cardinal Law of Boston who, according to investigative reporter John Allen, was "another cardinal with historic ties to Opus Dei." He had a friend from his college days, William Stetson, who became a priest of Opus Dei and worked closely with Law on several assignments in the Vatican. When Law was made a cardinal in 1985 he invited the prelate of Opus Dei to his honorary dinner in Rome.

Who and what is Communion and Liberation? It is another sect that, according to Michael Walsh, has surpassed Opus Dei in influence in the Catholic Church. It is less secretive and much more explicitly activist than is Opus Dei. One observer talks of its "militant interventionism in temporal matters, which has made it the highest-profile Catholic pressure group in Italy."

The founder of Communion and Liberation (CL) is Don Giussani, a diminutive Milanese priest who started it in the early 1970s as a conservative student backlash to the student unrest of the 1960s. (Notice the parallel with Joseph Ratzinger's 1968 "conversion" owing to student unrest.) A Spanish photographer interviewed Giussani and reported afterward: "He has an Opus air about him," meaning his spirit smacked of that of Opus Dei. Of course it is different also insofar as it is Italian and not Spanish in its origin and is younger and less structured than Opus Dei and does not favor whips or *cilices* in its spiritual practices. In addition, it is anything but secretive. "CL openly proclaims its intention to change Italian society, frequently taking the Italian bishops and the Christian Democrats to task." But like Opus Dei its philosophy is integralism, which means the imposition of Catholic doctrine on society through control of the government. Like the most radical fundamentalists in the United States, it harbors no distinction between church and state but wants the state to represent the church agenda in all matters. And like Opus it harbors a deeply authoritarian structure, and, as one former member put it, "spirituality was reduced to a hard choice between Catholicism and a corrupt world." This is the "secularism" that Ratzinger is so fond of invoking.

CL has been called "Wojtyla's lackeys," "Wojtyla's's monks," "samurai of Christ," and "Stalinists of God" because of their aggressive and fundamentalist promotion of traditional Catholic values and beliefs, and their devotion to the pope. Many Italian bishops have resisted it. "The movement has caused havoc within the Italian church and politics and has a vast network of secular operations throughout the country, including a number of influential publications and, until recently, its own political wing, the Popular Movement, regarded by many as a distinct Catholic party." Lernoux comments: "John Paul's open support of CL as a universal model for the laity frightens bishops around the world, who see it as an attempt to resurrect an integralist model of society." Cardinal Law very much supports this model in the United States.

Giussani's ideas and words "underlie every utterance of the movement and have influenced many outside it, including leading figures in the Church like Cardinal Ratzinger and Cardinal Biffi of Bologna." Giussani's perspective is called both "rigid" and "confrontational" regarding both church and secular matters. The CL publishing house Jaca Book is one of the major religious publishing houses in Italy, and it has published many of Ratzinger's books as well as Biffi's. In addition, Ratzinger has often appeared in interviews in their journal, *30 Giorni*.

Like Pope John Paul II and Cardinal Ratzinger, the Communion and Liberation philosophy takes a dour view of Western society, "perceived as teetering on the brink of a moral abyss," that is all about the "intrinsic moral evils" of contraception, direct sterilization, autoeroticism, premarital sexual relations, homosexual relations, artificial insemination, abortion, and euthanasia. These are all condemned in Pope John Paul II's encyclical *Veritatis Splendor*, in which he presents a world view that is "essentially dualistic." The movements he espouses are "the embodiment of a perfect society" while "outside is the world, which is evil." This dualism "became the dominant message of John Paul's pontificate"—and Ratzinger's too as is evident in his encyclical *God Is Love*. Nothing about pedophilia, however, is condemned outright.

Communion and Liberation is anti-ecumenical. Giussani finds the root for all these evils to arise from an "invasion of non-Catholic thought in the church" arising from "an influence which I would call protestant by which Christianity is perceived exclusively in the context of the relations between the individual and Christ." No such emphasis is put on the individual in his organization. The recruit should demonstrate no personal initiative. "Just one thing is required: 'He must follow. That different human presence he has encountered is an "otherness" that must be obeyed.'" Obedience is everything. Does this sound familiar?

The essence of CL's ideology is twofold. First, it is antimodern and finds its inspiration "in Catholic thinkers of the past—sometimes the remote past; second, its aim is not so much to formulate solutions as to denounce errors." CL sets itself up in opposition to today's "secular world." They support "a retreat from the conciliar view that grace is present throughout the world; instead, it promotes a return to the fortress mentality in which the Church is the repository of all truth and goodness, and all outside is error." In this context Karl Rahner's theology is crypto-Protestant because it says God and the grace of Christ are in all things. "They rejected Vatican II's call for Catholics to work with all men of good-will for a more just society."

Those who have lived in a group like CL tell us that an underlying conviction is that "the institution is infallible . . . the institution becomes totally identified with God." Comments Gordon Urquhart, Catholic journalist and former sect member in Focolare who wrote *The Pope's Armada: Unlocking the Secrets of Mysterious and Powerful New Sects in the Church*: "These are views which would shock and repel most Catholics yet they are the fundamental precepts of the movements that were presented by the Vatican in 1987 to the bishops of the world as the definitive model for the laity." A "crusading righteousness" follows, as Lernoux puts it, and particularly vulnerable are teenagers, who like the energy evoked by the message that "we are right and we will save society."

Paul Josef Cordes was the prime advocate and protector of the new movements in the Roman Curia. He was bishop of Paderborn in Germany until the late pope appointed him vice president of the Pontifical Council for the Laity in 1980. (He is now a cardinal and president of the Pontifical Council *Cor Unum*.) Cardinal Cordes sees the movements "as a new justification for the papacy—as their protector—and has developed a theory of *communio*, or Church unity centered on the pope." It became clear during the Lay Council in Rome in 1987 that he orchestrated that this and other sectarian movements derive much of their influence in Rome precisely because they represent "direct rivals" to the base community movement of Latin America. On a visit to New York in 1986, Cordes, ever the cheerleader, praised CL by saying, "You should trust Communion and Liberation. They are splendid young people. They have the pope's approval. The Holy Father hopes they will take charge of the whole university apostolate in the United States."

CL is a "bitter and vociferous" opponent of liberation theology that was only too happy to support Colombian Cardinal Alfonso Trujillo's campaign against progressive elements of the Catholic Church in Latin America and especially base communities and liberation theology. In 1981 CL launched a magazine, *Incontri*, to carry on this cause in Rome. This magazine later morphed into *30 Giorni*, one of Ratzinger's favorites.

At that gathering of the Lay Council in Rome the bishops from around the world "burst forth in their full fury" in denouncing CL. One Spanish-language group of bishops protested: "Some movements imagine they are going to save the world and behave as though they know the only way to be authentically Christian. They tend to self-sufficiency. Sometimes they have a spirituality of a pietistic kind which stresses personal satisfaction with not the slightest effect on life." Another Spanish group accused CL of rejecting the option for the poor, and still other bishops objected to the personality cults of the founder and "a tendency to become the self-appointed watchdogs in the local churches" as well as their fundamentalist theologies. Yet these objections never made it to the final report that the pope read. In fact, one year after the gathering the pope promulgated the encyclical *Christifideles Laici,* in which he praises such groups as models for laypersons.

Many bishops have been appointed from the ranks of CL. As one observer has put it, "in addition to members who have become bishops, CL has many highly placed friends." Pope Benedict XVI "wholeheartedly shares CL's negative view of the contemporary church and believes that the new movements are the *only* positive development of the period following the council . . ." Most welcome to Ratzinger's worldview is the fact that CL believes in "a hierarchical church in which authority is unquestioned and total obedience the pre-eminent virtue." He was "CL's greatest ally." They also fit a mold that, to put it benignly, "devalues reason . . . They are militantly anti-intellectual"—even though they recruit mainly among college students.

Ratzinger considered himself a longtime friend of Monsignor Giussani, and he personally celebrated his funeral Mass. According to Vatican reporter John Allen, during this time Ratzinger told a priest of CL that Giussani "changed my life." Allen also reports that the papal household of Benedict XVI is now run by consecrated members of CL (*Memores Domini*) and that Pope Benedict joins them weekly for their School of Community. He also chose to speak to their gathering while he was campaigning for the papacy.

The sordid stories of Escriva and Opus Dei, of Maciel and Legion of

Christ, and of Cardinal Law, who tolerated serial rapist pedophile priests in his diocese while all the time championing Communion and Liberation, should not be seen as a mere case of bad judgment on the parts of Pope John Paul II and Cardinal Ratzinger. It is much more than that. Behind their enthusiastic endorsement of these men and their uber-right sympathies and organizations is a well-thought-out strategy, a strategy in opposition to the letter and the spirit of Vatican II. Above all, they are reactions against an event of 1967.

In 1967, after the conclusion of the Second Vatican Council, Pope Paul VI convened a Third World Congress for the Apostolate of the Laity. Composed of delegates sent by the world's bishops, it "sent shockwaves through the church with its call for a degree of democratization and elected representation for the laity. It was the last gathering of its kind." Instead, the Vatican invested in the sect movements of Opus Dei, Communion and Liberation, Legion of Christ, Focolare, the Neocatechumenate, and others. Gordon Urquhart put it this way: "With the movements, the Vatican was putting its money on a new breed of layperson, tightly controlled by their respective organizations which vowed collective allegiance to the central authority of the pope." As for a creeping democracy in the Church, forget it! "The founders of the new movements have all spoken out vigorously against the idea of democracy in the Church—hardly surprise in view of their own hierarchical structures." Hierarchical structures and fascist sympathies, one might add.

In October 1987, a very different Synod of the Laity was convened in Rome. This time Cardinal Ratzinger spearheaded the event, and in his opening speech he "practically sanctions membership of the movements as mandatory for all lay Catholics." Joseph Ratzinger admits his bias in favor of these fascist sects, in which "we see certain kinds of movements which cannot be reduced to the episcopal principle, but rather draw support, both theologically and practically, from the primacy of the pope."

CL now enjoyed support "from the highest levels of authority in the Church. They had come of age. The proposal that they should form the Pope's shock-troops had been accepted. John Paul II was now their chief supporter and champion" and he gave an official speech at their second Convention in which he proclaimed the movements "indispensable and co-essential" with the hierarchy. While the pope protected them from the interference of local bishops, they took up his cause by stressing centralization in the church. As bishop of Krakow, the future pope Karol

Wojtyla had supported Communion and Liberation as well as other sects, "all of which were well established in Catholic Poland long before the fall of communism." What most appealed to Ratzinger and other centralists about these sects was "the total obedience the new movements professed to the successor to Peter's throne: they were prepared to carry out his will to the letter, and they had the resources to do it. They were conveniently centralized in Rome, with a disciplined and effective chain of command headed by charismatic leaders who were owed unquestioning obedience."

CL possesses "staggering wealth" verging on the "colossal," including an annual turnover of nearly 2,000 million lira and 200,000 partners in manufacturing, service industries, and privately run social services. An umbrella organization known as the Company of Works gathered more than five thousand companies under it so that it is possible for CL members to bank, shop, educate their children, receive health care, and take vacation within the structures provided by the movement. Its political philosophy is to privatize social services, including schools, hospitals, and employment agencies. CL stood strong against the Referendum on Divorce that passed nonetheless in 1974. The church saw this as a major defeat, "a watershed in the battle against secularization." An abortion referendum came to a head in 1981 in Italy, and CL went into action in a big way to oppose it. But only a third of Italians went along with them.

Today, with the pope's and Ratzinger's push, CL is present in more than eighty countries. In Italy it operates many primary and secondary schools throughout the country, especially since so many religious orders are dwindling in numbers and no longer staffing schools. It was Cardinal Law who so dutifully brought CL to the New World in his diocese in Boston. No doubt that move was not lost on Ratzinger and his other friends in the Vatican, who, among other things, rewarded Law when the American press, courts, and lay Catholics were out to hang him for his shutting his eyes to the pedophile priest scandal. Apparently it is more to Catholic doctrine's liking to resist abortion than to resist pedophilia.

A coworker with Ratzinger in pushing these sects has been Cardinal Paul Josef Cordes, formerly vice president of the Pontifical Council for the Laity. In developing their argument for centralizing everything in the papacy, Cordes, with Ratzinger's blessing, actually invokes the medieval Pope Gregory VII as an example of "extreme relevance" for our times. It was Gregory VII who claimed complete jurisdiction of the papacy over both spiritual and temporal matters. He famously decreed, "The pope is the only one whose feet are to be kissed by all princes . . . That he may depose emperors . . . That the pope may absolve the subjects of unjust men from their fealty . . . That he himself may be judged by no-one . . . That the Roman Church has never erred, nor never, by the witness of Scriptures, shall err to all eternity."

The following elements make up the strategy of those now running the Vatican.

Destroy, intimidate, and make uncomfortable and impossible the role of theologians.

Replace theology and critical thinking with sentimental appeals to the "deposit of faith" and to "the pope says this."

Centralize every decision possible, including the appointment of bishops and cardinals, and reserve all "magisterial" or teaching authority in the Vatican, thus ignoring cultural and political nuances and, of course, theological questioning.

Give special status in the church to those sects that report exclusively to the pope and bypass all episcopal conferences and bishops within their dioceses.

Intimidate and marginalize bishops' conferences.

Appoint bishops and cardinals who are yes-men.

Appoint bishops and cardinals who are members of these sect groups (such as Opus Dei) and who know how to obey above all else. (Currently about half of the bishops of Peru are Opus Dei, and the numbers are growing everywhere—including in the United States.)

Make morality almost exclusively about sexuality, and define sexual morality in the narrowest of ways ("no contraception," even in a time of AIDS and overpopulation; no divorce; no abortion) and make this and one's view on *Humanae Vitae* a litmus test for faith.

Substitute "charity" for the term "justice" wherever possible.

Reward those (such as Cardinal Bernard Law) who submit to this strategy. Punish those who do not.

Call these sects "lay groups," even when in fact they are all
   deeply clerically dominated.
Forbid even the discussion of women's ordination and
   excommunicate priests who support it, thus keeping
   the priesthood a "men's club" forever.
Make sure the College of Cardinals is dominated by people
   who submit to these rules and therefore will perpetuate
   things after Pope John Paul II and Pope Benedict XVI die.
Make symbolic gestures about ecumenism but change
   nothing and yield nothing. ("Protestants are not
   churches," says Ratzinger; Mohammad was "evil and
   inhumane"; Thich Nhat Hanh is the Antichrist; and
   yoga must not be practiced by Christians because
   it gets you too much in touch with your body and
   can "degenerate into a cult of the body and can lead
   surreptitiously to considering all bodily sensation as
   spiritual experiences.")

It is the height of naïveté to reduce theological silencing to "personality problems" or "disobedience," or to think that there is not a concerted
strategy by an extreme ideology to deconstruct Vatican II and reconstruct
a very different church, a church that does not think of itself as "the people of God," as Vatican II insisted, and does not put decision-making into
the hands of bishops' conferences, but instead thinks of itself as "Rome"
and tells the "people" to get in line and be quiet—and tells bishops to do
the same. In doing so, the papacy is dismantling one of the cornerstones
of reform established by the Vatican Council. Urquhart puts it this way:

> The council had emphasized the role of the local churches and
> hence the authority of the bishops. Collegiality, or the authority of
> the bishops as a body united with the pope, had been emphasized
> as a counterbalance to infallibility. John Paul did not see it quite
> in these terms. He spent the eighties bringing bishops and their
> national councils—the bishops' conferences—to heel. Central-
> ization was something the movements knew a lot about. They had
> no place for democracy in their own structures and were impas-
> sioned advocates of the idea that democracy has no place in the
> church. The support of the pope became the calling-card of the
> movements in the local diocese, especially handy where bishops

were hostile. In return, they preached the gospel of the new ultra-montanism (meaning papal absolutism).

Cardinal Ratzinger made it a special priority of his to attack the national and regional bishops' conferences "in an attempt to claw back the supreme authority of the papacy. It is no wonder, then, that he has been one of the most ardent supporters of the movements." Ratzinger goes on record supporting them 100 percent. He says: "The intense life of faith found in these movements does not imply they are introspective or sheltered but simply a full and integral catholicity . . . Our task—as those charged with a ministry in the church and as theologians—is to keep the doors open to them and prepare a space for them."

Urquhart evaluates the likely success of such a project when he writes:

Whereas the council marked the coming of age of a Catholic laity which was intelligent, able to think for itself, with is own special expertise to bring to church teachings, the movements are a sad return to a brainwashed, submissive flock whose only duty is to heed and obey. Trends within the Catholic Church towards changing the traditional clerical male-dominated power structure by modifying the compulsory celibacy rule, ordaining women priests or allowing the laity to participate in decision-making are violently repudiated by the new movements . . .

How committed was the previous pope to these movements? He fought bishops of Italy and other places tooth and nail to establish them. He hailed them as "among the most beautiful fruits of the council." And the present pope? Cardinal Ratzinger has called them the council's *only* positive results. Urquhart states:

Perhaps, as the architect of Restoration in the Catholic Church, he esteems them for other reasons. In fact, for all their pretence of "councilor values," the new movements could be the wooden horse through which pre-councilor practices are being restored on a vast scale.

They claim to be lay; in fact, they are run by priests or celibates and count large numbers of clergy, religious and "plainclothes" celibates among their members . . . Their members are encouraged to retreat from the world—the opposite of the council's desire.

They claim to be unstructured and spontaneous; in fact, they are organized into rigid but secret hierarchies on a multinational scale, exacting blind obedience from members, with a personality cult surrounding the charismatic founder who wields supreme authority.

One outstanding feature in all of these sects is that not one of them has produced a single theologian. Canon lawyers? By the hundreds. Theologians? No. One wonders if they even study biblical languages or biblical theology—or theology at all. As one probes deeper, one realizes that they have substituted ideology for theology and the basis of their ideology is not the Gospels, but two papal encyclicals—one on priestly celibacy and the second on birth control—that form the substratum of their Christian consciousness. These teachings reiterating Roman Catholic praxis about sexuality constitute their entire litmus test for orthodoxy—obey the pope about sex, no sex, and the female sex. This demonstrates a sick preoccupation with sexuality from an organization that has failed to rein in its pederasts—and indeed has *promoted* CEOs who failed to do so as long as they remained loyal to the club.

Vatican II encouraged thinking and professional Catholics to infiltrate the world with solid Christian values of justice and compassion. But these groups, very much in the image of Cardinal Ratzinger, love to discourse on the evils of the "secular world" and how one must keep clear of such places. As Urquhart reports, having lived within such a sect for a number of years: "If the Second Vatican Council introduced a new openness to the world, the new movements display a deep mistrust, even hatred, of the world. They are profoundly anti-progress. Like fundamentalist groups in other religions, the movements' attitude to contemporary society is parasitic: they make full use of the advantages it offers—such as the media and communications technology—while rejecting the culture which produced them. They contribute nothing to the progress of society." Urquhart comes to the conclusion that the papacy under John Paul II and Cardinal Ratzinger has created a message that the Catholic Church is "the new world leader of the far right," and that a church that has to sink to the level of holding up fundamentalist, fascist right wing-clubs and call them lay movements is an organization "in desperate straits."

CHAPTER 8

SISTER JANE BLOWS THE WHISTLE
ABOUT THE PEDOPHILE CRISIS

✠

THREE YEARS BEFORE THE
Cardinal Law pedophile crisis made ugly headlines in
Boston, Sister Jane Kelly found the
courage to speak the truth in the
diocese of Santa Rosa, California.
In exchange for doing so, she was
expelled from her order at seventy-
five years of age.

Sister Jane Kelly had been running a drop-in center for the homeless and poor in Ukiah, California,
for thirty-four years. In that time she
had raised more than $2 million to
keep the place going and in the style
and quality of life that honors her
clients. But she was thrown out on the streets by her religious order, of
which she had been a member in good standing (if occasionally a thorn in
the side of the powers that be) for fifty-eight years. Why would they expel
her after fifty-eight years? Why would they throw a seventy-five-year-old
sister out on the streets? What was her crime? Sister Jane, not by choice,
but by dead-end options, became a whistle-blower.

I sat down at her kitchen table to hear her story in greater detail. She
said enthusiastically, "This year is the twenty-fifth anniversary of our center, Plowshares. We opened the doors on Main Street with forty people.
Now, there are one hundred people." When they opened up, people said
to her, "Jane, we don't have poor and homeless in Ukiah." Her response
was: "Great, we'll open the doors and no one will come."

In its early days she asked the local ministerial association to endorse the program, but they responded, "You aren't preaching the Gospel." To which she burst into tears: "Feeding the hungry *is* preaching the Gospel." The needs of the homeless were endless, so they opted to focus on hunger. "All we could do was the hunger thing. Food. The needs are so great. We focused on that. Community too. It means more than the food! They'll take the hug more than the meal. They are respected and therefore they respect us. No problem ever." Once someone left a threat on her answering machine. The next morning two homeless guys were there sitting outside the center when she arrived early to be sure the man who threatened her did not come back. They were protecting her. Says Sister Jane, "The homeless are such beautiful people. I pity those who do not mix with them. I listen to their stories. 'I've been sober for five days,' one says. I say, 'Great, let's make that six.'"

She laughs when she says, "If Jesus were to come to Ukiah you'd see him at Plowshares, not the church, and certainly not the rectory." She tells how she herself learned how to cook for a hundred people when the volunteer did not show up one day. I asked Sister Jane where she got her strength. "My mother was a very strong woman. They turned our water off one day because we were poor and could not pay the bill, and she went out with an ax and broke the lock. She said, 'I have three babies. I can't be without water.'" Her father was a reporter who had a good sense of humor and had the habit of bringing street kids home to stay overnight. "We were brought up to respect people. It's in the genes."

Sister Jane observes, "All the homeless people have a story." You get to know them and their story. "I could have been born like that," she notes.

Ninety percent of the homeless she knows were molested as children and wanted to get out of their house as soon as possible. They did not get much education. Many of them succumbed to drugs and alcohol. This is the predominant reason for homelessness. Many were veterans, too, including a former Vietnam War helicopter pilot who did not want to show his face and smelled so bad Sister Jane would set him up at a special table to eat by himself at the back of the building. He would take three servings of the food. "Imagine his memories," she says. "He saw soldiers killing kids from his helicopter. Like they were prey or something."

As for herself, she confesses she misses her religious community and would like to grow old with her sisters. "I take what comes. Day by day." Her own evaluation of her eviction process was, in her typical no-nonsense way, blunt and to the point. Here is how she puts it in her book, *Taught to Believe the Unbelievable: A New Vision of Hope for the Church and Society*:

> In response to the choice of either relocating to the Mother House in two weeks, or requesting from Rome a dispensation from my vows, I chose the dispensation. I felt that I was being driven out of the congregation after fifty-eight years. I soon learned that when it comes to church authority, it is absolute. The person with the authority becomes the jury and the judge. There is no room for dialogue. In my case, authority spoke. I had no other option . . . It's frightening that one person has the authority to force a sister out, after fifty-eight years in the congregation! I felt that I was living the experience of the Inquisition when people were brought up before the tribunal and sentenced without any avenue of recourse.

At her final meeting with her superiors in the old mother house where she had first entered the Congregation of the Presentation Sisters fifty-eight years previous, there was no dialogue. She was forced to listen to a pre-arranged agenda. When they asked her to pray, she offered this prayer: "The Lord is my refuge, the Lord is my refuge, peace and justice have met and God has set me free!" Then she volunteered the following to her accusers and dismissers: "You have treated me cruelly and unjust. Not one of you came to Ukiah to see if indeed it was unsafe for me to live alone or drive a car. Two of you didn't even speak to me, yet you signed a letter demanding that I relocate to the Mother House in two weeks or request a dispensation from my vows. There was no process! I pray to God that you compose a process so that no Sister will have to go through what I went through."

Previous to this process Sister Jane was told to turn in her car keys and live without a car by her superior, who lived in San Francisco. Ukiah, where Sister Jane lives, is a small California town with great distances between places. Sister Jane had undergone a serious fall, and simply to get to the hospital to have her wounds dressed on a regular basis, or to go to Safeway for groceries, was a great ordeal without a car. After being caught in a rainstorm on a long walk to the grocery store and falling on the slippery sidewalk, she got angry and said, "This is ridiculous. No one in authority can order you to do something that threatens not only your physical health, but also your psychological health. So I called Ken Fowler, a car dealer in town that I had known for years and said, 'Ken, I need a car today.'" He found her a car with forty thousand miles on it at a good price. When her superior heard about her driving again, orders came down that she was to go to a psychological institute to be evaluated. While several programs were long-term (one offering a minimum of nine months), one program promised a six-day evaluation. She agreed to go.

The place was in Toronto. She had ruptured discs in her lower back but did not take pain medicine for them at the time since water therapy was working well for her. "When we arrived at the center I was interviewed and given a test to see if I was suicidal. I was also asked if I had any sharp instruments with me. I was tempted to say that I had left my guns at the front desk and that I would relinquish my knife at the front desk as well. However, I restrained myself since sarcasm would not benefit me at this time." Deprived of her water therapy, the pain in her back returned in great force. She agreed to take some medicine for her pain—which proved to be a decisive decision.

The interview with the psychologist who held the power to recommend she stay for six months of treatment began at 11 a.m. and continued for five hours. Sister Jane could barely seat herself because of her back pain. She had to leave the session early, and the next day the psychologist informed her that she flunked the test of playing with blocks (the test she cut short due to the pain in her back). Sister Jane comments, "The interview turned into an interrogation. All that was lacking was a bare light bulb overhead. He kept repeating that I could not remember." The psychologist seemed to have no sense of humor and was "forever moving in his chair and had an eye twitch."

Sister Jane felt it was time to evaluate the program itself and asked the psychologist for fifteen minutes of his time to do so. This is what she said: "Henry, when I came into your office, it was obvious that I was in a great deal of pain. You made no move to get up and help me into the chair. You started off by questioning me for an hour. I felt that I was in an interrogation rather than an interview. You proceeded with multiple tests that lasted for five hours. You never once made reference to my pain. Any psychologist knows that you don't test a person who is on pain medication. It impairs a person's reflexes. The staff is under constraints, since they have only one hour to ask the one hundred questions of the client. There is no time for dialogue."

The next day the psychologist offered his oral evaluation in the presence of the president of her congregation, who had flown in for it. It was a devastating opinion that concluded that she had no memory and had impaired motor skills. Her superior was pleased since it sounded like she ought not to live alone or to drive a car. Sister Jane could only think about getting home and starting up her water therapy for her ailing back again, but three days after arriving home she got a registered letter from her superior demanding that she either relocate to the mother house in two weeks or write Rome requesting a dispensation from her vows. "It was humanly impossible after living thirty-one years in Ukiah to move in two weeks! I had no choice but to petition Rome for a dispensation from my vows after fifty-eight years."

Sister Jane recalls, "She wanted me to come to the mother house. I had a bad back. I said, 'I can't. My ministry is in Ukiah with the poor. If I went to the Mother House, what would I do? Shuffle up and down the corridors waiting for my next meal? I can't live my life out like that.' But she had the power."

What was Sister Jane's crime that got her thrown out of her community? The story begins a few years earlier when a new bishop of her Santa Rosa diocese, George Patrick Ziemann, called her in to ask her to supervise a seminarian named Jorge Hume Salas, from Costa Rica. Sister Jane protested that she had no experience supervising a seminarian and asked if she could at least look at a psychological profile of him. Bishop Ziemann said there was none and waved that idea off. Her response was: "Bishop, without a psychological profile, Jorge could be a psychopathic liar or killer." Later she commented, "How prophetic these words would later prove to be! Reluctantly, I agreed to supervise Jorge. Little did I dream it would change my life forever."

Sister Jane and Jorge met weekly, often for three-hour conversations. She confronted him when he talked of opening a bank account to deposit youth program fees, admonishing him that all accounts go through the parish, not through a personal bank account. Jorge was very inflexible, insisting, for example, that parents of First Communion children must be at Sunday morning classes even in the case of a poor mother who worked on Sunday mornings. He dismissed her child from the class, but with Sister Jane's and the pastor's insistence later relented to let the child back in. He launched a youth group and a soccer team; sponsored more than one hundred adults commissioned as lectors, catechists, and Eucharistic ministers; and held large and impressive processions for special feast days, such as Our Lady of Guadalupe.

A complete surprise struck Sister Jane when Jorge announced to her one day that the bishop was going to ordain him a deacon—the final step before the priesthood. She was "astounded" because the bishop never consulted with her (his supervisor) or the pastor regarding his credentials for this advancement. Even more astounding was the announcement nine months later that the bishop was going to ordain him a priest. "It literally blew my mind. Jorge had never attended any classes on theology or liturgy and never made a retreat!"

After Jorge's ordination his entire work and personality changed. No more youth group. No more catechists or religious teachers; they were dismissed and replaced by two young Hispanic men, one of whom spent nights with Jorge on a regular basis. And Jorge, who had always been poor, all of a sudden had a new car, designer clothes, a computer, and more electronic gadgets. Sister Jane wondered where he was getting all his money and discovered he was stealing money from the Sunday collection and the selling of religious articles. It also became clear that Jorge was molesting young Hispanic men.

Sister Jane brought this information to the attention of the bishop, whose response was to meet with the parish council, finance committee, and the parish staff, with the chief of police in tow and to swear all people present to secrecy. Then he proceeded to whisk Jorge away. Sister Jane, suspecting in advance that the bishop's strategy would be to swear people to silence, boycotted the meeting. She comments: "The power of the bishop was evidenced in the fact that not one person spoke of the matter."

What did Sister Jane do? "For two years, I went through every church channel to have Jorge removed, but to no avail. I finally went public with the story." This was a very brave decision, to take on a member of the church hierarchy. Her action became a kind of rallying cry for other victims of priests, and Sister Jane ministered to other church people whose lives had been seriously affected by priestly abuse. Don Hoard was a father of a boy who had been sexually abused by a priest in Humbolt County, California. Eight days after she went public with her story, Hoard wrote a letter to the editor of the *Press Democrat* and said, "For this lady to do what she's done is mind-boggling. If you don't have a Catholic background, I don't think you can conceive of the amount of courage it took."

The story was picked up by the *New York Times,* the *Los Angeles Times,* the San Francisco *Chronicle,* and the Ukiah *Daily Journal.* The public outcry to Sister Jane's revelations was overwhelming and "100 percent positive." As Sister Jane read the responses to her situation, she drew a powerful conclusion: "People knew, either instinctively or through direct, painful experience, that the power and the authority of the Catholic Church had taken on a life of its own and that it did not always serve the best interest of the Church's followers."

In her book on the entire episode, Sister Jane not only described the crimes and the bishop's cover-up but also laid out her own spiritual journey deepened by the difficult process she had undergone. "In the Fall of 1999 I bumped into a wall of misconduct, denial, secrecy and self-preservation among church officials. When I failed in my repeated attempts to see that all clerics involved be held accountable, I soon found myself in the epicenter of a whirlwind of deceit and destruction that forced me to question the substance of the faith that had governed my life for fifty years . . . This whole experience forced me to re-examine everything I was taught, both as a child and an adult. It freed me up, and I wanted to free others up as I had been." A film emerged of Sister Jane's struggle and her whistle-blowing. In it Sister Jane analyzes her experience: "It's all about power; it's all about money. I have a simple solution; do what Jesus said: 'Go sell what you have, give to the poor, then come, follow me.'"

Later Sister Jane learned that the bishop was allegedly having sex with Jorge, and that was another source of Jorge's inflated income. When the bishop assigned Jorge to St. John's parish in Sonoma, Sister Jane wrote the bishop: "He's a con artist, he is stealing, he's having sex with young men. How can you do this?" She heard nothing at all. One year later, she sent a second letter. Nothing happened. She interviewed families of people Jorge molested. It is then that she decided to go to the *Press Democrat*. It was December and she was sick with pneumonia, and as the reporter started the tape recorder he first paused and said, "Why are we doing this, Sister Jane?" Her response: "Because it is right." They had no idea what would happen. "Would they condemn us or what?" Says Sister Jane: "I tried for two years to get Jorge out of active ministry. I went to the paper and it happened in two days."

A follow-up story was published about the sexual liason of the bishop and Jorge. He insisted it was consensual. Both were arrested, but they were let go because the police said they were lying and they did not have enough evidence to prosecute.

It is then that Sister Jane started writing Cardinal Joseph Ratzinger, because it was in the paper that the bishop had had consensual sex with Jorge. Ziemann was sent to Arizona at a monastery for counseling and, lo and behold, he was assigned to counsel young seminarians in that community. Sister Jane says, "I thought, 'That's a candy store. He has his own candy store.'" In her letter to Cardinal Ratzinger she said, "I don't understand that Bishop Ziemann is still in active ministry when he had consensual sex with Jorge and you said homosexuality is 'intrinsically evil' ["Which I don't believe," Sister Jane is quick to comment.]—how is it he is still in active ministry?"

The response from Ratzinger was to tell Sister Jane to look up the church's teaching on homosexuality in the Catholic catechism. "But this is not what I was asking, so I wrote a second letter: 'You did not answer my question. Why is Bishop Ziemann in active ministry?'" She waited for three weeks and still had no response. So she wrote Ratzinger a third letter in which she observed, first, "Undoubtedly your letter to me must have been lost in the mail because you were so prompt in answering my first letter and I'm writing a book and I am going to say that you did not respond to my question." Almost immediately by return mail she received a letter from Ratzinger saying, "I don't know anything about Bishop Ziemann. You will have to go to the U.S. Bishops' Conference and ask that question." Comments Sister Jane, "That was a lie. Of course he knew about Bishop Ziemann. I did not follow up with it. I was tired of it. I threw his letter in the wastebasket."

The response to her going public was so great that it became increasingly clear to her that "the incident I had confronted in my own parish was not a unique event . . . The pattern of abuse and cover-up that I had witnessed at St. Mary's Church and in the Santa Rosa diocese were echoed all around the country—in fact, all around the world. There was a solidly built clerical wall of silence that was firmly guarded not only by Bishop Ziemann and Monsignor Keys, but by officials throughout the hierarchy of the Church."

It is then that she wrote her book *Taught to Believe the Unbelievable*. "I examined everything I had been taught and saw so many discrepancies and so much that was not Christian. For example the virgin birth. Church revelations and cover-ups. I believe that when we come together at Mass that brings Christ together for us. Not the priest. It becomes the body of Christ because we believe it was . . . we need a presider. But we are all called to the royal priesthood (Peter's epistle). We already have women who can ordain. Ludmila Javorova in Czechoslovakia who was ordained when Communists overtook the country—and four other women were ordained with her . . . It's all about power. Women have no power. Can't make any decisions. We are a community of priestly individuals; we come together and that brings Christ in our midst. It happens when we come together."

The administrator of the parish called Sister Jane in and said to her: "You're a wonderful person. You can't teach the adults any longer. You are so far ahead of them." Sister Jane responded that "that's an insult to the adults." Clearly, she said, "I was silenced." It turns out that "I brought scandal to the church. Not the priests, but the one who exposed them. Don't bring scandal to the church." Bishop Ziemann died in 2009 but retained the rank and authority of a bishop until the end.

What lessons has she learned and carried with her from her ordeals? "I believe in the autonomy of the individual. We are called by the Lord, by the Holy Spirit. Sometimes it's in conflict with authority. I respect authority, but if they ask me to do something that will destroy me, that is suicide and that is against the law."

And what is she feeling now? "I am at peace. My biggest struggle is my infirmity. Day after day it prevents me from going to Plowshares because I can't hold off the medication. I can only go two times a week. My decisions were the right ones. I'm glad I had the gumption and courage to do it. Now I have a certain sense of freedom. No one I have to ask 'may I?' It's very freeing. When I can't take care of myself, I will go into a rest home. I'll administer to the people there. There's always a ministry to be had regardless of where you are."

Sister Jane's story with Cardinal Ratzinger and the matter of priestly pedophilia is not, unfortunately, so unique. Note especially the role that secrecy played in her diocese and the bishop demanding an oath of silence and how, by going to the newspaper, she violated the cover-up. (And how, quite cannily, she avoided the meeting with the bishop with an intuition that he would demand an oath of secrecy.) Note also the indifference on the part of Cardinal Ratzinger to the accusations against the bishop as well as the offending priest.

As I write this book in early summer 2010, countless stories about priestly pedophilia and Cardinal Ratzinger's role as prefect of the CDF are emerging. Almost every day brings a new revelation. I will list here just some of those stories and facts that we are certain about at this time.

Cardinal Ratzinger appropriated to himself as head of the Congregation for the Doctrine of the Faith all the cases of priestly misconduct. Part of his modus operandi was to employ a secret 1962 Vatican document called *Crimen sollicitationis*, which ordered bishops to enforce silence in sex abuse matters. On May 18, 2001, Ratzinger sent a document to all bishops dealing with severe crimes (*epistula de delictis gravioribus*) in which cases of abuse were sealed under special pontifical secrecy and its violation could entail grave ecclesiastical penalties.

We know that many such cases when brought to the attention of Ratzinger's congregation were never pursued, and many priests guilty of serious abuse of children were never called to task and never dismissed from the priesthood (even though at least ninety-one theologians and activists were being silenced, expelled, and even excommunicated). As Swiss theologian Hans King put it recently, "There is no denying the fact that the worldwide system of covering up cases of sexual crimes committed by clerics was engineered by the Roman Congregation for the Doctrine of the Faith under Cardinal Ratzinger (1981–2005)."

Case Studies

Now let us consider some specific cases.

Case One: Father Lawrence Murphy was in charge of the Deaf School at St. John's in Milwaukee, Wisconsin. He sexually abused about two hundred deaf children between 1950 and 1974. When the scandal was about to break open, he was simply moved to another location in Wisconsin. On March 5, 1995, a victim of Father Murphy wrote then–Vatican secretary of state Cardinal Angelo Sodano about his molestation over a period of years. He heard nothing. He wrote a second time and still got no response. In July 1996 the archbishop of Milwaukee, Rembart Weakland, wrote Ratzinger to say, "You need to take jurisdiction on this. We have to avoid scandal and remove this priest." Yet Ratzinger kept the priest in ministry and in good standing until his death in 1998. A lawsuit filed against the Vatican "suggests that the Vatican failed to discipline Murphy because he was a prolific fundraiser." Cardinal Sodano, as we have seen, is the cardinal who so vehemently supported Father Maciel and who at Easter Mass 2010 said the allegations against the church and Pope Benedict were "petty gossip." Sodano is currently dean of the College of Cardinals, and he was in fact echoing the words of the pope himself who had said in a sermon on Palm Sunday that one ought not be "intimidated by the petty gossip of dominant opinion." The person who was Ratzinger's deputy at the time of the investigation and who also knew about the case is the current Vatican secretary of state, Cardinal Tarcisio Bertone.

Countless victims and their families suffered in secrecy, shame, and silence. Ratzinger's argument was that to let the truth out would bring scandal to the reputation of the church hierarchy. Murphy wrote Ratzinger a personal letter, and the CDF did not pursue a trial but ruled that the alleged molestations occurred too long ago and that Murphy, ailing and elderly, should repent and be restricted from saying Mass outside his diocese. Murphy died a priest in good standing. Jeff Anderson, the lawyer on behalf of the victims of Father Murphy, came to the following conclusion: "when they discover a priest that commits crimes, they're more concerned about concealing the crimes and protecting that priest and protecting the reputation than they are about removing that priest or reporting them to the law enforcement authorities, which they never, ever, if rarely, do."

Case Two: Father Oliver O'Grady admitted molesting approximately twenty-five boys and girls in California from the late 1970s to 1991. He spent seven years in jail and was then deported to Ireland, his home. He demonstrates no remorse and ambles "freely among schoolchildren in Dublin as he recounts his patterns of abuse with almost cheery glee" in Am Berg's chilling 2006 movie on his case, *Deliver Us from Evil*.

Case Three: Father Stephen Kiesle of Oakland, California, confessed to tying up and raping numerous children. In 1981 his bishop wrote the Vatican to remove him from the priesthood. At least three times the diocese wrote Ratzinger, and Bishop John Stephen Cummins brought up the case on an official Vatican visit. Yet there was no response. A Vatican official wrote to say the file may have been lost and suggested resubmitting materials. Kiesle was returned to suburban Pinole, California, as a youth minister, even though he had asked to be dismissed from the priesthood. A 1985 letter signed by Cardinal Ratzinger says that for "the good of the universal church" Father Kiesle should not be defrocked just yet. Bishop Cummins wrote in 1982 that "it is my conviction that there would be no scandal if this petition were granted and that as a matter of fact, given the nature of the case, there might be greater scandal to the community if Father Kiesle were allowed to return to the active ministry." The case languished in the CDF for six years.

After finally leaving the priesthood, Kiesle married but was arrested and charged in 2002 with thirteen counts of child molestation from the

1970s—however, all but two counts were thrown out, owing to the statute of limitations. He was sentenced to six years in state prison in 2004 for molesting a young girl. More than a half-dozen victims reached a settlement in 2005 with the Oakland diocese for his molesting them as young children. Yet it took Cardinal Ratzinger more than six years to agree to remove him from the priesthood. "Cardinal Ratzinger was more concerned about the avoidance of scandal than he was about protecting children," observed Irwin Salkin, an attorney representing a victim.

Case Four: Boston priest John Geoghan molested scores of boys and girls. Yet he was not defrocked or arrested but rather moved from parish to parish by none other than Cardinal Law in attempts to hide the crimes. In 2002 it took a judge to force the release of eleven thousand pages of church documents that were kept hidden by Cardinal Law, in what Peggy Noonan calls an attempt "to hide the crimes." At one point this serial rapist was dallying with children in a public pool, and Law claimed "he was probably 'proselytizing.'" Law "left Boston just hours before state troopers arrived with subpoenas seeking his grand jury testimony in what the state's attorney general, Thomas Reilly, called a massive coverup of child abuse."

Case Five: Two bishops tried to get Cardinal Joseph Ratzinger to act on abuse cases involving two priests in Tucson, Arizona. In a letter signed by Ratzinger on June 8, 1992, he told them he was taking control of the case. Five years later no action had been taken. Bishop Manuel Moreno pleaded for years for the Vatican to defrock Father Michael Teta, who, a panel determined, had molested children as far back as the 1970s. This church tribunal, set up in the 1990s, claimed that "there is almost a satanic quality in his mode of acting toward young men and boys." He molested boys ages seven and nine in the confessional as they prepared for their First Communion. It took Ratzinger twelve years to remove Teta from the priesthood despite written pleas from his bishop to take action. "There's no doubt that Ratzinger delayed the defrocking process of dangerous priests who were deemed 'satanic' by their own bishop," an attorney of one of the victims said.

Bishop Manuel Moreno also wrote to Rome about Monsignor Robert Trupia and called him "a major risk factor to the children, adolescents and adults that he may have contact with" in 1995. Moreno warned that "we have proofs of civil crimes against people who were under his priestly care" and warned that he could "be the source of greater scandal in the future." Eight years passed. On February 10, 2003, Moreno wrote

Ratzinger again. There was no response. Being sick with cancer, Moreno retired early, but before doing so he wrote Ratzinger still another time. The new bishop, Gerald Frederick Kicanas, also sent requests to the CDF. Finally, in August 2004, Trupia was defrocked.

A lawyer for one of Trupia's victims says: "The tragedy is that the bishops have only two choices: Follow the Vatican's code of secrecy and delay, or leave the church. It's unfortunate that their faith demands that they sacrifice children to follow the Vatican's directions."

Case Six: Ireland has been the hardest hit of any country when it comes to child-abuse scandals. A nation of 4 million, it has paid out $1 billion to some thirteen thousand victims. Three investigations ordered by the Irish government from 2005 to 2009 documented the abuse of thousands of Irish children by priests, nuns, and brothers in parishes, boarding schools, and orphanages. A government commission set up to investigate these tales of horror reported that "the Dublin Archdiocese's preoccupations in dealing with cases of child sexual abuse, at least until the mid 1990s, were the maintenance of secrecy, the avoidance of scandal, the protection of the reputation of the Church, and the preservation of its assets. All other considerations, including the welfare of children and justice for victims, were subordinated to these priorities." Irish bishops "did not report a single case to police until 1996" when victims started suing the church. Already in the 1980s the bishops had taken out group liability insurance, so they must have seen the handwriting on the wall. In 1994 the Irish government was brought down when it botched the extradition of a particularly notorious pedophile priest.

Bishop James Moriarty of Kildare, Ireland, who served as auxiliary Dublin bishop from 1991 to 2002, resigned in April 2010 and confessed to going along with a practice of concealing child-abuse complaints from the police. "The truth is that the long struggle of survivors to be heard and respected by church authorities has revealed a culture within the church that many would simply describe as unchristian," he said in a statement on resigning. Two other Irish bishops have resigned, and two more have tendered their resignations. An Irish government–ordered investigation into child abuse by clergy in the Dublin archdiocese found that "all bishops until 1996 colluded to protect scores of pedophile priests from criminal prosecution."

As late as late February 2010, the Vatican refused to cooperate with investigators over sexual abuse by clergy in Ireland. Members of the

Murphy Commission Report tried to speak to the Vatican department that oversees sexual abuse cases "but was spurned." A Vatican official said the request had "offended many in the Vatican" and that the Irish government was failing to "respect and protect Vatican sovereignty." Nothing about respecting and protecting the young. For more than four years, an Irish bishop urged the CDF to remove Father Tony Walsh from the priesthood for numerous sexual attacks on children. The bishops, however, abiding by Ratzinger's rules, did not inform civil authorities and only after four years and numerous victims was Walsh removed from the priesthood. As an Irish journalist put it, "the cover-up of abuse during the final decades of the 20th century [occurred] in Dublin and at the highest levels of the Vatican." Andrew Madden, a former altar boy who was molested by a Dublin priest comments: "The only issue for the Vatican has been the supposed 'failure' of the Irish government to protect the Vatican from intrusive questions. Self-interest ruled the day when their priests were raping children."

In his response to Pope Benedict's letter to the Irish church that puts all the blame for the pedophile cover-up on the Irish prelates and takes no responsibility whatsoever for Rome and the CDF and its regulations, Fintan O'Toole comments: "The church's combination of temporal authority, spiritual control and a closed, internal hierarchy created the power that corrupted it. The backlash of the past few weeks has merely confirmed what was already overwhelmingly likely: that Benedict is entirely incapable of grasping this reality, let alone altering it. He has spent much of his career crushing dissent and rolling back the anti-hierarchical spirit of Vatican II. His solution, as he suggested in his pastoral letter, is more of the same— more obedience, more authority, more resistance to secular modernity."

Case Seven: In France, Father Rene Bissey was sentenced to eighteen years in jail for repeatedly raping a boy and sexually assaulting ten other children. Bishop Pierre Pican of Bayeux-Lisieux kept the priest in parish work in spite of the fact that he admitted committing pedophile acts. Yet Cardinal Castrillon Hoyos of Colombia, who was the Vatican official in charge of priests worldwide, praised the French bishop in 2001 for not revealing the sordid facts to the police. "I congratulate you for not denouncing a priest to the civil administration," Hoyos wrote to Bishop Pican. "To encourage brothers in the episcopate in this delicate domain, this congregation will send copies of this letter to all bishops' conferences." Hoyos has said he had the approval and support of Pope John Paul II in praising the bishop. "After consulting the pope . . . I wrote a letter to the bishop congratulating him as a model of a father who does not hand over his sons," said the cardinal. "The Holy Father authorized me to send this letter to all bishops in the world and publish it on the internet," he went on.

Barbara Dorris of Survivors Network of Those Abused by Priests (SNAP), a U.S.-based support group for victims of clerical sex abuse, comments about this confession by Hoyos: "In what other institution on this planet does a top official praise a colleague for hiding a criminal from the police?"

Case Eight: In Germany, when Ratzinger was archbishop of Munich and Freising, he allowed a child-abusing priest into his diocese for psychiatric treatment. During his treatment Father Peter Hullermann was assigned to a parish where he molested a boy. Vatican spinmasters want us to believe that Ratzinger knew nothing about this decision to appoint this priest back to parish life, but knowing what a keen eye Ratzinger has for so-called heretics around the world, it does stretch the imagination a bit to be told to believe that he was ignorant of the priest's conduct. The head of a newly formed abuse prevention task force reported that Ratzinger's former diocese is facing physical and sexual abuse claims on a daily basis. "It is like a tsunami," he said.

The Vatican spin was that Ratzinger left this decision entirely in the hands of the vicar of the diocese, Gerhard Gruber—but that story has been recently debunked by the vicar himself who, at eighty-one years old, refuses to take the fall for Ratzinger. Gruber has reported that he was "emphatically 'asked' to assume full responsibility for the affair" by the current archbishop Reinhard Marx. Gruber's friends say "he was apparently being used as a scapegoat" but "to everyone's surprise" he wrote an open letter denying that he "acted on his own authority" when assigning the priest to a parish. Newly discovered documents prove that "there could have been no doubt in Munich about the priest's previous history," a history that was fully relayed to the Munich diocese from the priest's previous diocese. It was only two weeks into his therapy that the priest was reassigned and this in a meeting that Ratzinger chaired. Hullermann continued to work in the diocese for thirty years and found many new victims in that period. Archbishop Marx has recently been made a cardinal by Ratzinger, the youngest German cardinal.

Der Spiegel comments that Ratzinger "even failed to take the problem of child abuse seriously when he was the archbishop of Munich" since he knowingly returned this abusive priest to parish work with children. Moreover, he kept it all secret within the church. A policeman's son, Ratzinger was well aware that no one had notified the police and that everything had been handled by the Church internally. Neither he nor his diocese reported the case to the authorities." This practice continued when he became head of CDF and the one responsible for issues of clerical sexual abuse. "For over 23 years—until his election as pope—he headed the CDF [and] missed countless opportunities to vigorously tackle the issue. . . . It wasn't until 2001, after a sexual abuse scandal had rocked the Catholic Church in the U.S., that Cardinal Ratzinger took action." But even then the action was limited to informing the CDF only and keeping the information "under strict secrecy." The action did not include informing civil authorities.

Also, in Germany, Ratzinger's older brother Georg, who was ordained with him in 1951, has admitted to slapping boys in his well-known children's choir. (He has not acknowledged knowing anything about sexual abuse that also occurred in that choir between priests and youth.) One German bishop, Walter Mixa, whom Pope Benedict XVI appointed head of the Augsburg diocese in 2005, has admitted that he physically abused children in a Catholic orphanage in the 1970s. At first denying the charges, he finally confessed to them and subsequently submitted his resignation to the pope. Mixa was one of the key members of the German national bishops' conference for more than a decade. A sixty percent increase in people leaving the church has been reported in Augsburg since this news broke.

In the Ettal Benedictine boarding school near Munich, an investigation revealed that hundreds of children were brutally beaten or tormented by more than a dozen monks and other staff, mostly before the 1990s. The result was "a regime of violence" in which some children had to be admitted to the hospital owing to the seriousness of their injuries.

An expert investigation has reported that "huge gaps" exist in the documentation of pedophilia in the German church that hints strongly of "a systemic system of cover-up" and "extensive destruction of files." Especially in the period from 1977 to 1982 when Ratzinger was archbishop were such matters "particularly poorly documented." Indeed, his diocese was "one of the worst hit in Germany" when revelations came to light in 2009. Recently a German woman who grew up in Ratzinger's diocese when he was archbishop there wrote me the following communication.

I grew up in a village near Munich as a girl with parents who had recently moved into this Bavarian culture and thus did not have traditional ties with the priest or the school. Both attributes, girl and newcomer, made me an easy target for the local priest. In spite of my parents' interference, and it being illegal at the time (in the 70s), it was common practice for the priest to give preferably girls a good beating with a set of rulers or a bunch of hazelnut-twigs bound together when ever he felt like it, but especially when we could not immediately recite the appropriate section out of the bible or had a question that was "not proper" (I was full of them in the beginning but learned quickly to shut up in fear). I remember clearly feeling the wrath of God sink into me forever, believing with every cell in my body that I would certainly end up in hell because I was a rotten sinful creature, a girl, condemned to suffer continuously. So I swore to God, the revengeful one out there somewhere, to never have fun, to always please others and work hard—and just maybe—I would not have to end up in hell. I still can recall the internal waves of fear-stricken shivers move through my body. My parents' complaints about the abuse never led to any improvement of the situation. Rather, they made things worse, and the teachers, supported by the priest, threatened to place me in a school for the mentally retarded because I was a "worthless case."

As a teen, God's wrath and punishment caught up with me again in a new form when a priest in Ratzinger's diocese who was doing "youth work" with my class pulled me in the woods to satisfy his human needs, turning into an animalist creature. I immediately felt at fault, especially after confiding in a teacher who did not believe me (priests do not do that!). It was confirmed once more that as a girl I was a sinner, at the mercy of God's wrath. I could not trust anyone in "heaven" and nobody on earth, especially not anyone in church.

I must have really had good guardian angels, because after many years of trying to find ways to kill and sabotage myself, I am still around, slowly discovering a totally "non-Ratzingish" way of connecting with God and discovering a life without nagging fear and depression but rather thrilling awe and curiosity about being a valued female participant of creation at almost 50 years of age.

. . . Matthew, this story may sound too much like many you

may have heard already but it does illustrate what was possible during Ratzinger's time, against all public laws. It was a dictatorship, not in wolves' clothes but in "church robes."

Case Nine. In Belgium reports are just emerging of a wave of sexual abuse of children by priests over the years. Archbishop Andre-Joseph Leonard, head of the church in Belgium, says "the report and the suffering it contains makes us shiver." Thirteen of the victims committed suicide. A stunning case concerned Roger Vangheluwe, bishop of Bruges, who resigned in April 2010 after admitting raping his own nephew over a thirteen-year period from 1973 to 1986. Cardinal Godfried Danneels, who was head bishop of Belgium previous to Leonard, covered up that abuse. The Vatican still has not defrocked the bishop. Members of parliament have called for an inquiry and the Survivor Network (SNAP) has stated that "the reforms offered by the church are but 'smoke and mirrors.'" In 1967, 42.9 percent of Catholics attended Sunday Mass; in 2006 it was 7 percent.

Church officials admit that the sex abuse cover-up is not unrelated to financial concerns. Bishop Guy Harpigny, chief spokesman for the Belgian hierarchy, concedes that Belgian church leaders have been slow to admit sex-abuse problems because, "if you apologize, then you are acknowledging moral and legal responsibility. Then there are people who ask for money and we don't know what lawyers and the courts will do about that."

Case Ten. A study of international scope has found that at least thirty cases of priests who were accused of abuse in their own country were transferred abroad by church prelates—some to escape police investigations. Many predators had access to children in other countries and abused again. The probe spanned twenty-one nations across six continents. One such incident involved Father Nicolas Aguilar Rivera, who was moved from Los Angeles to Mexico City. A Mexican citizen filed a civil lawsuit in U.S. federal court in California against him and the Roman Catholic cardinals of Mexico City and Los Angeles, claiming they moved the priest between the two countries to hide abuse allegations. The plaintiff reports that Rivera molested him in the mid-1990s when he was twelve years old.

In other instances a priest who admitted to abuse in Los Angeles was transferred to the Philippines; a priest convicted of sexual abuse in Canada was moved to France, where he was convicted of abuse again in 2005; a priest accused of attacking boys was moved back and forth between Ireland and England; a priest in Holliston, Massachusetts, was sent to Brazil and worked among the Kayapo Indians for thirty-three years; and Father Allan Woodcock molested at least eleven boys in New Zealand and was sent to Ireland. Woodcock was extradited to New Zealand in 2004, pled guilty to twenty-one sexual abuse charges, and was sentenced to seven years in jail. Transferring abusive priests has been called "the geographical cure" by Terry Carter, one of Woodcock's victims in New Zealand.

Case Eleven. We have already seen the Maciel scandal, the letters to Ratzinger attempting to expose him, and the silence from the CDF offices for decades. Now, as I write this, the pope has just accepted a report that confirms the horrors of Maciel's reign and has appointed an overseer of the Legion of Christ. This action comes only after he "belatedly reopened an investigation into" Maciel and refused to open an investigation for eleven years. This leads us to ask: How could so sordid a human being as Maciel receive such support from two popes for so long while ignoring all accusations against him? Were the present pope and the previous pope so inspired by his uber-right-wing ideology and love of dictators and authoritarianism and money-making prowess that ideology trumped all theology, all acts of justice? And the young suffered and still do to this day. Investigative journalists Laurie Goodstein and David Halbfinger conclude that Ratzinger, "it is now clear, was also part of a culture of nonresponsibility, denial, legalistic foot-dragging and outright obstruction. More than any top Vatican official other than John Paul II, it was Cardinal Ratzinger who might have taken decisive action in the 1990s to prevent the scandal from metastasizing in country after country, growing to such proportions that it now threatens to consume his own papacy."

The extent of the defensiveness of the CDF is highlighted in the case of an Australian bishop who resigned when he was attacked by the Vatican after saying to pedophile priest victims that he "was not happy with the level of support we were receiving from 'Rome.'" He received an official letter dated August 7, 1996, expressing "the ongoing concern of the Congregation for Bishops that you have in recent months expressed views that are seriously critical of the magisterial teaching and discipline of the Church." He was later informed that his actions were forwarded to the CDF, "implying that I was suspected of some form of heresy." Bishop George Robinson, auxiliary bishop of Sidney, resigned his office because "I could not continue to be a bishop of a church about which I had such profound reservations."

Sexual and Theological Abuse Linkage

These facts and stories are very sad to hear and distressing to write and read about. But they must be told (and numerous others as well). Only then can things be in any way cleaned up. What keeps coming up is the question of power and abuse. How different is it to cover up sexual abuse in an organization and to countenance intellectual abuse? More than ninety-one theologians and activists condemned under Ratzinger and Pope John Paul II are part of the abuse story of the past thirty years in the Vatican. Abuse comes in many forms. Many of the attacks against thinkers in the church were also secret and anonymous.

One such victim was Father Tissa Balasuriya of Sri Lanka, whose ministry was among the poor of his country. He was attacked, mistranslated, and eventually excommunicated by the CDF, and he says about his experience: "We can no longer accept secret, anonymous denunciations. Those who accuse others to Rome must be subject to reasonable norms of inquiry. If they defame or falsely accuse someone, they should be subject to punishment. This is operative in civil society." What does it mean to condemn thinkers? Balasuriya observes: "It strikes me that there is widespread fear among Catholics when they deal with theology and institutions such as the CDF: As a result, almost all of the structures of the Church become inoperative. At all levels—diocesan, national and even the international level—everyone becomes stymied. There is a sort of 'holy fear,' a kind of religious reign of terror, with threats of hell, excommunication and exclusion. These psychological weapons are used to frighten people, as the threat of torture was in the past by the Inquisition. That is why it is important to emphasise that where there is love, there is no fear. If we do not become a community of love and acceptance, people will just bypass the Church."

The deliberate attacks on thinkers in the church has morphed into the coddling of sexual abusers, because when obedience alone becomes premium, then you do not have people of strong conscience running an organization. You have ignorant, self-serving men who pull the wagons around them and denounce the "outsiders" as wanting to destroy the institution. You have silly talk about "petty gossip" (as if even one act of sexual abuse of a child is a petty matter) and blaming pedophilia on homosexuals (which is what Cardinal Tarcisio Bertone, the current secretary of state for the Vatican, recently did) or on the media (another ploy by Vatican characters during this crisis) or even on sex education (which bishops in Mexico declared recently). In reaction to the latter, the Mexican Association for Sexual Health, a group of professional counselors and educators, responded to the bishops' criticism: "Those of good conscience in the church should stop this absurdity and find good help. Blaming the problems that the Catholic Church has had with priests' sexually abusing minors on sex education makes no sense. It borders on the pathetic."

Yes-men, sycophants, do not make good leaders. And when a crisis arises such as pedophilia, they are at a loss to respond except to follow orders of silence that come from above. This is truly pathetic and absurd—especially coming a mere seventy years after the Nazi era, when obedience was elevated to a supreme virtue. One would think we might have learned something from that pathos by now.

Bullying and Bribery

English actor Christopher Frye recently called Ratzinger a "playground bully" for the ugly documents he has written against homosexuals. One psychologist who has studied bullying in depth points out that those who experience trauma as young children "are at much greater risk of becoming aggressive or even psychopathic later on, bullying other children . . ." For Ratzinger and his brother, growing up as they did under a very strict father and in dire times in prewar Germany, bullying may have been the order of the day. Like father, like son. Just as Georg beat up children in his choir and saw nothing wrong in doing so, so Ratzinger has beaten up theologians in his church, and apparently with a clear conscience. Walter Mixa, a leading conservative bishop in Germany and a key member of Germany's Bishops Conference, was forced to resign in April 2010 because of accusations of hitting children.

Martin Hoffman, a professor of psychology at New York University and a pioneer of empathy research (empathy being the opposite of bullying) suggests that "you can enhance empathy by the way you treat children, or you can kill it by providing a harsh punitive environment." A harsh, punitive environment has characterized Vatican Catholicism for decades. In fact, studies show that over the long term, routine use of corporal punishment not only fails to change behavior but also increases aggression in children. How aggressive was Ratzinger's father? Mary Gordon, founder of

Roots of Empathy, a school-based program designed to foster compassion, points out that children who suffer more abuse at home are more likely to become bullies. "It's not that they don't know what it feels like to be hurt; it's that they have learned that violence is the way to express anger or assert power."

Ratzinger's sense of empathy for children abused by priests has obviously been lacking for a very long time. His empathy for theologians and those they serve is grossly underdeveloped. His deeper empathy was clearly reserved for the image of the church institution and the priests, bishops, and cardinals who represented that image even when it was profoundly tarnished.

Dutch sociologist René Veenstra observes that bullies strategically pick victims they know few other classmates will dare to defend. Perhaps this helps explain the "in-group" mentality of the clerical and all-male system of the Vatican that Ratzinger and other in-house clerics demonstrate as they so vigorously defend one another and cheer one another on. One thinks of the bullying by Escriva that did not deter Vatican officials from canonizing him a saint. There seems to be no one thing that makes a particular victim a target of bullying—"one day, they just don't like a kid because that kids will wear pink, and the next day they might not like other kid because they're wearing blue, or they're tall, or they're small, or they wear glasses," comments Professor Young Shin Kim of the Child Study Center at the Yale School of Medicine. This might help explain why so many of Ratzinger's attacks on theologians are not theological at all, but simply attacks out of the blue, and why others are rallied to join in the campaign.

Very often, according to Kim, aggression and control are part of the bully's psychological profile. They may be abuse victims themselves. "Bullies want their behavior to be noticed," and 85 percent of bullying cases happen for the benefit of an audience. Indeed, "bullying is often used to maintain the social pecking order"—and, in a strictly hierarchical and all-male society like the Vatican creates, what a pecking order that is!

The social pecking order of the Roman Curia under Pope John Paul II was something to behold—and principal participants are still in important posts under Pope Benedict. We have seen how Cardinal Sodano, one of Maciel's chief cheerleaders and benefactor of his financial largess, was Vatican secretary of state from 1990 to 2006—and he is currently the most senior cardinal, as dean. Cardinal Somalo, a Spaniard, who was head of the congregation overseeing religious, never moved against Father Maciel even after nine seminary victims came forward in 1997 to accuse him of abuse. Somalo is said to have received numerous envelopes "thick with cash" from Maciel's priests, who would come to his home with their bribes in hand. From 1994 to 2004 Somalo oversaw any complaints about religious orders and their leaders, and he was made chamberlain and put in charge of the papal conclave that elected Benedict XVI. The current head of the congregation that oversees religious, Cardinal Franc Rode, was also a loud champion of Father Maciel and his now disgraced Legion of Christ.

William Black, who is a white-collar criminologist and the author of *The Best Way to Rob a Bank is to Own One*, comments on the phenomenon of bullying: "Bullies play a well known game. Their strategy is to intimidate. Sometimes they threaten us directly and sometimes they threaten those we care about. . . . They must be confronted . . . Bullies are cowards. . . . Giving in to bullies guarantees that they will act ever more abusively. . . . An adult who repeatedly gives in to a bully is a coward."

Bullying and control can be as much a financial thing as a sexual or an intellectual thing. After all, power is power. One Legion of Christ member, a priest who eventually left the order, has said, "Maciel wanted to buy power. It got to a breaking point for me over a culture of lying [within the order] . . . They lie about money, where it comes from, where it goes, how it's given." This priest was apparently a delivery boy for Maciel's money, which he took to various cardinals of influence. "It was a way of making friends, insuring certain help if it were needed, oiling the cogs." Another ex-Legionary commented that the idea was to get wealthy people to offer money "for works of charity." But what charities? "In fact, you don't know where the money's going. It's an elegant way of giving a bribe." How much of the incessant support of Legion of Christ, Opus Dei, and Communion and Liberation on the part of the Vatican the past thirty years has been, in fact, a quest for financial support from these engines of money making?

As I write this, the Italian government is investigating the Vatican for having "deliberately flouted anti-laundering laws with the aim of hiding the ownership, destination and origin of the capital." The police seized $30 million from the Vatican bank known as the Institute for Religious Works in September 2010. Twenty years ago the Vatican bank was involved in scandals and hired Sicilian financier Michele Sindona to manage its foreign investments. When Sindona's banking empire collapsed in the mid-1970s, his links to the mob were exposed and he was put in prison in New York, where he died from poison in his coffee. Roberto Calvi, a banker from northern Italy, then took over his job and his bank, Banco Ambrosiano, collapsed in 1982 after $1.3 billion in loans to dummy companies in Latin America were exposed. The Vatican had provided letters of credit for the loans and repaid $250 million on them. Calvi was found hanging from a bridge in London, his pockets stuffed with money; his wife reports he had met with Opus Dei prelates the day before.

Conclusion

What we are coming to know as the great "pedophile crisis" within the Roman Catholic Church is not only that. Pedophilia happens in many places and under many circumstances—not all in the church. The real crisis is the way the hierarchy handled the sick and criminal acts of their clergy. The real crisis is the cover-ups, sworn silences, ignoring of victims' suffering, lack of empathy, delay, and denial—in short, continued abuse. But the abuse was not only about sexual crimes. There was intellectual abuse going on in the same offices that condoned the sexual abuse and on a massive worldwide scale. The CDF that abused theologians is the same CDF that allowed sexual abuse of children to fester and fester.

To silence and bully more than ninety-one theologians whose vocation it is to help think through the church's tradition in light of historical and cultural evolution is no small thing. How does one count the millions of Catholics and others around the world whose lives were shortchanged because the Vatican embraced cults and right-wing dictatorships and anti-intellectual orders in the name of religion while condemning theologians and activists actually fighting for justice?

There was also financial abuse—not only the $3 billion that the American Catholic Church has so far lost to pedophile payoffs, payoffs that have rendered at least six dioceses bankrupt, but also the bribery and financial malfeasance that has made a mockery of the Curia and its powerful decision makers and invitations to morality and justice.

Fintan O'Toole comments on clerical abuse in Ireland, "The truth is that child abuse and cover-up are not primarily about religion or sex. They are about power. The bleak lessons of human history are that those who have too much power will abuse it. And that organizations will put their own interests above those of the victims." He points out that the Irish Amateur Swimming Association gave coaches unlimited power with their charges and the results were, "on a much smaller scale, essentially the same as that of the bishops." The lesson? "The problem is not swimming, any more than it is Catholicism. It is power."

But power has become a dominant theme in Catholicism ever since the Second Vatican Council adjourned. Power is the issue, and Ratzinger's life journey since 1968 at least has been in pursuit of power, "seeking the purple." Authoritarianism is the constant common denominator in his and Pope John Paul II's unbounded admiration of the Opus Dei, Legion of Christ, and Communion and Liberation organizations and founders.

It is time to introduce a new term: ecclesiolatry. Ecclesiolatry is making an idol of the church, its structures, and its offices. It is a severe form of idolatry for it conjures up evil spirits of ego and ambition, willful ignorance and arrogance, deceit, abuse of power, and small-mindedness. It substitutes human structures for divine realities. Jesus preached the kingdom/queendom of God. Substituting Church for kingdom/queendom of his teaching is simply inaccurate and idolatrous and can easily be self-serving.

All this is the bad news. The good news will now follow when we discuss how, given so much destruction in a once proud tradition, the Catholic Church might resurrect from its own grave. The Holy Spirit may have something up its sleeve in all this rancid story of Vatican malfeasance. Maybe it is preparing us for a post-Vatican Catholic*ism*, a truly *catholic* Christianity that is respectful of the contribution theologians and laypeople make to the community and truly respectful of the varied spiritual traditions of the world and of global cultures and their marvelous diversity.

Maybe the church is not meant to be a noun or an institution, but a yeast, to use Jesus' expression. Here is how Bishop Casaldáliga puts it: "For me the church is not even a society. The church is the *ferment* of the new society God wants. The church is light, it is salt, it is the seed in humanity. The only society that exists is human society."

The End of the Catholic Church as We Know It

AND

The Birth of a Truly Catholic Christianity

✠

Many are the cries for justice and renewal of the Church in the face of the shameful scandals we have dealt with in this book. The scandals are trinitarian, a kind of shadow mirror of the traditional three vows of celibacy, poverty, and obedience: They are about sexual power and its cover-up, about financial power, and about governing power and whom to obey: an Ecumenical Council and the full magisterium of teachers and lay sense of the faithful, or the Curia eager to take back its power and dictate to others their meaning of Church? Included in this battle is intellectual envy and bullying of thinkers and the preaching of an "ideology of submission," the very distortion of obedience that totalitarian regimes everywhere promulgate. Included in this struggle are these immortal words from a curial member uttered during the council: "This accursed council is ruining the church."

We know which side won in the short term. In the short term the curialists got their Church back and with it the promulgation of strange, so-called lay organizations whose only theology is ideology and where obedience trumps all other virtues. And with it condemnations of most thinkers and activists and the brave, brave souls who risked life and limb to support the struggle for justice in Latin America and beyond.

But what the curialists have won is disintegrating before our eyes. It is dying from a thousand cuts on television and in Internet news daily. The Church as we know it—that is, in its institutional form of many centuries—is dying. It has lost its moral and spiritual credibility such that one thirty-four-year-old can say to me: "There is nothing left to reform. The only issue is: Who gets the buildings?" None other than Bishop Casadáliga has observed that "the Vatican, as it has crystallized over the course of history right up to the present day, is the greatest enemy of the mission that Christ entrusted to Peter. After all, it is an internal enemy. It is a structure hostile to the witness, service, and evangelical form that Christ obviously wanted for his church."

So the question is: What next? What is worth saving from the burning building? Is the Holy Spirit, so full of imagination and willingness to "make all things new" behind all of this turmoil, disappointment, and struggle? Are Cardinal Ratzinger, Pope John Paul II, Father Maciel, Father Escriva, and Cardinal Law all part of an effort by the Holy Spirit to clean house in the most radical way? To press the restart button? To start over for the twenty-first century? To invent all new wineskins to hold the rich and delightful wine of Jesus' authentic teachings and actions? Have they so devastated the playing field that it is level again? Are we ready for new actions and a new birth of generosity, courage, and imagination?

I think so. And if so, it means that it is time for all Catholics and indeed all Christians to get involved in rebirthing Christianity. Protestantism, while not reeling from the scandals of Vatican Catholicism, still has a need to be renewed. Not only the Church is at stake but good and afflicted people everywhere and the earth herself, with her bountiful and beautiful creatures, suffering so much at the hands of our species.

In this section we will deal first with letting go of some myths, with taking treasures from the burning house (what is worth saving?), with what a post-Vatican Catholicism would entail, and last with dealing with the grief that betrayal by Church structures and leaders has wrought—and suggestions for practical actions.

CHAPTER 9

SOME MYTHS THAT CATHOLICS
NEED TO SURRENDER

✦

OR A TRULY *CATHOLIC* CHRISTIANITY TO EMERGE, there are some myths that have to be surrendered. When this happens, some alternative new (and some very ancient) myths can emerge. For religion, like morality and most important human enterprises, runs on myths. Remythologizing requires some demythologizing. Emptying precedes filling.

Following are some of these myths that can and need to go, and the myths that are emerging anew.

The Myth of Celibacy

When celibacy is truly lived out and fully embraced, it has a role to play. It can allow a person to focus more on one's service and less on the daily requirements of making a living, changing diapers, providing for bread on the table for others, paying for children's schooling, and more. I have known a number of celibates—both Catholic and Buddhist—who have demonstrated by their generosity and life choices that not everyone needs an active sexual (defined as genital) life to be useful, happy, and engaging. It can also serve to provide a path to deep exploration of consciousness such as a true monk or nun is committed to explore.

But—and this is a big "but"—celibacy needs to be a choice, not a requisite for leadership. Given the success of contemporary birth control techniques (the Augustinian refusal to allow birth control not withstanding), the rediscovery of sexuality as an altogether beautiful and organic way to express love for another human being and for God—just as the Song of Songs says in the Bible—is well within the Jewish tradition. Thus it is within the tradition of Jesus, the rabbi.

Seeing sexuality as a blessing and not a moral problem is a necessary part of remythologizing Christianity.

What is clear from the emergence of facts about priestly celibacy in the past forty years is that much of it is mythical. Some of the finest priests I have known—the most caring, generous, and intellectually alive—also had a lover in their life. This is how the practice has been divorced from the story. It is time to change the story. Celibacy as a requirement needs to go. It is not a myth grounded in reality. The new myth, an ancient one, that sexuality and mysticism go together, that making love is an experience of the divine and a taste of theophany—this needs to supplant the excessive preaching of celibacy as a primary goal of priestly discipline.

In an excellent article titled "Celibacy and the Catholic priest," author and former priest James Carroll makes many important points about celibacy and how "power was the issue." There was a time, he points out, in the "Bing Crosby glory days," when celibacy stood for an "all-or-nothing bet on the existence of God." Celibacy carried a magnetic pull—but "the magnet is dead." The monastic vow of "chastity" which takes place in a community of support was imposed on all priests in the Western church in the twelfth century as "celibacy" and this destroyed the freedom behind the choice. The Second Vatican Council was preparing to consider both birth control and celibacy (after all, a council had declared celibacy a rule for priests in 1139, why should not a council discuss it in 1965?), when Pope Paul VI got jitters and intervened on both issues, reserving the decisions for himself. He delivered an encyclical on each that allowed no change in practice. Both teachings "plunged the whole church into a culture of dishonesty" as Catholic lay people ignore birth control mandates and priests often find their way around celibacy rules. And a preoccupation with sexual issues—"a screeching, single-issue obsession with abortion," for example, swamps far more pressing issues of social, economic and eco-justice matters.

The Myth That the Vatican Is the Only Teacher (or "Magisterium")

The idea that all truth resides in one central place is a relatively recent myth, reinforced by television as much as by the odd declaration of Vatican I (1869–1870) that the pope, in teaching *ex cathedra* (that is, from the seat of his authority), is infallible. Furthermore, this questionable teaching has undergone an ever more odd effort by Cardinal Ratzinger, now Pope Benedict, to expand the notion of infallibility, a "creeping infallibility" or even a "galloping infallibility" doctrine that may serve the interests of Vatican potentates but does not serve the interests of other believers worldwide. Garry Wills writes: "The Pope alone, we are now asked to accept, is competent to tell Christian people how to live. No one else can have any say in the matter—not a Council, not the college of all bishops, not the national synods of bishops, not the Christian people. The Holy Spirit now speaks to only one person on earth, the omnicompetent head of the church, a church that is all head and no limbs."

I believe that the modern view of physics, namely that there was a center to the universe somewhere if we only found it, greatly embellished the notion of papal (Vatican) infallibility. That physics has been proven wrong. There is no center of the universe. Our universe is multicentric. So, too, intellectual thought is multiple, diverse, and debatable. We need to demythologize the notion of one central magisterium (the teaching authority within the church) and remythologize the ancient and premodern understanding that there are many theologies and many thinkers, all of whom ought to be listened to, discussed, and debated, and that very few answers are absolute. Questions are more important than answers. Isn't that why Jesus preached in parables and not in legalistic norms or lists of moral dos and don'ts?

The late and esteemed Father Bede Griffith wrote a fine article on the true meaning of "magisterium," saying: "Many people today think that the magisterium consists of the pope, and the Roman Curia, but this is mistaken. 'Magisterium' comes from the Latin *magister*, a master, and signifies authority to teach. Strictly speaking there is only one such authority in the Church and that is the Holy Spirit whom Jesus promised to his disciples to 'lead men into all truth.'" He goes on to name four "organs of the magisterium" including the pope and the Roman Curia, which deals with day-to-day administration of the church; the second is the bishops. The pope is "subordinate to the authority of the bishops in communion with the pope who constitute the magisterium properly speaking. This was made clear at the Second Vatican Council." The third organ is the "periti" or expert theologians who advised the bishops. "In a sense it is to the theologians that the word magisterium properly applies, since a theologian is a master of sacred doctrine, who has been commissioned to teach theology in the name of the Church."

But the "most important" organ of the magisterium is the laity, "the people (*laos*) of God . . . Strictly speaking, it is the laity, the people of God, who constitute the Church, while popes, bishops and priests are 'ministers' chosen from among the laity and commissioned by the Holy Spirit to act in the name of the Church." The whole church is called "a holy nation, a royal priesthood," and all members of the church share equally in the gift of the Holy Spirit The idea that authority comes from above, from the pope and the bishops, is not the ideal of the church as found in the New Testament. Such a "command structure" smacks much more of the Soviet Union than of New Testament church. Popes and bishops "are responsible to the laity, the people of God, for their teaching and their actions. Just as the pope has no authority apart from the bishops, so the pope and the bishops have no authority apart from the people from whom they are chosen and whom they represent."

Bede wrote these words at the time of the collapse of the Berlin Wall. His prayer was that Eastern Europeans' newly found freedom might also extend to the Roman Catholic Church. Cardinal John Henry Newman, who has recently received the dubious honor of being named a saint by the same organization that called Escriva a saint, would very much support this analysis of teaching authority in the church. Newman said this about the papacy in his day: "It is anomaly and bears no good fruit. He [the pope] becomes a god, has no one to contradict him, does not know facts, and does cruel things without meaning it." He called the papacy of Pius IX a "climax of tyranny" that was heretical, and decried the fact that an "extreme centralilisation . . . now is in use." Newman believed the laity should participate fully in the life of the church, and when a bishop objected he said: "The church would look foolish without them." Newman favored individual conscience over groupthink and blind obedience.

The Myth of the Pope as a Celebrity, a Contemporary Version of Idolatry

"Papalolatry" is a contemporary form of idolatry, fanned and whipped up by the nature of television and other electronic media, which like nothing more than to zero in on one "star" figure, especially if that star figure is robed attractively in, for example, white robes and bright red slippers, kisses the ground on occasion, and blesses large throngs of people. There exists a very unholy marriage between the star power of television and the papacy today that can easily fall into a cult of personality and a cult of papalism.

This is especially dangerous when the papal forces desire such a cult to bolster the power of their centralized bureaucracy or their needy ego. This grave danger exists, and it has been abused time and time again in the past forty years. Adulation replaces authenticity and can feed the most dangerous forms of projection. Idol worship, star worship, is always a temporary thing. True spirituality does not condone it or seek it. A cult of personality is not what makes authentic religion happen. It is the opposite of authentic religion, as the Epistle of James warns us: "Pure, unspoiled religion, in the eyes of God our Father is this: coming to the help of orphans and widows when they need it, and keeping oneself uncontaminated by the world" (James 1:27).

The Myth Enshrined in the Cupola of St. Peter's Basilica

That myth comes from the Gospel of Matthew (and only Matthew's Gospel), chapter 16, verse 18. It says: "Thou art Peter and upon this Rock I will build my church." This line has been very foundational to the petrine version of Christianity, namely that of the *Roman* Catholic Church. The problem is that scholars today agree that the historical Jesus did not in fact say these words. They came later as the Christian community began to build itself up globally. Here is what the scholars tell us: "The commendation of Peter is a construction of Matthew. The play on Peter's name (*petra* in Greek means 'rock') makes him the foundation on which the congregation is built (v. 18): this undoubtedly reflects Peter's position in Matthew's branch of the emerging Christian movement. (Peter's assignment is confirmed by verse 19: 'I shall give you the keys of Heaven's domain, and whatever you bind on earth will be considered bound in heaven, and whatever you release on earth will be considered released in heaven.') All of this is Christian language and reflects conditions in the budding institution."

Of course, Jesus did not speak Greek or know Greek, so how could he make this play on the name "Peter"? By common consent, the scholars of the well-regarded Jesus Seminar agreed that "Jesus did not say this; it represents the perspective or content of a later or different tradition."

This teaching may come as a shock to some Roman Catholics, but it is necessary to return to the facts of Jesus' teaching, to demythologize in order to remythologize. Historical circumstances led to the Roman Empire persecuting the early Christians in Rome and beyond (and both Peter and Paul were most likely martyred in Rome along with many other followers of Jesus in the early centuries). But eventually, as we know, the empire collapsed of its own sheer weight and extravagance in the fourth century and the Christian church picked up its pieces. Many compromises were made between the message of Jesus—which was anti-imperial, as whenever he talked about the "kingdom of God" he was distinguishing it from the kingdom of the empire—and the needs of the empire.

Paul too, like Jesus, set up his teaching in contradistinction to the empire. Biblical scholar John Dominic Crossan reminds us of how in his letters Paul used the phrase "in Christ" countless times, but that for Paul and his listeners this was understood in contrast to being "in Rome." Crossan writes: "In a world where identity was often shaped by one's relationship to Rome, by being, as it were, 'in Rome,' insisting on a self-definition exclusively by being 'in Christ' was subversive at best and treasonous at worst." No right thinking Christian would confuse today our being "in Christ" and being "in the Vatican."

Emperor Constantine in the early fourth century gathered the bishops from all around the empire to fashion a creedal statement that could at last end the warring sides of religious polemic and bring peace to the kingdom. But much of that creed was less Jesus' teaching than it was an institutionalizing of organized religion. It smacks somewhat of being "in the empire" more than of being "in Christ."

An authentic remythologizing, therefore, would once again set the values of Jesus in contrast to those of empire and would rely less on one figure (Peter) and one place (Rome) to symbolize Christian unity, which may account for some of the fierce resistance to liberation theology that has emerged in our lifetime from the extreme right wing of Latin America and of the CIA in our own country. Empires do not freely or happily relinquish their power—and certainly not to spiritual values. (Of course, Gandhi proved how one might dismantle an empire without engaging in fierce military warfare but using what are essentially spiritual tools and tactics, tactics that Martin Luther King Jr. would also pick up on in his struggle against a segregationist ideology and empire.)

The Myth That the Roman Curia Will Reform Itself or Wants to Reform Itself or Is Serving the Larger Church, the "People of God"

Consider the following statement by a particular victim of the Roman Curia: "I do not see any means of reconciling with the spirit of the Gospel a system that condemns someone as a result of secret denunciations, that gives that person no way of defense, and that provides no way of knowing the context of the condemnation." This observation was made by Father H. M. Feret, a French Dominican theologian in 1954. Yet it could be made again today, in 2010. Supposedly there was a reform movement more than forty years ago—a very complex and elaborate Vatican Council II that brought together the best minds and leaders of the church to reform and renew the church. Here it is fifty-six years later and nothing has changed in the Vatican bureaucracies. The reasons are obvious.

Curialists are padding their nests of power and privilege. They let the Council happen (fighting it all the way) and then they took it all back to serve their real religion. Their "theology" (which is in fact an ideology of power) is completely suspect. They have learned nothing from decades of deep biblical, historical, anthropological, and spiritual scholarship. They have learned even less from the generous living of the Gospel by many around the world and especially in the Latin American church. And they learned nothing from the council. Thomas Aquinas teaches that willful ignorance of what one ought to know is a mortal sin.

Peggy Noonan put it this way: "I know this from having seen it: Many—not all, but many—of the men who staff the highest levels of the Vatican have been part of the very scandal they are now charged with repairing. They are defensive and they are angry, and they will not turn the church around on their own." Gandhi observed that people do not relinquish power and privilege voluntarily. The Curia has had forty-some years since Vatican II to get it right. They have failed completely, and their failure is the scandal that is making a mockery of the Church. Their simony alone stinks to the highest heavens.

Cardinals were invented fifteen centuries ago; they can be replaced and new inventions can happen today. One church historian reminds us that cardinals appeared "long after the apostolic age" and for several hundred years were generally laymen. In the ninth century three classes of cardinals were made: cardinal bishops, cardinal priests and cardinal deacons. "All were tied directly to the pope and the papacy." Only in the twelfth century were cardinals appointed outside Italy. Bishop George Robinson made the following point at the Australian Council of Priests Conference recently: "Most bishops would be in favor of bishops electing the cardinals . . . What happens at the moment is the pope appoints the cardinals who then elect the pope who then appoints more cardinals and on and on it goes . . . So it's a vicious circle. And it is deliberately designed to ensure we do not have another Pope John XXIII." A vicious circle indeed.

Bishop Pat Power of the Diocese of Canberra-Goulburn comments: "In responding to sexual and other forms of abuse within the Church it is not enough to concentrate on the sinfulness and failure of those guilty of abuse. It is not just a question of individual repentance but *a total systemic reform of Church structures which is needed.*"

The Myth That Unity Must Sacrifice Diversity

There is unity and there is unity. There is diversity and there is diversity. There is unity with diversity and there is unity that countenances no diversity. When one looks at nature, one sees everywhere so much unity and yet so much diversity. Nature is biased in favor of diversity. We now know that our species is one species that has traveled from one homeland in Africa, some sixty thousand years ago or more, to fill the earth. But we come in diverse colors, languages, songs, rituals, religions, ways of seeing the world. It is important—indeed vital for survival—that we both honor the richness of diversity and look for our common roots and common values. (I have done the latter in my book *One River, Many Wells*, in which I name eighteen themes that all our religions share in common.) We need to dance the dance and find the flexibility to celebrate unity *with diversity*—not a unity that clubs differences, denounces them, or tries them as heretical.

The early Church, we now know, was profoundly diverse. There were the "branches" that followed James, the brother of Jesus and a leader in Jerusalem; one that followed Peter; the branch that followed Mary Magdalene; the branch that followed Paul; and many more throughout the world of the first century. They argued among themselves. Can you have Christ without Moses? Paul, for example, brags at one point that he stood up to Peter and said he was simply wrong. They had their petty differ-ences; Peter seemed especially envious of Mary Magdelene, and within a few decades the female leadership of the original movement seemed to have been pretty snuffed out by the men. Bruce Chilton writes: "By class, temperament, cultural bias, and religious custom, Christianity was a fractured movement from the moment people started using the term 'Christian.'" Diversity was a part of Christianity from the get-go.

Once we have demythologized the simplistic notion of unity as "everyone obey one voice" and move on to the more organic and natural understanding of unity—a unity of form that sets out in different direc-tions and through trial and error creates its own expressions and ideas, leaders, and practices—then we have a healthy remythologizing process unfolding. Today Christianity has morphed into many varied expressions from Greek Orthodox to Egyptian Coptic, from Petrine Roman Catholi-cism to Anglican Catholicism, from Lutheran to Presbyterian to Baptist to Methodist, and so on. And there are distinctive Christianities in South and Central America, in North America, in Africa, in Europe, in Asia—all creating an authentic and valuable expression of the variety of traditions that informed Christianity from the beginning.

The new mythology, therefore, says something about unity *and* diver-sity and celebrates the many expressions of language, liturgy, teaching, and practice that exist. What binds it all together is not shouting "heretic" from one central command center, but rather the beauty and truth that is found in one "mystical body of Christ." As M. D. Chenu put it, "Uni-formity is a caricature of unity. Unity implies diversity. Today pluralism is necessary for theology and for pastoral work. I think the new churches of the Third World should have autonomy."

The Myth That St. Augustine's Teaching Accurately Represents the Teachings of Jesus of Nazareth

Augustine of Hippo lived four centuries after Jesus, in northern Africa. He never met the man except as we do—in the Scriptures or in Christ experi-ence. And yet the Western church (certainly not the Eastern traditions of Greece and Russia) burdens believers with teachings of Augustine that are unique to him—and that Jesus would never recognize. His writings were often used to buttress a Christian empire. Among these mistaken teachings is that we are born with original sin and that this is what Jesus means—he has come to wash us of original sin. Jesus never heard of original sin; no one of the time had. The fall? Yes. But not original sin. Since my book *Original Blessing* was published in 1983, I have learned more and more stories from mothers, native peoples, and others who cannot believe that their children come into the world damaged and unlovable. It is a very dangerous teaching.

The great Jewish psychologist and spiritual writer Otto Rank posits that humans come into the world with an original wound, and I find that language much more sensible. He names the wound as that of separation, a deep separation we feel from our mother on leaving the womb and a button that is pushed every time other separations such as death, divorce, sickness, or distance affect us in the course of our lifetime. And he says only the *unio mystica*, the mystical union we experience in love and in beauty, can heal that wound. In that understanding we can recognize what a reunion Jesus and the Christ bring us.

So let us demythologize Augustine's original sin notion and remythologize around original blessing (meaning all beings in the universe are essentially good, including ourselves) at the same time we acknowledge the reality of our wounds, including our most primary wound of separation.

Another teaching from Augustine that Jesus would deny is that women are inferior to men. Augustine actually said, "Man but not woman is made in the image and likeness of God." In doing so, he was building on a couple of centuries of ecclesial patriarchy, including lines such as these: "Women are the gateway to hell" (from Tertullian, a third-century theologian).

Any follower of Jesus has to renounce such patriarchal nonsense and demythologize such lies. Part of the revolution of Jesus' consciousness was his respect for women and his holding women in a place of responsibility and intelligence. It was a woman who first told the Easter story, after all, and it was the women, and only one man, who were present at the crucifixion, according to the Gospels.

Another teaching from Augustine that does not come from Jesus is that sex must be justified by having babies. Augustine taught that all lovemaking is at least a venial sin because "one loses control." Funny, I think losing control is pretty much what a mystical experience entails. If control is one's god, then losing control is a negative thing. But if love is one's God, then losing control in lovemaking or in other creative acts may well be a path to spiritual union. Augustine's fear and shame about sexuality has haunted the Western consciousness for centuries, and it is still behind papal teaching that even in a time of AIDS and a time of excessive human reproduction, birth control is always wrong. Augustine's teaching also reinforces homophobia, for homosexual love cannot be justified by promising to make babies. This mythology needs to go, and with it can arise a healthy mythology of sexual love.

The Myth That Jesus Wanted a Church Leadership of All-Male Celibates

Did the Lord endorse forming a kind of boys' club sworn to secrecy (and hearing one another's confessions)? One wonders. And making all decisions about everyone else's lives? Doubtful. We have seen from the earlier portions of this book what a dangerous thing unbridled power can be in the hands of men who want to please their tiny little circle, how power corrupts and absolute power corrupts absolutely. Would the horrible events around priestly pedophilia have occurred and also been covered up so fully if women were on board to question all-male decision makers? Most of Jesus' disciples were married men, and a number were women.

All human gatherings today need to bring back the healthy balance of yin and yang, feminine and masculine. The church is no exception. Without that balance we will perish. The issue to bring alive is the divine feminine but also the sacred masculine (as opposed to the ill and diseased masculinity that reigns when an empire mentality dominates).

The Myth That the Church "Is Not a Democracy" (Cardinal Ratzinger's Words) but Ought to Be a Monarchy, the Last Monarchy on Earth

The forms the church takes to present itself to the world and to govern its own existence can and will evolve with time and cultural changes. Everything humans do is of that ilk since every being and system in the universe is subject to nature's rules of living, dying, and rebirth of form. Evolution happens. Why would the church be exempt? The fact is that after centuries of imperial rulers and of monarchical rulers, the human race discovered democracy and has made many attempts to establish some form of representative governing by and for its citizens. Why would a religious body not want to participate in some way in this advanced consciousness? The Anglican Church, for example, deserves credit for developing a parliamentary system whereby not only the clerics but also laypersons have a say in choosing church leaders (bishops). Each religious body has its way of choosing leaders. The idea that an all-male group of supposedly all-celibate cardinals were appointed by Jesus to lead the church is, of course, silly. Jesus never heard about cardinals (they emerged in the late fifth and early sixth centuries), just as he never heard about the Vatican or the pope.

Jesus did know about imperial potentates and monarchs, and he was not impressed. He rejected them. And yet the Roman Catholic Church has slid back into the monarchical and imperial way of leadership even though Jesus taught that "the last shall be first" and the Second Vatican Council strived mightily to decentralize decision making and urged national bishops' conferences to lead their respective churches and laypeople to take responsibility, especially at the local parish level. All this was stripped away by the *coup d'eglise* of the past two, in my mind, schismatic papacies.

The Myth That Confuses Jesus and Christ and Calls Jesus the Exclusive Son of God

Another myth that derives from the time of the marriage of empire and church under Constantine in the fourth century, and the Nicene Creed that was established to render that marriage effective, is the teaching that confuses Jesus and Christ. As if "Christ" was Jesus' last name and that only Jesus is a son of God. Jesus did not talk about himself as the only Christ; in fact he urged his followers to do the works he did and greater ones. He teaches all of us to take in the Christ nature and to live accordingly. Or, as Meister Eckhart put it seven centuries ago, "We are all meant to be mothers of God. What good is it to me if Mary gave birth to the son of God and I do not do the same in my time and culture and person?"

Authentic Christianity flies on two wings—that of the historical Jesus and that of the Cosmic Christ, the light in all things and also the wounds in all things. Jesus woke us all up to our Christ-hood, to our likeness to God and our responsibility for God-like actions such as justice making and compassion.

Nor did Jesus teach that he was the exclusive way to God. Biblical scholar Bruce Chilton writes: "Readers today think exclusively of Jesus when they hear the words the 'Son of God.' But the phrase had a life of its own before it was applied to Jesus, . . . referring to angels (Genesis 6:2), the whole people called Israel (Hosea 11:1) and the kind in David's line (Psalm 2:7). Direct revelation extends God's favor to people and angels; each is 'the Son,' 'the beloved,' as Jesus became in his vision at his baptism (Mark 1:11). It was at Baptism that God sends the Spirit of his Son into every believer who cries, as Jesus did, 'Abba, Father' (Galatians 4:6). The believer becomes a Son, just as Jesus called upon his father; as Paul says in the same sentence, God sends his Spirit 'because you are Sons.'" We all need to recover our awareness of our divine sonship and daughtership.

There are many ways to God and Jesus found and taught ways that God also comes to us. As Meister Eckhart put it, "All ways lead to God for God is on them all evenly for the person who knows." I have known Buddhists who were more Christ-like than Catholic popes, and they followed Buddha's ways. I have known Native Americans who were more Christ-like than Christian leaders, and they derived their spiritual strength and integrity from following Native ways. So let us not confuse Jesus with Christ or make an exclusive way of Jesus' way. The Spirit "blows where it will," and the Spirit has always worked through all cultures and all times. This teaching from the Second Vatican Council is a breath of fresh air that deserves our attention and meditation. Christians need to practice some humility and observe—rather than judge—the ways of other faith traditions and how the Spirit has been busy at work in them and continues to be so. I call this "deep ecumenism," and it is a myth that needs to be brought alive in this time of global connecting and mixing of the marvelously diverse religious traditions of humankind.

We can learn so much from one another about what matters most deeply to ourselves and what mattered most deeply to our ancestors. But that learning will not come to us if we are living in a boxed-in attitude that ours is the only way. Such thinking is profoundly adolescent. It is stuck in ego-identity. It is not at all adult.

The Myth That God Is Exclusively Male

To this day the present pope and the previous pope require that the pronoun "she" never be used at the altar of God. The divine name is not relegated to one half of the human race. When we render our images of God to be exclusively male, we do great harm to ourselves, our institutions, and our children. Meister Eckhart warned that "all the names we give to God come from an understanding of ourselves." Thus it is something of a Rorschach test when the Vatican forbids images of the divine feminine. Such actions are sinful excuses for prolonging sexism and reinforcing punitive father images of an avenging, angry patriarchal deity. Such images support a society and organization that is more likely to be part of the "dominator complex" than one of partnership. What are the lessons here for our children, whether they are boys or girls? That God relegates girls and women to secondary status? Is that a healthy lesson for boys or girls to receive?

The divine feminine is present in our deepest biblical traditions, such as the wisdom tradition that nurtured the historical Jesus, and also in our great medieval mystical traditions of such teachers as Hildegard of Bingen, Meister Eckhart, Mechtild of Magdeburg, Julian of Norwich, and many others. Is the Vatican so out of touch with its own tradition and so married to an all-male projection onto divinity that it can remain blind and ignorant to this important dimension of our tradition? The Holy Spirit is feminine, as is wisdom, in the biblical traditions. And scholars today agree that the historical Jesus himself came from the wisdom tradition.

It is a dangerous thing to leave out one half of our psychic wholeness, to offer a yang view of the universe and of divinity with no yin to balance it. Such teaching endangers the souls and the institutions that we develop from our soul state by rendering them one-sided. Boys and girls, men and women, need to hear of the great balance and dance between the masculine and the feminine that is found everywhere in nature, in ourselves, and hopefully in our institutions and in divinity itself.

CHAPTER 10

TREASURES FROM THE BURNING
BUILDING: WHAT IS WORTH SAVING?

☩

O NE OF THE GREATEST MYSTERIES, if not miracles, of Christian history is how there is still a lineage to Jesus and of the Christ that has survived the onslaughts of the church itself. Howard Thurman is not alone in making the observation that "Christianity has betrayed Jesus." Martin Luther King Jr., Mahatma Gandhi, and so many other great souls have lamented church history versus Christ history. Albert Schweitzer offered this opinion of church history: "What has been passing for Christianity during these nineteen centuries is merely a beginning, full of weaknesses and mistakes, not a full-grown Christianity springing from the spirit of Jesus." What would it take to develop into a "full-grown Christianity springing from the spirit of Jesus"?

One of the great gifts Christianity has not been able to destroy completely or to betray is the truth and beauty of many stories and images or archetypes that Jesus revealed in his teaching and that the early community also created to tell the story of Jesus and the Christ.

Recall that an archetype is by nature universal (i.e., catholic, in its true and original meaning). That means it applies to people's lives, whether young or old, male or female, black, red, brown, or white, East or West, North or South, Christian, Buddhist, atheist, Muslim, goddess worshipper, or whatever. An archetype awakens energy—indeed, like a thunderbolt, it ignites energy. As Marian Woodman, a Jungian analyst from Toronto puts it, if you think of an image as awakening 1,000 volts of electricity, an archetype awakens 100,000! Archetypes come from a deep, common well in individual and cultural circles. This is why they are so universal.

They also arise at different times in our personal and collective histories. Timeliness is everything. I offer fifteen very useful and perennial archetypes from the Christian lineage for your consideration. There are many more in addition to these, but in such a book as this, there are limitations of time and space. Surely these are metaphors worth saving from the burning building of institutionalized Christianity.

The Paschal Mystery of Life, Death, and Resurrection

In the ancient Celtic monument in New Grange, Ireland, built even before the pyramids of Egypt, there lies a great stone at the entrance. This stone holds an ancient and common symbol—that of three spirals. This symbol echoes that of the Paschal mystery of Christianity, namely the circles of life, death, and rebirth that we all undergo.

It is Christian practice to apply this Paschal mystery to Jesus and to Christians' life, death, and rebirth that occurs by entering into that same mystery with Christ. However, the depths of this archetype suggest that this lesson applies to far more than Jesus and his followers. Look about you. We know that plants live, die, and get reborn as fertilizer for other plants. The same is true of every animal, fish, and bird. After all, what we call "fossil fuels," including oil and coal, were once plants and animals. Every time you fill up your gas tank you are participating in this same ritual. Evolution sheds light on the living, dying, and rebirthing of entire species. And today's cosmology teaches us that stars, too, as well as galaxies and supernovas, all live, die, and spread their elements in explosive resurrections and rebirths. Thus the Paschal mystery is a cosmic habit.

"Incarnation," God Taking on Flesh

The idea that God need not be relegated to an etherial, ghostly, superior arena of pure spirit but can actually be present in and set up the divine tent and dwell among and in places, mountains, rivers, valleys, trees, whales, animals, flowers, and us—this is what incarnation means. God taking on flesh. God blessing flesh. Flesh as not being the obstacle to spirit but the companion to spirit. The end of scapegoating flesh and matter as the origin of evil or the enemy of spirit is real to the extent that incarnation is taken seriously. Whatever God is and wherever God manifests or reveals the Godself, flesh can truly be God's home and dwelling place. Taking good care of our bodies and the food that enters our bodies and the exercise we bestow on our bodies are all part of honoring the temple of God that is our bodies and within which the divine dwells. Divinity is not oblivious of history or of matter but integral to both. This teaching honors our bodies and the reality of our everyday lives and the very history of ongoing evolution of our world, our earth, our cultures, and our personal stories.

God as Light

"I am the Light of the World," says Christ (not the historical Jesus, but Christ). How important a statement is that? Especially if we are all other Christs. Are we also "lights of the world"? How are we doing in that regard? "Do not hide your light under a bushel," suggested Jesus. How are we doing in that regard? He is called the "true light that enlightens all people" (Jn 1:9).

My research teaches me that the symbol, metaphor, or archetype of Light is the oldest symbol we have as a species for divinity. The sun was not impersonal for our earliest ancestors. They knew intimately, lacking as they did light switches and indoor heating, the gift of the sun rising daily, and the difference between cold and heat, dark and light, day and night. The sun was required for survival then just as today. But it was probably felt more deeply and intimately and taken less for granted than we do today.

The sun brings light and warmth, food and seasons. Who cannot appreciate light? And that is why when the Christ says, "I am the Light of the world," he is speaking of how divinity manifests itself in the gift of light and how widespread and universal is the experience of this reality.

Today's science adds another, powerful, and anciently understood truth to the role of light. When the physicist David Bohm says matter is frozen light, he is challenging every temptation of rationalistic and dualistic philosophers who continue to pit matter against spirit or body against soul or matter against God. The scientific truth is that for every particle of light that is matter (i.e., incarnated) in the universe, there are a *billion* particles that are not matter. This means that we beings who are flesh and incarnated light are *rare in the universe*. We are unique. Far from being a drag on our spiritual aspirations, matter already celebrates the divine incarnation as light.

"Do It to One of These, the Least of My Brethren, and You Do It to Me"

These words from the mouth of the historical Jesus tell the great and universal truth that we are all part of one another. This is the meaning of compassion. We celebrate and we suffer not as isolated individuals but as companions. The light that is God in you is the same light that is God in me. So to relieve your suffering is to relieve my suffering, and vice versa. And all of it is relieving God's suffering as well. To rejoice at your light is to rejoice at my light, and vice versa.

We are all Christs, not just on the good and happy days of joy and light, but also in the dark times of suffering, loss, grief, and oppression. Solidarity is the acting out of the archetype of the Christ being in all of us. The ability to see Christ in everyone is the beginning of authentic compassion.

The poor will resurrect in this lifetime. In Luke's gospel Mary is said to say: "He has pulled down princes from their thrones and exalted the lowly / The hungry he has filled with good things, the rich sent away empty" (Lk 1:52f.). Many are the promises that justice and hope will prevail.

> The spirit of the Lord has been given to me, for he has anointed me.
> He has sent me to bring the good news to the poor, to proclaim liberty to captives
> And the blind new sight,
> To set the downtrodden free,
> To proclaim the Lord's year of favor. (Lk 4:18f.)

The struggle for peace and justice is everyone's struggle. Jesus was in the heart of it in his time and place. He invites us to be also.

The Cross: Redemptive Suffering

We all go through it—suffering, loss, abandonment, betrayal, sickness, and death. Buddhists teach that all beings suffer. Thus the wrenching of the one great continent millions of years ago when the earth broke into seven continents was a suffering. Animals suffer, plants suffer, and even supernovas and galaxies and the original fireball suffered.

Certain teachings of Christianity have distorted the cross and left the notion in peoples' heads that we as individuals caused Jesus to suffer. Even if we did not exist, Jesus would have suffered. Why? Because all beings suffer. Yes, our mistakes and errors, jealousies, and temper tantrums, greed and envy, selfishness and lack of compassion do add to the suffering in the world. Sin does add to suffering. But even without sin there is suffering and death and destruction and loss.

So instead of exaggerating our role in Jesus' suffering on the cross, we should be reminded by this archetype that this good man underwent his suffering and death, misunderstanding and betrayal, in a most cruel fashion, being crucified like a common rebel. But he did so with courage and knowing that his teaching of compassion would somehow, someday, triumph over killing and empires.

In this way suffering redeems. Some power, some force, some spirit recycles our pain and loss and grief. But we have to acknowledge it, enter into it, yield to it. When we surrender, we learn deep wisdom and in that way too suffering does not have the last word. Death gets recycled as new life, Good Friday as Easter Sunday.

The Dark Night of the Soul

In the Christian Scripture there are some wild stories told about what happened when Jesus died in the afternoon on the cross. One source says the day turned into night. Another that the temple veil was ripped apart. Another that the dead came out of their graves. All this is apocaplytic language. Dramatic and memorable. What is that about? What are they trying to tell us?

Maybe that we all undergo these deep deaths more than once in a lifetime: divorces, deaths of loved ones, suicides, loss of jobs, being diagnosed with a serious illness, losing our homes or jobs or family, wars, depressions, and deprivations—the list goes on. Christian mystics have called these experiences the "dark night of the soul." And they are for real. There is a tendency in our culture to trivialize such episodes by taking an antidepressant pill, for example. Or to flee to some allurement, be it gambling, alcohol, drugs, sex, shopping, or some other addiction.

But the mystics urge us to stick around and learn what we can learn from this deep time of grief and bereavement. In doing this we are purified, our desires and intentions get purified, and we eventually move on stronger and wiser for the experience. We also learn compassion because we learn what others are going through in their grief. Your grief is also my grief, and vice versa. The dark night is not a private journey. It is communal, something we all undergo, something we all taste.

Creativity: Impregnation by the Spirit

One of the most celebrated teachings in the Christ story centers around the moment of conception of Jesus in the womb of Mary. According to that story (which is not a historical account but a Cosmic Christ story), the Holy Spirit impregnated Mary. The angel Gabriel said: "The Holy Spirit shall come over you." Does this impregnation by Spirit occur only to Mary? Does the story stop there? Or are we dealing with a universal story, an archetypal story? What is that story?

Perhaps it is that we all become impregnated with Spirit whenever we are being creative. We are all creative. We all give birth to the Christ as we give birth to our own persona, our own values, our own uniqueness. All the decisions we make in life about relationships, children, earning a living, being a citizen, recycling our trash, the food we eat, what we do with our money, and how and where we worship—all of it is a Spirit experience.

We saw above the teaching of Meister Eckhart that "We are all meant to be mothers of God." The Holy Spirit did not retire after the Jesus story ended. The Holy Spirit is busy impregnating us all to give birth to the Godself in all of us in the communities of which we are a part.

Another story of the omnipresence of Spirit occurs at the Pentecost event when the Holy Spirit pierces through doors and walls to fall upon the heads of the scared and frightened disciples following the tragic crucifixion event. They emerge strong and bold, courageous, and speaking in many languages.

Thomas Aquinas in the thirteenth century celebrates this promise of the Spirit bringing creativity to us all when he writes: "The same Spirit that hovered over the waters at the birth of creation hovers over the mind of the artist at work." What we give birth to is bigger than us. It is the work of Spirit. It is another Christ.

Justice

In his sermon on the mount Jesus is reported to have taught: "Blessed are those who hunger and thirst after justice, for they shall be satisfied." The entire prophetic tradition of Israel is passionate about justice. Hungry for justice. Demanding of justice. Jesus is from that same tradition. Love and justice cannot be separated. How can you say you love someone to whom you are unjust? How can we love one another outside a sphere of justice making and of fairness and balance? What is unjust does not last; it falls apart; it is not sustainable. Indeed, the psalmist teaches that the whole earth stands on a pillar of justice and righteousness, and when there is injustice the whole earth is off-kilter.

History shows that people must struggle for justice. Justice is not handed out for free. There is little "cheap justice" to be had. The elimination of apartheid in South Africa; of segregation in the United States; of child sweatshops; of sexual servitude; of homophobia; of economic, racial, gender, and ecological injustice—this is the work of all of us. But it begins, as Jesus observed, with hunger and thirst. A great desire has to be tapped in to in order to sustain the struggle for justice. Moral outrage must be tapped in to in order to carry on. Anger inspires us to persevere in the long struggle for justice. Desire must be lit, and an intelligent weighing of options must occur.

That we are capable of justice, that we can live in justice, are great and enduring myths. Justice offers hope. It keeps us going. Those who fought and died for justice are our heroes, and for good reason. Justice is a great and universal yearning looming deep inside the recesses of each of us. We are born with a sense of justice and fairness. We have to return continually to that Source.

God Is Love

God has been called many things: Father, Mother, Deity, All-Powerful, Judge, Creator, Destroyer, Avenger, and Savior, among countless names and descriptions. But to say ever so simply and ever so bluntly—and ever so directly—that "God is love" is a game changer. Almost any other name for God melts away (or ought to). There is something penultimate about calling God "Love." Something we have all been waiting to hear, especially if we have been victims of abuse by parents or adults or authority figures in any way in our lives. There is a washing and a cleansing that happens with the naming of God as *love*.

Howard Thurman puts it this way: "The religion of Jesus makes the love-ethic central. This is no ordinary achievement." To love one's neighbor as oneself, as is taught in the Good Samaritan story, means that "every man is potentially every other man's neighbor. Neighborliness is nonspatial." This is the ultimate in deep ecumenism for it challenges us to go beyond class, race, gender, nationality, religion—all barriers melt.

Notice, too, that the Letter of John, where this naming occurs, does not say: "God is heterosexual love." Or that "God is Platonic love." But simply that God is love, which to me includes both homosexual and heterosexual love. It includes love of nature and love of self, love of the cosmos and love of music, love of poetry and love of children, love of parents and love of the deceased ancestors, love of self and love of beauty everywhere. Love of justice. Love. Look for it. Make it if you can't quite find it already made.

Christ Is Born in a Manger

The archetype of Christ being born in a manger is never going to go away. It is too profound and reaches too deeply into our collective desire. We all want to see the poorest of the poor entertaining the divine. A manger is a feeding trough for animals, dirty, smelly, attracting flies and bugs, and offering food for animals. There is where we will find the Christ, the Divine One, the Holy One: among the four-legged ones (see Isaiah 1). Among the outcasts and the homeless. And in the simple corners of our own souls where there is no varnish to advertise to those with excess.

The birth story unfolds with shepherds (lowly and smelly workers living among the sheep), angels, and eventually Magi, or wandering scientists, also enter the picture. It is quite a picture. Quite an archetype overflowing with fantasy, all of it touching some powerful points in our yearnings. We all yearn to visit a place of "great tidings," of good news, of breakthrough, of the marriage of the divine and the human that takes place not in the splendor of papal or princely palaces, but in the places of straw and humility where the four-legged ones are at home.

Wisdom Sets Up Her Tent and Dwells among Us

We are all hungry for wisdom. Knowledge is not enough. Information does not satisfy. Only wisdom satisfies. Wisdom "plays with God before the creation of the world." We all need play in our lives. And in the lives of our God however we name God. She is "the artisan of all." We all want to be around creativity, and wisdom rides in on creativity. She was there "before the creation of the world." Thus she has been around for a long time. She always shows up when something is being born. She cares about justice for she is also a "friend of the prophets," and the prophets were committed to see justice replace injustice.

She comes as female generally. And in Jesus' case she came incarnate as male. She speaks to our hearts, not just to our heads. "When you have found her never let her go." She is the object of our search and our many wanderings. She is the mother of us all. She balances the masculine energies of divinity. She provides the yin to the Bible's yang. We lost her in the modern era when patriarchy so enveloped society and soul. She is coming back. She insists on justice. She loves the earth. She is Gaia. She is Mary. She is the goddess. She is Christ. She is everywhere.

In the Jewish tradition wisdom is learned from nature, for nature is her special dwelling place. Scholars today agree that the historical Jesus came from this wisdom tradition of Israel. It is less about books than about drinking in the sacredness of nature—all of it—from body to rocks, from cycles of the seasons to plants and herbs, from sexuality (Song of Songs) to stars and galaxies. She is everywhere. She is a cosmic presence. She is the divine dwelling, the Godhead, the mystery that precedes history, the silence that precedes words, the darkness that precedes light, the quiet that precedes sound. We can access her in a special way through silence and quieting the mind and heart. We connect to her when we learn to listen.

Resurrection: "And the Stone Was Rolled Back"

There is much in the human psyche that yearns to hear that death is not the final word. That we reincarnate or return or resurrect in some way or another. In the view of the genius psychologist and cultural historian Otto Rank, the quest for immortality is what most drives human culture and human decision making. Consider the pyramids of ancient Egypt, for example. The issue was immortality: If the pharaoh was properly buried, everyone else would participate vicariously in his eternal salvation. What an immense effort the Egyptian civilization went to in order to make the giant pyramids just right. Imagine all the science, all the sweat and hard work, that went into building the pyramids. It was all about immortality. That quest is what drove the project. Rank believes that soul itself is our human quest for immortality.

Little wonder then that Rank, though a Jew and not a Christian, teaches that Jesus and Paul's stories of resurrection are the "most revolutionary ideas" of humankind. Why? They democratize immortality. No pyramids needed. Nor palaces (papal or otherwise) required.

Now we can get on with living because we have broken through our fear of death and our denial of death. Resurrection is not just about the next life but an invitation to live this life fully. Easter's celebration in springtime is not accidental. Nature herself is resurrecting after a winter's burial. We follow suit. The Paschal mystery continues. No beauty, no warmth, no love is lost in the universe. It all gets recycled, whatever form it takes.

"Do This in Memory of Me"

Remembering is vitally important. Connecting to the ancestors is important. Though we need to "live in the now" and the "kingdom of God is among us," nevertheless the ancestors need to be remembered. Rabbi Abraham Heschel taught that all of Jewish liturgy can be summarized in one word: "Remember." This would seem to underscore Jesus' deep intention in speaking of remembering him, an intention to replace the elaborate rituals of the temple priests with a ritual supper much more simple, direct, person-to-person, without class distinction or bureaucratic intermediaries. In Islam too, *zikr*, the core of Sufi worship, means "remember."

To remember our ancestors is to make them present, to call on their courage and vision and care for us, whether they knew us or not. It is also to see ourselves as ancestors, to embrace our responsibility to care for the children and the earth of the future. In Jesus' case it is to remember the stories and the teachings, the decisions and the actions, yes, the archetypes that he unleashed, some in his own words, some in the words of those who would follow him.

There are many ways to pray and many ways to pray as communities. One thinks of the silence of the Quaker form of praying, the silence of a monk in meditation, the dance of a rave or the Cosmic Mass, the drumming of a sundance ceremony, the scriptural sharing and storytelling of a base community, the echoes of a gospel choir, the reading or chanting of Scriptures, or the sounds of a Bachian Mass. These are many and diverse forms of prayer and worship. Which ones work best today? It is important to test and see. For worship, an opportunity to thank and praise, to grieve and be fed, to become community together, is archetypal. It is a great act of remembering therefore. We need—and deserve—forms that solicit the best in us.

Breaking bread and taking communion together is a profound way to pray together. It sacralizes all other rituals of eating, drinking, and dining as a community. It is a reminder that we are here both to eat and to be eaten. The teaching that Christ is the light in all things that is also cosmic food is profoundly erotic. That we can eat the divine presence that is found in every photon and therefore every atom in the universe makes for a meal that is both intimate and immense.

"Be You Compassionate as Your Creator in Heaven Is Compassionate"

Laying the groundwork for the later teaching that God is love, the historical Jesus teaches that God is compassionate. That is ancient Jewish teaching since in the Jewish tradition "compassion" is the secret name for God. "Compassionate" is also the preferred title for Allah in the Qur'an. It is essential to Buddhist teaching, namely that compassion is the heart of what we are about. The Dalai Lama claims that we can do without all religion but not without compassion, that in fact compassion is his religion. Thus Jesus' instruction taps into a universal teaching, an archetype. In doing so he reminds us of our own dignity, our likeness to divinity, that we too have the divine power of compassion in our midst, within each one of us. We can all do it.

Science tells us that we humans carry three brains within us. The oldest (420 million years) is the reptilian brain, the next (210 million years old) is the mammal brain, and the most recent (some 200,000 years) is our intellectual, cognitive brain. Compassion has much to do with the mammal brain: Mammals carry their young for long times before they are born, the young suck at the breast of the mother, intimacy is required, and family and kinship are survival mechanisms. No wonder in both Hebrew and Arabic the word for womb is the basis of the word for compassion. Womb-people, mammals, bring compassion to the world in a special way. That is our destiny—or should be.

Unfortunately, much in human society rewards the reptilian brain at the expense of the mammal brain, action and reaction at the expense of caring and compassion. That has to change if we are to survive. Buddha taught that. Isaiah taught that. Muhammad taught that. Black Elk taught that. Jesus taught that. How are we doing?

The Cosmic Christ

In this time of ecological destruction happening upon the earth, when extinction spasms are more frequent than any time in the past 65 million years, it is time for all people to rediscover the sacredness of all creation. The gift of Christianity in that regard is the archetype of the Cosmic Christ, which we have referred to previously in this book. The Cosmic Christ represents the divine image in all things, the light in all things, but also the wounds in all things. To destroy a rain forest is to crucify the Christ. To support a child is to support another Christ. The sacred is everywhere. This represents the deep mystical tradition of Christianity. We need to bring it back to life.

I have listed but fifteen archetypes that Christianity gives the world. There are many more. They are surely worth saving from the burning building, saving and applying anew to our twenty-first-century needs.

In my book *One River, Many Wells: Wisdom Springing from Global Faiths,* I propose eighteen categories or "myths" that all the world religions share and that are essential for our survival as a species. These are deep ecumenism and the universality of experience; sacredness of creation; light; community and interdependence; names for God; the feminine face of divinity; wisdom: another feminine face of the divine; form, formlessness, nothingness; the divine 'I am': humanity's share in divinity; meditation and mindfulness; holy imagination; joy; suffering; beauty; sacred sexuality; dying, resurrection, reincarnation; service and compassion (including justice and celebration); and spiritual warriorhood. Certainly Christianity speaks profoundly to them all. These too are very much worth saving as we leave the burning building.

The last one out, the one turning out the lights in the Vatican, please don't forget these gifts to the world.

Chapter 11

Toward a Truly Catholic Christianity and a Post-Vatican Catholicism

✛

The late Leonard Bernstein once said, "I hate music, but I love to sing." In expressing this seeming paradox, he was underscoring the vast divide that can occur between spirit (singing) and structure (music). I believe the same divide can occur—and does occur at certain historical periods—between religion and spirituality. Many people have come to hate religion but still love to pray, to praise, to thank, to celebrate, to heal, to do justice, and to practice compassion. Our time in history seems to be such a period.

Pentecost and the Prophecy of Joel with Its Promise of Catholicity

As I sit down to write this chapter, it is Pentecost Sunday 2010. Pentecost is that holiday in the Christian tradition when all celebrate the coming of the Holy Spirit over the fearful disciples of Jesus after the trauma of the crucifixion left them so bereft and wandering in the dark—and so scared. The story goes that the Holy Spirit appeared to them both in the form of a "violent wind" ("breath," "wind," and "spirit" are the same words in biblical languages as well as in many other languages of the world). In addition, a flame came over each of them (yang energy for their spiritual warriorhood to take root?), and all were touched by it. This Spirit transformed the disciples from being afraid and overly meek persons to being brave, standing up and preaching the story and teaching of Jesus, and indeed preaching in the various languages of the thousands who had gathered in Jerusalem for the special feast day of the Jews. The Acts of the Apostles names a number of countries, regions, and tribes from afar whose representatives were present and heard the words of the apostles in their own diverse languages.

Peter rose to give a sermon, and it culminated in these beautiful and evocative words from the prophet Joel, words that are as inviting to the human heart today as they ever were in Peter's day or in Joel's day.

> In the last days it will be, God declares, that I will pour out my Spirit upon all flesh, and your sons and your daughters shall prophesy, and your young men shall see visions, and your old men shall dream dreams. Even upon my slaves, both men and women, in those days I will pour out my Spirit; and they shall prophesy. And I will show portents in the heaven above and signs on the earth below, blood, and fire, and smoky mist. The sun shall be turned to darkness and the moon to blood, before the coming of the Lord's great and glorious day. Then everyone who calls on the name of the Lord shall be saved. (Acts 2:17–21)

Notice the promise of universality in these words: The Spirit will pour out upon "all flesh" and all generations and all social classes. Pentecost is often called the "birthday of the church" because Christians yearn to believe that the Holy Spirit has inspired their gathering or *ekklesia* (from which we derive the word "church") and that the Holy Spirit still guides it. Indeed, in the Nicene Creed, which as we have noted above is a flawed document, still there are these words: "We believe in the Holy Spirit, the Lord, the giver of life, who proceeds from the Father and the Son . . . He has spoken through the prophets. We believe in one, holy, catholic, and apostolic church."

Five Pentecosts ago, shortly after Cardinal Joseph Ratzinger became Pope Benedict XVI, I, who had known this man and his works for years, had a dream that urged me to go to his homeland, Germany, and do what Martin Luther did five hundred years previously—namely, to pound a number of theses on the door of the church in the name of a New Reformation. I sensed then, as we all can see today, that something dark was unfolding in the history of religion and of Christianity in particular. The darkness was not just a Vatican issue—the rise of fundamentalist Christianity is as fierce in Protestantism today as it is in the Vatican. I called for a New Reformation and a New Coming of the Spirit, and I spelled out directions in the ninety-five theses I nailed at the very door where Luther nailed his theses.

One might think, from the contents of this book and the daily news coming out about clergy sex abuse and its widespread cover-up, that now is hardly the moment to celebrate the church's birthday. But in fact, I would argue that this is precisely the moment to celebrate a new birth of Christianity. The deliberate betrayal of the Second Vatican Council that Pope John XXIII envisioned as a "new Pentecost"; the silencing of thinkers; the expulsion of social justice activists; the vows of secrecy shielding priests, bishops, and cardinals from telling the truth about pedophilia; the pay-to-pray syndrome of the late pope's personal secretary (now a cardinal); the cozying up with groups such as Opus Dei, the Legion of Christ, and Communion and Liberation, saying nothing of their scurrilous leaders—all this is evidence that a new kind of church is needed. New forms. New relationships.

The time is ripe. This is, after all, the beginning of a third millennium for Christianity; a twenty-first-century form of church is needed. A postmodern form. A renewed and cleansed form. Even Pope Benedict XVI has called for cleansing of the sins of the church after finally admitting some of the horrors that have ravaged it. I agree wholeheartedly. But the cleansing is far more than "six Our Fathers and six Hail Marys" (the familiar penance Catholics receive at the sacrament of confession)—it is a renewal and a birth of new forms that only Spirit can give. But Spirit needs our help, our hands, our voices, our courage, our imaginations, and our hard work.

The Meaning of "Catholic"

The creed that we cited above speaks of a "one, holy, catholic, and apostolic church." In a previous chapter we spoke of how "one" does not mean uniform. Oneness and diversity go together. Unity is not sameness. Unity is likeness and commonality in the midst of diversity. What do we mean by "holy"? Spiritual terms are often best understood by going to their opposites first. What is the opposite of "holy"? Distancing oneself from the sacred, perhaps? Being entrenched in egoism, lies, greed, bullying, abuse of others, perhaps? I think we could all agree that pedophiles and those who cover up for them do not fall into a category of "holy" people. At least not yet. Nor do those addicted to power and those who imagine they are the only thinkers on earth.

Let us consider the word "catholic," then. This word comes from two Greek words, *kata* (by or according to) and *holos* (whole). To be catholic is to be whole. Synonyms in English for "catholic" are "comprehensive" or "universal," according to Merriam-Webster's Collegiate Dictionary. "Catholic" means "broad in sympathies, tastes, or interests." In religion it has come to mean "of, relating to, or forming the church universal; of, relating to, or forming the ancient undivided Christian church or a church claiming historical continuity from it."

It is hard to imagine a time—surely not in its time of origin—when the church was "undivided." There have always been a variety of versions, expressions, and interpretations of the message of Jesus and indeed of the earliest Christian followers of Jesus. Even the four Gospels step on one another's toes at times. Paul was not always in agreement with Peter, nor James with Paul, nor Peter with Mary Magdelene. But the word "catholic" in, for example, "Roman Catholicism," urges the church to err in the direction of diversity, not in the direction of uniformity.

The Encarta Dictionary of North American English speaks of "catholic" as meaning: "1) all-inclusive, including or concerned with all people, 2) useful to all—useful or interesting to a wide range of people, and 3) all-embracing: interested in or sympathetic to a wide range of things." A church that was all-inclusive, useful to all, and all-embracing—now that would be much welcomed, wouldn't it? Vatican II in the early 1960s was surely tacking in the direction of more universality, more ecumenism, more true catholicism in its opening in theology and in liturgical practice and to work in the modern world. But such outreach is sometimes subtle, for example, in liturgy. One might argue that liturgy in Latin was more "universal" because it was one language for everyone. But truth is that it was an increasingly dead language that was "for everyone" in the sense that it was equally unknown by Africans, Asians, Latin Americans, North Americans, and so on. The council's response was to invite liturgy to be present in the unique and specific vernaculars of varied cultures and societies. This allowed for more, not less, catholicity or universality, for it allowed various languages to sing and dance in their own unique tones. The extreme right-wingers in the church, such as the late Archbishop Marcel-Francois Lefebvre and his schismatic followers (whose excommunication was lifted by Pope Benedict in 2009), resisted the vernacular liturgy fiercely to the end. Their Catholicism was uniquely wrapped in Latin—or else it was not the real thing. Their notion of "culture" began and ended with a Latin-based history and ethos. There was very little about it that was universal or catholic. Their virulent anti-Semitism (one of the bishops rehabilitated by Pope Benedict actually denies the Holocaust happened) is anything but "catholic." The decision of Pope Benedict to bring back old prayers for Good Friday, for example, that are explicitly anti-Semitic and blame the Jews in general for Jesus' death, is more evidence of a shrinking, not an expanding or catholic, Christianity.

Another area where Vatican II clearly came out in favor of catholicity was in its decree of the Pastoral Constitution on the Church in the Modern World, where Christians are urged to contribute their deepest spiritual values to remaking society through their work and professional contributions. Pope Benedict and the loud right wing seemingly are not on board with this emphasis, since they begin their theologies with a dualistic division between the "sacred" and the "secular" spheres—as if the Spirit does not work where it wills and through all professions and spheres of work, and as if serious evil (such as pedophilia and its cover-ups by prominent church prelates) is not present in so-called sacred institutions.

Still another area where Vatican II consciously chose catholicity is that of ecumenism, first by inviting Protestant, Orthodox, and Jewish "observers" at the council, but then, in a document that speaks of how the Holy Spirit has always worked through all cultures and all religions, the thrust of Vatican II was to acknowledge truth and wisdom wherever we find it and that includes religions other than Roman Catholicism.

But the past thirty years of Vatican actions and documents have not advanced ecumenism in the least. Indeed, the present pontiff has said that Protestants are not churches, that yoga should not be practiced because it gets one too much in touch with one's body, that Buddhist monk (and saint) Thich Nhat Hanh is the Antichrist, and more. One Anglican bishop responded to the put-down of Protestant churches by Pope John Paul II's decree, *Dominus Jesus*, by saying: "Ecumenicity and interfaith hopes died as Rome went so far as to warn its own bishops against referring to other Christian bodies as 'sister churches,' for fear that this language might be misunderstood to confer some degree of legitimacy on these bodies."

Recently Ratzinger called Pope Pius XII "one of the great righteous men" who "saved more Jews than anyone else." In the U.S., a Holocaust survivor spokesperson responded that such comments "fill us with pain and sorrow and cast a menacing shadow on Vatican-Jewish relations," while a French-Jewish leader said this opinion "wasn't shared by any serious historian."

One has to consider the following reality: The term "Roman Catholicism" is surely an oxymoron. How can one be both Roman-based and catholic or universal? Isn't that like using a term like "dry water"? I think it is high time to leave the term "Roman" out of the "catholic" equation. The world is truly catholic today and growing more so as the outreach of iPods, phones, and texting reach a global dimension. Young people today are in deep and broad communication with their peers on six continents with the flip of a finger. There is something catholic—that is, all-embracing, universal, and expansive—behind what is happening. Of course, in an expanding era, one also needs roots, and in fact ever deeper roots. But the roots, if one is a Christian, do not begin with Rome. (Jesus never even went to Rome, nor did he speak the imperial language of Latin, and he died never having heard of the Vatican.) I sense an invitation today from the Sprit itself—the same Spirit that hovered over the waters at the beginning of the world and that hovered over the disciples at the first Pentecost—to become more universal, not less; more catholic, not more Roman; more all-embracing, not more defensive; and more ecumenical, not more sectarian.

The widening of community that is called for is not just about the religious community or the Christian community, or even merely the human community. It is about a rebirth of kinship with *all* the creatures of the earth in all their beauty and diversity and wonder—and precariousness. Together we face a global crisis of creation's demise that can and should unite all of us in authentic practices of compassion and healing and generosity. This is what it means to be truly catholic today. It calls for a recovery of the sense of the sacred in creation itself. For creation is truly universal. Catholicity, as Joel points out, involves all flesh.

Now the questions arise: How do we get there from here? What paths do we take? What forms are appropriate? This is where the Holy Spirit, with its vast and universal imagination, is making the path easier for us. By so melting the forms we now have, such as the morally, intellectually, and spiritually discredited form of the Vatican, the Holy Spirit has taken the scorched earth left behind by today's inquisition to make ready a new field of play. That new field of play is a vast field, a truly global and catholic field, and we are invited to play our games of worship and community building, of healing and praise, of celebration and compassion, of justice making and creativity, of grief and of awe, of praise and memory of our ancestors, on that field that has already been plowed up and prepared by the dark forces that this book demonstrates have taken over institution-alized Catholicism in the past forty years. The field is prepared. Are we?

Swiss theologian Hans Kung is a man due considerable respect. He and Father Joseph Ratzinger (then a mere professor of theology) were the two youngest theological advisers at the Second Vatican Council (1962–1965). Since then, Ratzinger has risen in the hierarchy, and Kung has been denounced by Ratzinger as being "not a Catholic theologian" for teaching such matters as suspicion about papal infallibility. But Kung has kept on trucking and recently, following the awful scandals emerging in the European church, has written strongly about the failed papacy of Ratzinger with whom he has, strange to tell, kept up a certain friendship over the decades in spite of deep theological disagreements. (In fact the two dined together shortly after Benedict's election.)

In a recent public letter to the bishops, Kung criticized the many failures of Pope Benedict XVI, including his "missed opportunity for rap-prochement with the Protestant churches" and for the "long-term recon-ciliation with the Jews" among other things. Kung offered as a concrete solution that a Third Vatican Council be convened. Immediately, a blog-ger, whose background I do not know, responded that this made no sense since the Second Vatican Council was totally co-opted by the powers that be in Rome. What would prevent that happening still another time?

I could not agree more with that blogger. This is hardly a time for another council, when we have not even been allowed to live out the previous council. Furthermore, since theology has been effectively shut down within church circles for decades, where are the theologians to help us steer our way? Also, where are the bishops and cardinals who could help lead, since all these years that entire body has been dumbed down as well? Practically the sole criterion for bishop selection by Rome for the past three generations has been to be a loyal yes-man. No, I do not think that another council is a way out of our deep morass. We must go deeper than that.

The problems revealed by the news of this papacy call for more grassroots change than another council. We have to move from religion to spirituality and from anthropocentric salvation-based Christianity to a creation-centered Christianity, and from top-down ladder thinking to a more circle-based celebration. We can do this. Here I outline certain steps we can take to accomplish that kind of truly *catholic* Christianity.

Steps toward a Truly Catholic Christianity

LISTEN TO THE SILENCED ONES

One concrete step we can take to awaken the Christ consciousness is to listen to those who resisted the overly institutional forces and were involved in creating new forms, involved in ecclesiogenesis, and who paid a price for that involvement. We have met some (but by no means all) of those persons in the pages of this book. There are many more to be listened to as well. Many of these heroes have already left us and those who remain ought to be filmed and interviewed and listened to before they leave us. What wisdom are they harboring? What good secrets do they carry inside their minds and hearts that the rest of us ought to celebrate and live out? Why is the Vatican so afraid of them?

I am currently involved in a film project called *The Silent Ones* to do exactly that—to let the Silenced Ones speak, to make known to the world and future generations of Christians their visions for church and society. There is so much to learn from those who bear the scars of ecclesial inquisitions and silencing. We need to be curious and eager to tap into the legacy of these fallen ones and to honor their sacrifices and their generous work on behalf of the Spirit.

Scholar Peter Kingsley has recently written a book on the shamans of Mongolia and how they made a four-thousand-mile trek to Greece and profoundly influenced Pythagoras and other giants of Greek civilization. Speaking of the thirteenth-century Buddhist leader Karma Pukshi, he says that his task was to "transfer the realities of the past into the present and make them real again." I think that is a fine definition of what a real theologian is called to do. Many of the Silenced Ones were indeed transferring the realities of the past into the present to make them real, and for that reason they were silenced.

Kingsley speaks to our times, I believe, when he observes that "just as civilizations have to come to an end, there can even be times of global extinctions. But always there are people who know how to gather the essence of life and hold it safely, protect it and nurture it until the next seeding." We look to these people at times like ours, when we are "between times" and when the church is very much a part of the collapse of the modern civilization and in a quandary where to go. Kingsley goes on:

Not only are these people needed to bring new worlds into existence. They even are needed to bring them to an end so as to help make way for the new . . . They are the ones who are entrusted to turn the pages of life, to open the book of a culture and close it. They are the ones who are given permission to sound the note that will bring a new world into being and then sing the song that will bring it nearer to its close. They are the watchers who know the real meaning of responsibility and compassion—who are needed to witness the beginning and ending because without the simple power of their attention nothing can ever be done.

All the more reason to give the Silenced Ones in the church a voice before they leave us.

It is one thing to be silenced—which is a grave and external act of violence. But it is another to cherish silence from the inside, where the Spirit so often speaks, and one can presume that the Silenced Ones have had time to ponder and listen to the Spirit's words deep inside. We need to invite that same Spirit out and into the daylight while we can.

MEDITATE AND TEACH MEDITATION

Developing the notion of healthy silence and listening to the Spirit who speaks in silence, it is vital that we recover our capacity to meditate and teach meditation. It is no small gift that many lineages from Hindu yoga to Buddhist sitting, from Lakota sweat lodges to Muslim rosary beads, are more and more available to all of us at this time in history to find ways to calm our busy "monkey" brains and learn an inner silence again. Meditation comes in a variety of forms—there is walking meditation and sitting meditation, there is the silence that comes from running or chanting, from music making to music listening, from yoga stretching to sitting in a cave or other dark place. Every spiritual awakening includes an awakening in deeper listening, therefore in silence. We need to calm our reptilian brains through meditation. Otherwise the crocodile in us will run away with our lives and our planet. Without meditation, the compassionate brain, our mammal brain, goes unattended and dries up. No healthy spiritual path can ignore the role that silence plays. It, along with joy and grief, are the sure highways into the deep human heart. Adults—parents and teachers alike—must be themselves at home with silence and with ways to it so that they can instruct the younger ones.

And, very likely, the younger ones may turn around and instruct the older ones as well.

REVIVE HOME CHURCH AND WITH IT A GRASSROOTS ECCLESIAL REVOLUTION

Christianity did not begin in million-dollar church edifices. It began in home gatherings (often of wealthy converts) and closely after that in catacombs, underground dwellings where the living and the dead could be hidden from the forces of the empire. Paul was very involved in home churches, for example. And evidence from the Gospels is irrefutable that Jesus himself felt the suppers he shared with persons of varying social classes was an antidote to priest-dominated temple worship (that was itself so linked with political and economic powers of his day that he felt the need to drive moneylenders from the temple and overturn their wares). The Last Supper was an extension of these home meal gatherings. To this day, the Sabbath is celebrated at the dinner table in most Jewish homes. In a home setting, participation is respected and invited so that the sharing of story as well as the breaking of bread can truly happen. Neighbors and friends can gather for a group sharing of depth. We should never underestimate the power of home church.

Might the new media offer a fresh opportunity for the home church to deepen and to flourish? For example, a home church gathering might pipe in a Webinar from a solid theologian and open that occasion to discussion. Or alternative rituals (see below) might be put on the Web offering music and insight that could be simultaneously replicated and danced to and prayed to within a smaller, home church setting. A film like *The Silent Ones*, to which I alluded above, might be downloaded and provide grist for discussion and debate in small, home communities. And the day may come, sooner than we think, when a version of reality TV might occur wherein lively discussions with and of healthy theological thought could be shared and debated and filmed for others to participate in quite broadly. In other words, a kind of grassroots ecclesial revolution could spring up complete with blogs, Webinars, e-mail exchanges, and more. None of this depends on permissions or censorship from ecclesial hierarchies.

Scholars also tell us that in addition to house churches, other Christians met regularly as guilds, professional groups that accepted common worship along with their shared craft; others gathered in tenements. And the greatest numbers gathered in synagogues. We should not underestimate places of work as potential places for spiritual gathering to take place.

PRACTICE COSMOLOGY AND ECOLOGY

What is truly "catholic" is, as we have seen, universal. In other words, it is cosmological. It thinks and acts with the whole universe in mind. Does this sound odd or extremely difficult? Only if one is stuck in a cultural mind-set (such as the modern Western mind-set) that tells us the universe is a machine that we cannot relate to and that we ought to hunker down, obey, and fit in. Such a perspective is itself very odd, one that is in no way taught during the times of indigenous teaching and wisdom and a way that in no way coincides with current, postmodern science and thinking. As the late physicist David Bohm put it, "I am proposing a post-modern physics which begins with the whole." ("Cosmos" means "whole" in Greek.) Bohm is reminding us that to put the modern consciousness behind us, cosmology has to be on a front burner for us.

The earliest Christian thinkers were profoundly cosmic in their understanding of the Jesus event. One scholar says that "no Christian thinker before or since has thought on so cosmic a scale, linking God's Spirit to humanity's and both to the transformation of the world," as has St. Paul, the very first writer in the Christian Bible and the very first theologian.

Today, it should not be so hard to think cosmically once again. The Hubble telescope's amazing imagery and the many forays into space, photographing stars, galaxies, supernovas, and planets being born and dying and resurrecting—this is becoming everyday stuff we can see on a regular basis in our newspapers or online. Cosmology is now reentering human consciousness and practice. And ecology is its younger sister.

Therefore a catholic Christianity will put cosmology in the forefront. It will link arms with contemporary science and be eager to learn more and more stories of the universe, how it works, what its patterns are, how we translate that into human relationships and human ethics and patterns of behavior (what previous generations might have called "natural law"). How can one be "catholic" or universal and embracing of the whole and ignore cosmology?

A *catholic* Christianity will honor the earth and the ecosystems of the earth and the amazing creatures of the earth from rivers to oceans, from fish to amphibians, from birds to four-legged creatures, reawakening a sense of awe and gratitude for all that is and how we are—quite mysteriously—so fully a part of it all. True cosmology awakens gratitude, awe, wonder, and a passion to defend what is so beautiful and fragile as our earth, its inhabitants, and its systems of support. The great twelfth-century mystic and prophet Hildegard of Bingen called Jesus a "green man." Today, given the crisis of ecological trauma facing our species on all fronts, can anyone be a human being without being a green man or a green woman? Surely no follower of Jesus, who grew up in the green part of Israel (Galilee) and who built his teachings around the stories of nature and natural processes, can possibly ignore creation as central to a faith consciousness. God the Creator awaits a creation-based spiritual awakening.

FIND AND CREATE POSTMODERN FORMS OF WORSHIP

The most obvious and most tested way to celebrate and remember our creation stories and our place in the cosmos and the ecosystems of the earth is through ritual. Ritual by definition is a marriage of psyche and cosmos, of microcosm and macrocosm. This is what gives ritual its energy and its drive. When cosmos is lost in ritual, worship gets reduced to lots of words on a page ("whoops—wrong page!") or personality cults built around a particular preacher or icon. That will not do. True worship comes from the cosmos itself. Praise for what is. But we must honor "is-ness" for worship to happen.

At a time when so much is disintegrating around us, it should come as no big surprise that we need to question, among other things, the very forms in which we are doing worship. Are the forms valid? Do they inspire? Or are they crushing and soporific, and therefore rejected by many who are voting with their feet to stay home from church on a Sunday morning? Modern forms of worship emphasize words—words on a page, words in a sermon, words read from the lectern, words read from a prayer book. Words, words words! Text, text, text! (After all, the modern age began with the invention of the printing press. That was its strength and its liability.)

Postmodern forms of prayer will put less emphasis on text and more on context, less emphasis on words from a book and more emphasis on "every creature as a word of God." It will be more democratic, therefore, and more cosmic, universal, or catholic, just as Walt Whitman prophesied 150 years ago when he called for a spiritual democracy that was all-embracing and included all of creation, all human tribes, and all human traditions. Worship will include body, not exclude it. It will include dance, not shun it. In many African languages the words for "spirit," "breath," and "dance" have the same root. To dance is to bring spirit in. To dance is to demand our breath's participation. This premodern wisdom will permeate postmodern worship.

Another dimension to postmodern worship is using postmodern languages and art forms to elicit the sacred. Many DJs today are eager to bring their art and skills to worship. Consider how image making from VJing and the creating of fractals along with other expressions of image sharing can happen today with contemporary multimedia. Invite art forms like rap and other living forms of poetry. This is how to integrate context and our bodies, imagination and prayer. I know because we have been involved in this ritual revolution for fifteen years and have seen profound results flow from our work with the Cosmic Mass. Our conscious effort to awaken worship through body and participation and imagery and grieving has truly paid off. New forms of worship *are* possible today—and needed and appreciated.

Such ritual opportunities are a big part of a truly catholic Christianity.

Practice Deep Ecumenism

Another dimension to a truly catholic—that is, universal—Christianity is a great respect for and curiosity about various world spiritual traditions. Let us begin with the variety within Christianity itself. Western Christianity, what we call the Roman Catholic and Protestant traditions, can easily ignore or forget Eastern Orthodox Christianity and its great cultural and national traditions (such as the Russian or Greek Orthodox churches). We can also easily forget the Coptic tradition, which is very ancient indeed in Africa, or the traditions of India, which go back to very ancient times, or Celtic Christianity, which, while smothered in the Council of Whitby in the seventh century, nevertheless was so deep and authentic an adaptation of the story and teaching of Jesus and of the Christ who was found in all of nature.

Within the West, we can and ought to come to terms with the immense diversity of practice and approach within many Protestant traditions, whether Methodist or Anglican, Lutheran or Presbyterian, Congregational or Baptist. And there is the Unitarian tradition and the Quaker tradition. There are also twentieth-century Christian movements, such as Religious Science and Unity churches, and Ernest Holmes and other authentic mystics, whom it is useful to imitate and emulate.

Within Roman Catholicism, there was in the past the diversity of the various orders and their unique charisms and cultural contributions whether Benedictine or Trappist, Dominican or Franciscan, Jesuit or Oblate, Carmelite or Augustinian. Where is that diversity today? There is also the energy of the base communities and liberation theology of Latin America, of Africa, of Asia, of North America, and more.

A truly catholic Christianity honors and respects and learns from these various and evolving traditions. There is no one way, no one flavor, no one song in dancing to the story of Jesus and the spirit of Christ. When it comes to worship and to the shared work of ecological and social justice, there exists a certain *oneness* that underlies and organizes our passion of praise on the one hand and moral outrage on the other. Very little appreciable differences need exist when it comes to these ethical matters.

But being truly catholic is not just about Christians respecting one another and our various lineages. It is about intrafaith but also interfaith. It is also about Christians respecting other forms of spiritual practice and spirituality. A truly catholic Christianity will not be shy to learn from Buddhists, Taoists, Muslims, Jews, indigenous peoples, and worshippers of the goddess. An important spiritual practice today is to study and pray the various wisdom traditions of the world—one is by no means wasting one's time studying and praying the Upanishads or the Vedas of Hinduism, the mystical texts and commentaries on the Buddha, the Tao Te Ching, the Hebrew prophets and wisdom writers of the Kabbala, the Qur'an or the great Sufi mysics such as Rumi and Hafiz of Islam, sweat lodges, vision quests, and sundances of indigenous peoples, and even more. The Dalai Lama's most recent book is devoted to deep ecumenism and lays out the issues and the consequences with considerable wisdom. We are all called to be catholic or universal today. Each tradition has its gifts to share with the rest of us. The day of religious wars is behind us—or ought to be.

We all face so many survival and ethical issues together at this time in history that sectarianism and living in our private religious worlds is a luxury that makes no sense. Would Jesus, who struck up a conversation with the Samaritan woman at the well, who praised a Samaritan man as a hero of compassion, who cured a Roman soldier's daughter, refuse to speak to Muhammad had he met him? Or Buddha? Or Lao Tzu? Or Black Elk? Think about it. I think he would have been eager to dialogue with any of them, just as we know he was communicating in depth with his ancestors, such as Isaiah, Micah, and Abraham. So why would those who claim to follow Jesus be any less spiritually curious, any less eager to learn, any less open in mind and heart to wisdom wherever it is found?

Living a life of deep ecumenism allows us to learn from other traditions that can assist us in renewing our own. I offer a few examples here. Buddhist meditation practices have helped many Jews and some Christians as well to learn to meditate and to calm the reptilian brain. This is no small accomplishment, no small gift that Buddhism extends to others. Consider how Thich Nhat Hanh has taught many people of diverse faith traditions or none at all to "walk in peace" and to lessen stress in their lives.

Consider how joining Native Americans in sweat lodges, in sundances, in powwows, and vision quests—and learning anew to dance and pray—has helped many European Americans to bring the body back to their worship (and to overcome addictions as well). Yoga practices from the Hindu tradition help hundreds of thousands of Westerners to become more conscious of healthy bodily awareness. Ernest Holmes of the Church of Religious Science tradition and the Unity Church in America both emphasize meditation practice and learning the mystical traditions. That is a great gift to mainline churches, which are so often out of touch with their mystical lineage.

The Anglican Communion (including the Episcopal Church USA) has much to teach those of the "high" Catholic traditions with bishops and archbishops about integrating women in all the priestly ranks (including bishops) and integrating gays (gays have always been integrated but often not explicitly). The fact that the Anglican Church as a whole is debating these issues so fiercely and publicly is a healthy thing—and I admire the American Episcopal Church for taking a strong stand in favor of women and gay clergy. It is far better than inviting sexist and homophobic clergy into the Roman Catholic Church as the present pope has committed to doing. Also, there is much to learn from the Anglican Church for its very real accomplishments in creating a church structure where laypeople and not only clergy vote on bishops and hierarchy. There is a kind of parliamentarian balance in the Anglican churches between lay and clergy that is played out at large gatherings that both set polity and elect leaders. The Roman Catholic Church could learn much from these mostly successful efforts at egalitarianism.

BRING BACK DIVERSITY

The latest historical scholarship on the early church underscores how diverse the early movement of Christianity was from the beginning. We have seen above how Bruce Chilton reminds us that "Christianity was a fractured movement from the moment people started using the term 'Christian.'" The compulsion for order and emulating the patriarchal Roman culture in which it was immersed in fact came later. For at least sixty years after Jesus' death, diversity reigned even among the most important issues in the Christian story, stories such as the fact and meaning of the resurrection.

We sometimes imagine that the Gospels were written by a disciple of Jesus sitting at a desk someplace in Jerusalem or Galilee. But of course this is not the case at all. The Gospels emerged in four very different cultural contexts and at different times and were assembled by varied teams of persons, each with their own constituencies and issues to address. As Chilton points out, "The Gospels emerged a generation after Jesus' death in major centers of Christianity . . . A consensus of scholars agrees that Mark was produced in Rome around 73 C.E.; Matthew in Damascus around 80 C.E.; Luke in Antioch on the Orontes around 90 C.E.; and John in Ephesus around 100 C.E. . . . They are composite editions of differing sources that different communities put together in the generations after Jesus' death."

Furthermore, the early stories emanating from the Jesus event were not all written down. Most people of the ancient world were not literate, after all. Oral stories and traditions often trumped the written word (a difficult concept for people born after the printing press to get our minds around). There was no "oneness" in many of the teachings we find in the Gospels. As Chilton puts it, "Primitive Christianity was an oral movement, not a book club, and therefore some of its deepest truths were not committed to writing. The identity of the nameless anointer is a case of Mark intimating more than is literally said. Mark's Gospel displays a mastery of the rhetoric of the unspoken." Confusion and chaos often marked the early church and even some of its most central beliefs. Abstractions were not at the top of the believers' list of things to think about. "Christianity became highly philosophical and often abstract from the second century onward, but Jesus and his Judaic contemporaries did not share the abstractions that have become common currency in the language of the divine world. For Rabbi Jesus, the word God conveyed not a philosophical idea but the ultimate reality—beautiful and fearsome and overpowering."

If you look at the Gospel stories about the resurrection, for example, profound differences emerge. Jesus, Paul, and Mary Magdalene refer to a spiritual resurrection, but Matthew and Luke talk of a physical one. Luke ignores altogether the Galilean stories of the appearances of the risen Jesus and speaks exclusively of Jerusalem appearances. Luke's resurrection is, like Matthew's, very physical and indeed more material than any of the other Gospels. In addition, Luke's account leaves Mary Magdalene, and the anointing stories associated with her, entirely out of his resurrection account, and the Acts of the Apostles, influenced by Luke's school, does the same. This fits a pattern in Luke's Gospel wherein male dominance is very much in evidence. Why is this? Because this Gospel is "focused on the unique authority of the male apostles in Jerusalem."

So we see that diversity of ideas—even around important events like Jesus' resurrection—are in evidence from the beginning in early Christian practice and teaching. There was an almost immediate adaptation to the needs of the listeners in the grand story. This would seem to argue for a large-minded acceptance of diversity in today's Christian discourse, especially as the Gospel becomes more globally dispersed and more readily available to varying cultures, languages, and needs.

The very name "Christian" is a late designation. Chilton reminds us that the early followers of Jesus "didn't think of themselves as 'Christians' yet. That word had not yet even been coined. They persistently called the teaching of their resurrected rabbi 'the way' (*hodos* in Greek . . .), the equivalent of the rabbinic term *halakah* (literally, how God commands Israel to 'go'). In the years before there was any formal division between Judaism and Christianity, Jesus' followers saw their master as the fulfillment of Israel's destiny, and most of them worked out their peculiar vision in peace with their Jewish neighbors." Only around 80 C.E. did leaders of the churches in Damascus see themselves apart from the synagogues there and cease using the term "rabbi" in Matthew's Gospel. Earlier Gospels do use the term "rabbi" to describe Jesus.

Promote Women as Leaders

Women were leaders in the early church (as they are in many Protestant denominations today). For those who study the facts, there can be no excuse for continuing ecclesial misogyny. Indeed, the historical forgetfulness by Rome of the facts we present here constitutes a scandal in itself. It demonstrates that fear and ideology trump history and church practice. Does keeping an all-boys club trump the reality of the early church practice and belief? If women had an authentic hand in decision making and knowing the goings-on in the church, would criminal cover-up of pedo-philia have been tolerated?

If the early church had followed the structures and values of their Jewish and Greco-Roman counterparts, women "would have been rele-gated to marginal roles in early Christianity," as biblical scholar and theo-logian Elisabeth Schussler Fiorenza reminds us. But this is not at all the case. The early Jesus followers held a radically different view of women and their role. "Women, in this egalitarian movement, were not marginal figures but exercised responsible leadership . . . The earlier countercul-tural and later extraecclesial groups accepted women as equal members with equal responsibility and leadership." In the Letter to the Galatians Paul promises that no distinction any longer holds between Jew and Gen-tile, free and slave, male and female. Indeed, this radical idea was part of the baptismal formula (Gal 3:27ff.). As Fiorenza puts it, this "Christian egalitarian creed was formulated over and against this commonly accepted ratification of social discrimination in Judaism and Hellenism." That Gen-tiles, slaves, and women could be active and equal partners to men in this new Christian community was an eye-opener for citizens of the empire. It was part and parcel of the arrival of a "kingdom of God" on earth that Jesus promised.

Much church history since has tried to forget, undo, and deny this radical breakthrough that early Christianity provided. But more and more scholarship recognizes the reality of this revolution that Jesus unleashed. Consider how Jesus himself drew women to him and trained them as leaders. This is at the heart of Bruce Chilton's study on Mary Magdalene. He is convinced that Jesus entrusted her with a special healing ministry. "Jesus, Mary, and the other disciples practiced anointing, which was asso-ciated with exorcism and healing . . . there is excellent evidence that oiling skin was a routine ritual in Jesus' movement and that Mary Magdalene was its preeminent practitioner. Over the course of his last weeks in Jeru-salem, Jesus designated Mary as his movement's paradigmatic anointer. Christianity in its modern form has all but forgotten this sacrament of unction as well as its indissoluble link with Mary Magdalene." Not only did we forget Mary Magdalene, we nearly forgot the sacrament of healing and anointing altogether!

Anointing was a "key ritual action" among the early followers of Jesus, and it was applied not just to the living but to the deceased. Mark's Gos-pel talks about Jesus' burial this way: "And when Sabbath elapsed, Mary

Magdalene and Mary of James and Salome purchased spices so they could go anoint him." Comments Chilton: "Mary is the indispensable character in Mark's account of the Resurrection, the pivot of the action around whom the final events turn. She, by name and by action, embodies the connection between Jesus' interment and the angelic announcement to the same Mary Magdalene (16:6–7) that Jesus has been raised from the dead. She connects his death and Resurrection, not only by who she is but also by what she does: Mary Magdalene established the place of anointing as a central ritual in Christianity, recollecting Jesus' death and pointing forward to his Resurrection."

In playing out this role of anointer, Mary Magdalene was in fact fulfilling an ancient practice in Judaism, one that was especially linked to her region of Magdala. "Women in Jewish antiquity, particularly within the folk mysticism practiced in Galilee, exercised a prominent role as anointers." In the first century a book circulated called *The Testament of Job*, which developed the portrait of the biblical Job and designated his daughters as heirs of his mystical practice. What is that practice? "He becomes . . . an expert in the practice of the mystical chariot of God, the *Merkavah* that conveyed the swirling energy of divine presence to those who meditated on this master symbol of Judaic mysticism." Furthermore, Job's three daughters are said in rabbinic literature to have settled and then to have died in Magdala, Mary's hometown. In Chilton's opinion, "*The Testament of Job* completely overturns the modern assumption concerning women's roles in Judaism, especially in the context of mysticism."

Remember too that in Acts 21:8–9 the daughters of Philip play the role of women prophets in the Christian community. "Ancient Jewish literature permits us to see that women pioneered the popular practice of the Merkavah and that Magdala was an important center of that tradition. Along with her vessel for unction, Mary Magdalene carried with her a mystical teaching of the Spirit that her anointing art conveyed." Women were healers and carriers of the Spirit, anointers of the living and the dead.

In the early Christian movement, observes Fiorenza, women played an "important role in founding and promoting house churches. Since the house church was a decisive factor in early Christian development, it provided the leadership and determined the form of church life." In the house church early Christians "celebrated the Eucharist (Acts 2:46; 20:7) and preached the gospel (Acts 5:42). The assembly was called the 'house of God,' the new 'temple' because the Spirit dwelt in it." Wealthy women converts often oversaw these gatherings (cf. Acts 17:4, 12). Acts 12:12 speaks of a prayer meeting in the house of Mary, the mother of John Mark. Paul acknowledges Apphia as "our sister," "who together with Philemon and Archippius was a leader of a house church in Colossae (Philemon 2). A businesswoman convert named Lydia from Thyatira founded a church in Philippi (Acts 16:14). In Colossians the author references Mympha of Laodicea and the "church in her house" (Col 4:15). Paul refers at least twice to a missionary couple Prisca and Aquila and "the church in their house" (1 Cor 16:19; Romans 16:3–5). The woman Chloe oversaw a house in Corinth that provoked Paul's first letter to the Corinthians (1:11). Fiorenza concludes: "We have no reason to assume that women were excluded from the leadership of the house churches or from presiding at worship."

Furthermore, Paul mentions women as his missionary coworkers on many occasions. He commends Mary, Tryphena, Tryphosa, and Persis in Romans 16 for having "labored" hard in the Lord. In Philippians 4:2f, he acknowledges that Euodia and Syntche have "contended" side by side with him. Fiorenza concludes: "The texts indicate that these women missionaries commanded the same authority, esteem and respect as their male co-workers in the missionary communities." Paul credits Prisca and her husband, Aquilas, with founding and leading house churches in Corinth, Ephesus, and Rome. Prisca is given credit for being the catechist and teacher of the convert and coworker of Paul, Apollos. Junia and Andronicus are another missionary couple; they converted to Christianity before Paul and were called "apostles" by him. In Romans 16:1f Paul speaks of Phoebe who is called a "deacon." Such people "served in a recognized official capacity as teachers and preachers in the Christian community." Paul also calls Phoebe *prostatis*, which "designates the function of the bishop, deacon or elder" in 1 Thessalonians and 1 Timothy. "Phoebe thus had a designated role of leadership and teaching in the community of Cenchreae. She was a person with great authority for many and for Paul himself."

Following is a summary of the role of women in the early Christian community offered by Elisabeth Schussler Fiorenza: "Paul's letters indicate that women were among the prominent and leading missionaries in the early Christian movement. They were co-workers with Paul but did not depend on him or stand under his authority. They were not excluded from any missionary function. They were preachers, teachers and leaders of the community . . . Their ministry was not limited to the ministry to women nor to specific gender roles and functions. The prominence of women in the early Christian movement is confirmed by examining the list of names in Romans 16. Of the thirty-six persons mentioned, sixteen are women and eighteen men. The Pauline letters thus give us a glimpse of the egalitarian early Christian missionary movement."

Another important leadership role in the early Christian movement was that of prophets. "Paul regards prophets as second only to apostles in the leadership of the church, and they were still regarded as the normative church leaders in some Christian communities in the mid-second century," comments Fiorenza. Do women act as prophets? Indeed they do. "Paul takes for granted that women also act as prophets in the Christian assembly" but that they recognize gender differences between men and women (1 Cor. 12:2–16). Prophets established "schools" and "Asia Minor continued to recognize women as prophets even in the second and third centuries."

The church gradually began to mirror more and more the ways of the surrounding culture, and patriarchy raised its head in opposition to women leadership as time went on. Battles ensued. Gradually, however, women leadership was displaced by all-male leadership, contrary to Jesus' teaching and the church's earliest practices.

Fiorenza writes further, "Women were prominent in the church even after the middle of the second century. They participated in church leadership, not only as widows and deaconesses, but also as prophets and teachers. Women actually dared 'to teach, to debate, to exorcise, to promise cures, probably even to baptize.' Their leadership and initiative were, however, more and more rejected by the patriarchal church. 'No woman is allowed to speak in church, or even to teach, to baptize, or to discharge any man's function, much less to take upon herself the priestly office.'"

In Rome there is a fresco in the St. Priscilla catacomb that pictures the earliest visual image we have of Christians celebrating Eucharist. The person breaking and distributing the bread is a woman. She is "acting as a priest would act today," and women were "natural leaders of the Eucharist" in the early church. Indeed, as Chilton reminds us, "unknown to the general public and often ignored even in scholarship, the women *presbyterai* [priests] exerted a deep influence in the Church until the fourth century of the Common Era." Why did we lose these facts? "Christians wanted to appear more Roman than the Romans in the control they exercised over their households . . . Appeals to the tranquility of a male-ordered household became more and more insistent in Christian literature."

Every reformation talks of going back to the sources and the spirit of the founder. The earliest sources we have, as shown above, demonstrate the reality of women leadership in the earliest church. How can there be renewal or reformation without women returning to leadership in the church? The argument I offer here is merely an historic argument. It does not even touch on issues of cultural evolution, of how women are playing every possible role in leadership throughout culture today from astronauts to presidents, from CEOs to media and government leaders, or about issues of blatant injustice. These arguments also reach the same conclusion: There will be no healthy Christian experience that does not acknowledge women and their roles as issues of justice and equality and common sense—just as it was in the early and radical days of the first Christian communities.

As I write this, an amazing new insult to women has appeared from Ratzinger's church. A new document devised to finally control priestly pedophilia at the same time declares that the "offence" of ordaining women is on a par with the sex abuse of minors. To ordain women is a "grave crime" according to this document and is comparable to desecrating the Eucharist. Some people are saying it is a journalistic faux pas to have sexual abuse and women's ordination condemned in the same document but I suspect the thinking runs deeper than that. This is how sexists think; it is how bullies think; it is how a dominator mentality operates: To let women into the clerical club threatens that club as much as a sexual predator threatens a child victim (that is what they are telling us). Ceri Goddard, chief executive of the Fawcett Society responds with "abject horror at the Vatican's decision to categorise the ordination of women as an 'offence' in the same category as paedophilia."

The document has also come under fire from victims of priestly pedophilia who point out that "the new rules make no mention of the need for bishops to report clerical sex abuse to police, provide no canonical sanctions for bishops who cover up for abusers, and do not include any 'zero tolerance' policy for pedophile priests."

The dominator paradigm is passé. The future calls for a partnership paradigm—yet again. How can any tradition call itself "catholic"—that is, universal—if it excludes half of the human race from its leadership?

Reinvent Pastoral Leadership Training

I am not impressed at current attempts to train persons for either the Catholic or Protestant ministry/priesthood. Among "liberal" seminaries, there is often too uncritical an approach to getting an accredited degree such that seminaries sacrifice their souls on an altar of rationalism, oblivious to the lack of mystical development and acumen in the priest-to-be. Fundamentalist seminaries usually suffer from the opposite problem—too little critical thinking and too much simplistic "Jesus saves" messaging. A truly authentic Christian message, following in the spirit and teaching of Jesus, will prepare future spiritual leaders to be both mystics and prophets in order that their primary job, which is to awaken lay Christians to be the mystics and prophets they can and ought to be, can be accomplished.

Biblical scholar John Dominic Crossan informs us that Paul, the first Christian theologian and the first writer in the Christian Bible, was a mystic through and through—and that for him one cannot be a Christian without being a mystic. "Paul is a mystic. He thinks mystically, writes mystically, teaches mystically, and lives mystically. He also expects other Christians to do likewise . . . Does Paul think, therefore, that only mystics can be Christians or that all Christians must be mystics? In a word, yes." This is striking because I do not know one seminary in the West that teaches future church leaders to be mystics.

Can one bring alive the mystic and the prophet in an accredited educational system in the West today? That is an altogether valid and essential question. This I know: You cannot do it if you ignore any of the seven chakras; you cannot do it if you teach only from the neck up in a blind quest for rationalistic accreditation. Mysticism is not about fleeing the body, but about finding the essence and heart in the body, the moral outrage in the body, our connection to the earth in the body, our sexual powers in the body, and our voice in the body, our left and right brains working in tandem in the body, and our connection to the cosmos in the body and to the ancestors and spirits in the body. I have just named the seven chakras. They are essential to authentic spiritual training and leadership today.

In addition, authentic spiritual formation must include the avenues to prophetic consciousness and action (yes, theory and practice). Beginning with the moral outrage felt in the third chakra and extending to the inherent compassion in the fourth chakra, leaders must be able to both analyze the sins of society and create alternatives to them. This means studying

the great prophets of recent times (Gandhi, King, Romero, Chavez, Dorothy Day, Heschel, Thurman, and others) and of ancient times. Jesus, after
all, derives from both the prophetic and the wisdom traditions of Israel,
and they are closely aligned since we are told in Scripture that "wisdom
is a friend of the prophets." If Rabbi Heschel is correct that the primary
work of the prophet is to "interfere," then training must teach the next
generation of leaders how to interfere effectively.

As we have seen, authentic Christianity flies on two wings: that of
the historical Jesus (the wisdom and prophetic tradition) and that of the
Cosmic Christ (very much an earth-based mystical tradition such as one
finds in the wisdom tradition). Clearly, then, wisdom teachings must
be uppermost in the training of mystical and prophetic church leaders.
The lineage of "creation spirituality" is very much the wisdom tradition
of Israel. It is very important to study the new cosmology and new science in light of the experience of awe and wonder that lies at the heart
of wisdom spirituality. "Awe," after all, we are told, "is the beginning of
wisdom." Wisdom is feminine in the Bible and around the world. Thus
leadership training must incorporate feminine aspects of learning and
especially creativity.

I have learned from more than thirty years of conscious effort to
reinvent education so that spirituality can be taught there, that the key to
spiritual education is creativity and cosmology. Hildegard of Bingen was
correct when she said, "There is wisdom in all creative works." What we
call "art as meditation" is key to healthy spiritual education. Wisdom literature, which holds the essence of the wisdom tradition that so nourished
Jesus, must become the center, not the periphery, of spiritual training. But
the *practice* of meditation cannot be ignored either. And there must be
room for the body, not only in body-based worship, but also in all efforts
at training the imagination.

Consider for example the role of mantras or chanting. Instead of just
teaching left-brain analyses of biblical texts, it is important to chant biblical phrases and phrases emanating from healthy mystics as well. Chanting
puts you into a meditative state. It is not enough to analyze our sacred
texts—we need to chant them as well. For example, the phrases "the kingdom of God is within you" and "the queendom of God is among you,"
when chanted, have a profound effect on people. Or the phrase "love your
enemies." Or "God is love." Or "walk humbly, do justice." Or "blessed
are the peacemakers." Or words from Meister Eckhart: "God is justice,"

or "Isness is God," or "I pray God to rid me of God," and so on. Chanting employs an entirely different side of the brain (the right hemisphere) than does analysis. Both are necessary—right and left hemispheres of the brain. Intuition and intellect, the verbal and the more-than-verbal. But Western Christians are far more schooled in left-brain practices than in right-brain practices.

When I led a group of about 350 students, many of them Protestant clergy, in chants such as these at the Vancouver School of Theology a few summers ago, a profound thing happened. Eighty percent of the clergy were up all night! This proved to me that even Protestants can chant! We can *chant* the Scriptures and not just read them. This is a revolution. It should begin in our leadership schools.

To be candid, I do not hold much hope out for the traditional "seminary"—operating under guidelines from accrediting bodies that don't have a clue or give a damn about mysticism *or* prophecy—being converted to a place of learning where, for example, Jesus and his disciples would feel at home. Who accredits the accreditors? What are their credentials as mystics and prophets?

I suspect that something more radical has to happen in so-called seminary training. We might begin by shutting seminaries down for a semester to teach all there—faculty, administrators, staff, and students— the basics of spirituality, that is, mysticism and prophecy. I know how to do this. I did it successfully with adults for twenty-nine years. We need wisdom schools more than we need seminaries, as such. The training and retraining that is needed cannot be done in the old wineskins of Western academic agendas. As I put it in my Thesis Number 77 that I pounded to the doors of the Wittenburg Church in 2005: "Seminaries as we know them, with their excessive emphasis on left-brain work, often kill and corrupt the mystical soul of the young instead of encouraging the mysticism and prophetic consciousness that is there. They should be replaced by wisdom schools." Amen.

This is a revolution *sine qua non* for the future of the Christian communities. The future cannot be held up and sustained without a thought-out and practiced educational conversion.

GRIEVING, THEN ACTING: TWENTY-FIVE CONCRETE STEPS TO TAKE CHRISTIANITY INTO THE FUTURE

✛

RECENTLY I WAS WITH A PRIEST FRIEND who is vicar of priests in an East Coast diocese. A fine priest himself and now in his early sixties, he said he can "hardly wait" to retire and get away from it all. Sadness and anger is everywhere among the clergy, he said. "Even the retired ones are at each other's throats"—and the few young clergy are "from another planet," wandering about relishing the titles of their offices like Stepford wives playing out a clerical role or clones of the two past popes. Morale is low among laypeople too, many of whom are voting with their feet. A new term has been coined: "the 'had it' Catholics." Anger is rampant and understandably so.

The dark days of the thirty-year Inquisition, orchestrated and wielded by the same powers that chose to look the other way when crimes against children surfaced and that also chose to excuse, keep secret, hide, and obfuscate these crimes and even promote bishops and cardinals who countenanced them—what can one say?

What can one say of these same powers who encourage and react to fanatics and spies everywhere who report on any sign of life or creativity among theological thinkers, base communities, lively liturgies (for example, in Holland), healthy forms of shared leadership, gender justice, respect for homosexuals—and yet still find the time to hound, persecute, condemn, expel, and make life miserable for those with vocations to offer the charism of theology to the people? What shall we say about that? A church denuded of thinkers. A church in the hands of persons "neurotic for orthodoxy" (a bishop's phrase) and in bed with fascist dictators. What shall we say? What shall we do?

The last meeting I had with the late Father Schillebeeckx took place at the Dominican House in Nijmegan, Holland, and I remember him saying to me, "I and many European theologians believe the current papacy is in schism." It was about 1993. (The Brazilian church has raised the same question, according to Lernoux.) I immediately replied in my American fashion, "What are we going to do about it?" He had a benign smile on his face that said to me, "These Americans, they think they can do something."

In 1054 the "great schism" occurred when the Eastern and the Western Christian churches separated. Ecumenical Patriarch Athenagoras I and Pope Paul VI lifted mutual condemnations on December 7, 1965. The "Great Western Schism" occurred from 1378 to 1417, and it was marked by the Western church having three popes at once. The Council of Constance ended the schism by firing all three popes and creating a single pope. The Protestant Reformation might be seen as another schism-like break within the Western Church.

Schism—a structure break—may already have happened, as Schillebeeckx pointed out. The curialists, who, in their grave fear, have co-opted the Second Vatican Council, are in schism since a pope is to be obedient to a council (notice it was the Council of Constance that put popes in their place). Vatican II was clear on the basic issues dividing today's church, and it is Vatican II that must be obeyed in preference to curialist canon lawyers and the sects they spawn. Thus, it seems that a schism has already occurred. The past two papacies are illegitimate. The Gospel and Jesus' teachings, not the pope and church, are the proper objects of faith. A great simplifying of Catholicism is at hand and with it a potential resurrection of Spirit both within and outside the church.

The coup d'eglise and the schism that has occurred by the betrayal of Vatican II is not just an internal, theological debate among Roman Catholics. It is about the future of Christianity and affects Protestants and Eastern Catholics. Moreover, one could make the case that it concerns the survival of our species and our planet as we know it since it is hard to see how our species can survive without healthy spirituality and religion willing to stand courageously for justice and eager to bring forth the most profound elements of its traditions in union with other spiritual traditions. Love versus fear; trust versus control; hope versus despair; human rights versus rigid legalisms; conscience versus blind obedience: These are issues running through all human choices and communities.

This is no ordinary church squabble or theological debate or ho-hum schism. This is about Jesus' witness and his authentic teachings and how they will or will not continue to flourish and get incarnated in history. One might put the question this way: *Does Jesus need the church? If so, what form or forms would that gathering take?* And, equally important: *What current forms of church would Jesus reject outright? What forms have proven so immoral and a-spiritual that Jesus would, once again, turn over the money lenders in the temple (Vatican basilica) in his own outrage at their abuse?*

Paying Attention to Our Grief

There is great grief in the church that needs to be acknowledged. Since the first stage of grief is anger, that anger can and needs to be directed in healthy and life-giving directions. The next stage of grief is sadness. We must acknowledge the sadness. We need rituals to lead us through our grief so we can move on and let the creativity flow that Spirit requires at this time. People can get stuck in grief. When they do, creativity gets bottled up. And if the anger is allowed to fester, bitterness results. That will not do, for our species needs all the creativity it can muster at this time if we are to survive. And religion needs creativity if it is to be part of the solution and not just the problem.

Why is there so much grief? Because betrayal is everywhere. One feels deep feelings with betrayal. Betrayal is never superficial. Betrayal is a rupture of trust between people who once loved each other. A schism is a betrayal. Betrayal happens between friends—not between strangers or enemies. That is why betrayal breaks the heart wide open. Yet when the heart breaks, Spirit can flow through more fully than ever before.

People are feeling real betrayals such as the following:

The betrayal of Vatican II's promise of freedom of conscience
The betrayal of Vatican II's promise of collegiality
The betrayal of Vatican II's sharing of power and decision making with national and local synods of bishops who would presumably represent the people
The betrayal of Vatican II's promise to share decision making with local churches and lay leadership

(remember Father Diekmann's phrase "the Magna
Carta of the laity," which we cited earlier?)
The betrayal of the promise to work closely with other faith
traditions
The betrayal of a renewed liturgical practice, worship that
honored and celebrated local artists, musicians, and
traditions
The betrayal of genuine Ecumenism among religious bodies
The betrayal of respecting the work of theologians and
encouraging intellectual debate
The betrayal of the very meaning of canonization by rushing
into canonization an egomaniac fascist priest who
abused women and admired Hitler
The betrayal of the admonition to heed "the signs of the
times"
The betrayal deriving from defining the church as "the
people" instead of a centralized bureaucracy
The betrayal of a rich tradition of intellectual richness and
spiritual depth
The betrayal of fidelity to solid contemporary Biblical and
theological scholarship
The betrayal of young people who are sexually abused
The betrayal of the promise of lay leadership
The betrayal of the martyrs of the church of Latin America
The betrayal of the Gospel and the teachings of Jesus and
the very invocation of the person of Jesus

There are many broken hearts amid the wreck of Catholicism today.
Mothers and fathers, priests and sisters, laypeople galore are voting with
their feet. Churches are closing in unprecedented numbers (one mod-
est-sized diocese on the East Coast is busy closing forty-two churches).
Nationwide 174 Catholic schools closed in 2009, and Catholic school
enrollment has declined 20 percent in the past decade. Churches are
hemorrhaging. For the first time in recorded history, Ireland did not ordain
a single priest last year.

The triple betrayal—sexual and governance, financial, and
theological/political—is not something that can be erased by the principal
perpetrators hearing one another's confessions and granting each other
absolution, or by canonizing one another in swift, uncritical fashion.

Ecclesial incest is part of the religious perversion we are witness to in our time. The scandalous revelations emerging daily for all the world to see about Vatican Catholicism thoroughly discredit any claims to moral legitimacy or spiritual truth.

It is time therefore to move on. To listen to the Spirit, who "makes all things new" and to envision, at this critical time in human and planetary history, a more authentic incarnation of the Spirit and teaching and intentions of Jesus of Nazareth and the many heroes and prophets, mystics and believers through the centuries who deserve to be remembered and honored as coworkers and cotravelers on the journey. We are blessed today with excellent biblical scholarship to help show us the way as well as with authentic recovery of spiritual traditions of liberation and creation. We are also blessed to be living at a time when science itself is offering not only a new creation story but new stories of our common interdependence that can both inspire us and offer us new guidelines regarding the wisdom of our actions, and when women are emerging with new and deeper questions for our path.

It is time to move from religion to spirituality. To take what is valuable from the burning building, but to do so swiftly. To travel lightly, more lightly than religious organizations are accustomed to traveling. There is much to leave behind.

It is important to tap into the valuable energy field that grief and moral outrage can generate. Future generations await a generous and courageous response. "Let the dead bury the dead" and move on.

Twenty-five Concrete Steps to Bring Christian Communities Alive Again

Very simply now, having examined myths we need to let go of and myths we need to enhance, and having examined some of the great archetypes we need to rescue from the burning building of Christianity, and having considered the meaning of a truly *catholic* Christianity, I wish to address steps to take in implementing a living spiritual community from the remains of Roman Catholicism that are worthy of Jesus and the Cosmic Christ tradition.

1. Look to the grassroots churches and be willing to move beyond the Vatican. It is important to look to each other for answers to

church leadership, direction, theology, and spiritual practice—
and to cease looking to "big daddy" in Rome, surrounded
by all-male, all-celibate (or supposedly celibate) clerics for
direction. Would Jesus be at home with that kind of hierarchical
decision making? Far from it. Jesus was a grassroots guy, a base
community guy, who said, "The first shall be last and the last
first," and who talked of leaders as "friends" and "servants." He
was very critical of hierarchical pomposity and authoritarianism.
The projection onto pontiffs of ecclesial stardom would not sit
well with Jesus.

And it is not working today. It has put unbearable burdens
onto a tiny administrative bureaucracy that it cannot uphold
with any sense of moral integrity. That is a proven fact. Power
corrupts and absolute power corrupts absolutely, as the nineteenth century Catholic historian Lord Acton commented upon
hearing of the papal infallibility decree of the First Vatican
Council.

Jesus never heard of the Vatican. For the first sixteen centuries of its existence the Catholic Church was not synonymous
with the Bernini columns and the giant Michelangelo-designed
dome of the basilica we know as St. Peter's. It is time to let that
go. Let it stand along with the other very fine museum at the
Vatican for what it once was: a modern edifice of great pomp
and immensity that has today become a distraction from true
spirituality, that is, the living out of lives of integrity, mysticism,
justice, and prophecy. Let all that begin anew at the grassroots.

If you are the "people of God" then it is time to start acting
like it. Be aware that from within church structures, the concept of "people of God" is valuable for it tells the truth that the
church is yours, not the pope's or the bishops'. A good example
of this is the bishop emeritus of Sacramento saying recently
that "the church is not the priests and the bishops. The church
is the people." But from the point of view of the larger communities to which we belong, both two-legged and more than
two-legged, "people of God" is an offensive term. It implies that
other people and other religions and other beings are not God's
people, which could not be further from the truth. So this term
is useful internally but needs to be outgrown in respect to those

outside church structures and traditions and indeed those who have more than two legs.

2. Cease paying money into the coffers of prelates who violate the spirit and law of Vatican II and the Gospels.

3. Do what eighty-year-old Jennifer Sleeman, who is a mother of a monk, did this past month—she called for a boycott of all Catholic churches in Ireland on Sundays. And keep the boycotts going once a month if necessary, until the laity are listened to again. Or at least wear armbands of protest when you go to church.

4. Support and even join those lay organizations that are trying to return the church to authentic gospel values such as Catholics United, Call to Action, Voice of the Faithful, National Survivors Advocate Coalition, Corpus (a gathering of married priests), Catholics United for the Common Good, Creation Spirituality Communities, and so on. These organizations represent the rise of authentic leaders for birthing real social and ecclesial change.

5. Instead of a "Vatican III" or a so-called lay synod that is gerrymandered by clerical curialists, let the various lay leadership groups hold national and then international gatherings among themselves—synods that are worthy of the name. Let them give marching orders to church officials instead of the other way around. Let the church officials listen to the laity for a change. Let the laity choose the theologians they wish to be their *periti* at such synods (if any).

6. Insist that whoever finds himself or herself pope simply and immediately sign four documents that grant the following: (1) Married persons can be priests. Leadership in the earliest church was mostly married people though they were not called priests. (2) Women can be priests. Leadership in the early church included women, as we have seen. (3) Gay people can be—in fact, have always been and will always be—called to priestly ministry. How can any tradition be "catholic" if it excludes 10 percent of the human race—homosexuals—from its leadership? How can there be spiritual depth if gay people— who carry a special charism of spiritual insight—are excluded? (4) Dispose of the Curia.

7. Don't ask for permission to make worship alive again. Just do it. Learn how to sponsor Cosmic Masses and Ecstatic Dance worship integrating community prayer and dance and do meditation retreats. Learn to meditate and to chant our Christian sacred texts. Do worship in small, home settings with an emphasis on sharing common stories and food and mutual blessing of the bread and wine. Learn from base communities. But also renew public worship à la the Cosmic Mass, thereby including dance and contemporary art forms such as DJing, VJing, rap, and more, but also as regards contemplative (or Buddhist) kinds of Masses and other expressions of diverse cultural charisms (for example, drumming and dancing as in African and Native American traditions of worship). Start your own version of the Spiritus Christi church.

8. Be strategic. Look for allies in your own or other traditions. Use the media SNAP—Survivors Network of those Abused by Priests—is doing a good job of this currently, and of course Opus Dei embeds itself in the media. Why can't healthy religion do the same? Tell your local journalists what you are doing. Use YouTube and the Internet and the social media, Facebook, Twitter, and more. Protest! Keep a watch on your local Opus Dei bishops and houses and let them know they are being watched and don't be afraid to blow the whistle.

9. If you can no longer take the lies and theological deadness of the Roman Catholic church, then do as Jesus said to do: "Shake the dust from your feet" and find another community that nurtures you and where you do not have to give out more energy than you receive back. Be assured there is life after Roman Catholicism, lots of it. Become a "had it" Catholic if your conscience so tells you. Do not settle for denial of what the truth tells us is truly happening in the Vatican church today. Do not waste your precious time or your soul trying to build up or reform that which your gut tells you is unreformable.

There will be some who, upon praying about it, will be called to stay, and others who are called to move on. Support one another in the overall spiritual vocation of invigorating an authentic spiritual renewal. There is no one path to church renewal. When you pray about staying or leaving, ask yourself the following questions: What does all this have to do with Jesus? With his teachings and life? What best enables me to live out his authentic teachings? Is this what Jesus would have me do? Even if you choose to exit, do not imagine you are "out of the church." You are reforming it from another place of leverage. The church is not a box or even a noun. It is where Spirit lives and comes alive.

10. Call back priests who have left active ministry to marry or simply to practice intellectual integrity and let them assist in leadership but share the leadership with both ordained and unordained. Mix them as we do in the Cosmic Mass.

11. Let the training and formation of leaders include the full tradition of Creation Spirituality, that is, wisdom, mysticism, and the prophetic tradition. Retrain *all* clergy in the Creation Spirituality tradition, including the new cosmology. Those who cannot adapt ought to retire.

12. Invite all bishops and cardinals appointed under what I deem the schismatic popes of the past thirty years to hand in their resignations and let those who wish to return to serve in ministry first undergo retraining in the wisdom tradition of Jesus and the Cosmic Christ tradition.

13. Let celibacy be optional for leaders, priests, and sisters, and encouraged for monks and nuns.

14. Move beyond moral pronouncements on sexuality to teach about the ecstatic and mystical dimensions of sexuality, and realize that limiting births is a moral and ecological obligation today, as is AIDS prevention. Practice safe sex and teach your children to do the same. Get over homophobia. Do not be put off by sexual diversity—praise it!

15. Deep ecumenism—do it! Join or start interfaith and intrafaith dialogues, practices, prayer, and social justice marching. Consider the spiritual progressive network of Rabbi Michael Lerner. Celebrate the diverse traditions and cultural expressions in the Christian church, east and west, north and south, Protestant, Catholic, indigenous, Celtic, Coptic, Aramaic, Russian, Byzantine, and more. Part of this celebration is to accept and recognize the authenticity of other ordination traditions.

16. Implement the ninety-five theses that were pounded on the Wittenburg Church door in 2005 into all theological education.

I reproduce just a few of them here: (i) God is both Mother and Father; (iv) God the Punitive Father is not a God worth honoring, but a false god and an idol that serves empire builders; (xii) "Jesus does not call us to a new religion, but to life" (Dietrich Bonhoeffer); (xix) sustainability is another word for justice, for what is just is sustainable and what is unjust is not; (xx) a preferential option for the poor, as found in the base community movement, is far closer to the teaching and spirit of Jesus than is a preferential option for the rich and powerful, as found, for example, in Opus Dei; (xi) economic justice requires the work of creativity to birth a system of economics that is global, respectful of the health and wealth of the earth systems and that works for all; (xxxvi) Dance, whose root meaning in many indigenous cultures is the same as *breath* or *spirit,* is a very ancient and appropriate form in which to pray; (lxi) interconnectivity is not only a law of physics and of nature, but also forms the basis of community and compassion— compassion is the working out of our shared interconnectivity, both as to our shared joy and our shared suffering and struggle for justice; (lxviii) pedophilia is a terrible wrong, but its cover-up by hierarchy is even more despicable; (lxx) Jesus said nothing about condoms, birth control, or homosexuality; (lxxvi) consumerism is today's version of gluttony and needs to be confronted by creating an economic system that works for all peoples and all earth's creatures; (xc) God is only one name for the Divine One; there are an infinite number of names for God and the Godhead, and still God "has no name and will never be given a name." (xcii) The grief in the human heart needs to be attended to by rituals and practices that, when practiced, will lessen anger and allow creativity to flow anew.

17. Insist that the Vatican open up its finances to scrutiny. (As this book is going to press, the Italian government is investigating the Vatican bank.)

18. Insist that the Vatican abolish the discredited movements known as Opus Dei, Communion and Liberation, and the Legion of Christ and retrain the participants in Creation Spirituality, the New Cosmology, and healthy biblical theology, one that honors justice making and healing ahead of obedient subservience.

19. Restart local appointment of leaders (bishops) and parish councils as proposed by Vatican II. Hold elections!

20. Have a ritual ceremony to bury anti-Semitism and imperial ambitions left over from the Roman Empire scars and to bury St. Augustine's dualistic consciousness, including put-downs of women, sexuality, and "matter," supplementing it with today's understanding of women, of sexuality, and of the marriage of matter, light, and spirit. In other words, bring the real meaning of "incarnation," the divine becoming flesh, alive again.

21. Know about the priesthood of all workers that I write about in my work *The Reinvention of Work,* and know that where you are doing good work you are a midwife of grace, that is, a priest. Work to bring spiritual values of courage and justice and joy to your profession. One journalist has observed that if the day comes when "the Church manages to purge itself of its shame—its sins, its crimes—it will owe a debt of gratitude to the lawyers, the journalists, and above all, the victims and families who have had the courage to persevere, against formidable resistance, in holding it to account." Without the commitment of these professionals doing their job, "the suffering of tens of thousands of children would still be a secret." Ironically, this is the very democratic and "secularist, liberal, pluralist modern world" that the past two papacies rail against—but it is thanks to the priesthood of these workers (my phrase) that the truth is finally being told and some healing can begin. Think and act far beyond church structures and religion itself to bring ecological justice and sustainability to our planet. Educate yourself and encourage your children to think beyond religion to the realities of justice and compassion, healing and celebration, creativity and simple living that are the real tests of an authentic spiritual existence in our critical times.

22. Encourage and trust theologians to think and to criticize one another and to offer service as a living magisterium—interpreters of the teaching—to the larger church. Instead of silencing thinkers—as tyrants, bureaucrats, and regimes of control have done throughout history—support and encourage them, enter into lively debates, and put their best ideas into action. It is an insult to the Creator to abort one's intellectual

life or allow another to do so. How can we have a conscience without training the mind?

23. Call a spade a spade and a schism a schism. Call out the schismatics who have defied the teaching of Vatican II in both spirit and letter. But do not spend a lot of time or energy in righteous indignation—rather, get on with the great task of birthing Christianity for a third millennium. Plant new seeds of community and fun, yet deep, worship experiences.

24. Work closely with the young and listen to them and their spiritual needs and give them roles in leadership. Practice intergenerational wisdom. Share elements of monastic practice with the young. Also encourage councils of grandmothers to meet regularly to scrutinize and comment on the directions that local churches are choosing to go or not to go.

25. Insist on downsizing the Vatican, and do not confuse the residence of the bishop of Rome with some kind of megachurch headquarters when, in fact, in these postmodern times, science teaches us that there is no one center of the universe, that the cosmos is multicentric. Believe in the power of the Holy Spirit to recreate things in church and society and put trust in the Spirit above compulsions to control and before trust in ecclesial dogmas or bureaucracies. Let the Spirit rise from grassroots Christianity and base communities to serve the poor, the dispossessed, and those suffering, whether humans or more-than-humans.

    Let the local churches and grassroots churches unfold as loving and prophetic and alive communities in the spirit of Jesus and the Spirit of creativity, who blows where it wills.

When we accomplish all these things, then we will know that the devastation wrought by the recent schismatic popes was not in vain. The Holy Spirit is busy making "all things new" and preparing the way for an authentic Christian practice, one that follows the path of Jesus and provides practices of spirituality for new generations to follow.

Wailing Wall of Silenced, Expelled, or Banished Theologians and Pastoral Leaders under Ratzinger

✝

I T IS GOOD THAT WE REMEMBER those who tried to serve but were banished in doing so. This list is only partial, and of course it continues to grow. As one editor of a Catholic newspaper wrote me: "Some theologians are not publicly disenfranchised but nevertheless are marginalized and in effect banned. Friends in these jobs tell me moral theology is basically dead in RC institutions because of the chill." It is a strange organization indeed that fires its thinkers and leaders, those who respond to the "signs of the times."

The work of these various persons varied as did their sentences. For example, some were fired from their jobs as editors of Catholic journals, others were expelled from their orders or expelled from their teaching positions, and some were hounded. All were tainted by the accusations from Rome, and many had to withdraw from their ministries. Some were rendered homeless; others died of heart attacks under the pressure. It is the people they served who were punished the most by the detour of distraction from their work that it took to defend themselves and ultimately by their absence. That is why a wailing wall is appropriate—a grieving ritual to remember and process all we have lost, all that might have been. And as a thank-you for their generous service.

1. Jon Sobrino, S.J. (El Salvador, but born in Spain)
2. Bernard Haring, CSSR (Germany)
3. Sr. Lavinia Byrne, IBVM (UK)
4. Jacques Dupres, S.J. (France)
5. Thomas Reese, S.J. (USA)
6. Professor Michael Buckley (USA—denied promotion to full professorship

even though Buckley was president of the Catholic Theological Society of America)

7. Fr. Philip S. Keane, S.S. (USA)
8. Fr. John McNeill, S.J. (USA)
9. David Hollenbach, S.J. (USA)
10. Anthony de Mello, S.J. (Indian Goan priest)
11. Michael Morwood (Victoria, Australia)
12. Bishop Thomas Gumbleton (Detroit, USA)
13. Archbishop Paulo Evaristo Arns (Sao Paulo, Brazil)
14. José Antonio Pagola (Basque)
15. Fr. Hans Küng (Switzerland)
16. Fr. Edward Schillebeeckx, O.P. (Holland)
17. Fr. Charles Curran (USA)
18. Fr. Leonardo Boff, O.F.M. (Brazil)
19. Fr. Anthony Kosnik (USA)
20. Fr. Gustavo Gutiérrez (Peru)
21. Fr. Karl Rahner, S.J. (Germany)
22. Fr. Matthew Fox, O.P. (USA)
23. Sr. Mary Agnes Mansour, RSM (USA)
24. Sr. Elizabeth Morancy, RSM (USA)
25. Sr. Arlene Violet, RSM (USA)
26. Archbishop Raymond Hunthausen (Seattle, USA)
27. Fr. Ernesto Cardenal (Nicaragua)
28. Fr. Robert Nugent (USA)
29. Sr. Jeannine Gramick (USA)
30. Sr. Barbara Ferraro, SND (USA)
31. Sr. Patricia Hussey, SND (USA)
32. Miguel d'Escoto, Maryknoll (Nicaragua)
33. Fr. Edgar Parrales (Nicaragua)
34. Uriel Molina, O.F.M. (Nicaragua)
35. Jean-Bertrand Aristide (Haiti)
36. Fr. Tissa Balasuriya, O.M.I. (Sri Lanka)
37. Fr. Eugen Drewermann (Germany)
38. Sr. Ivone Gebara, SND (Brazil)
39. Bishop Jacques Gaillot (France)
40. Fr. Fernando Cardenal, S.J. (Nicaragua)
41. Fr. Roger Haight, S.J. (USA)
42. Sr. Margaret McBride (USA)
43. Fr. André Guindon (Canada)
44. Bishop Remi DeRoo (Canada, forcibly retired)
45. Bishop Pedro Casaldáliga (Brazil)
46. Fr. Paul Collins (Australia)
47. Sr. Jane Kelly (USA)
48. Bishop Hélder Câmara (Brazil)

49. Fr. Gyorgy Bulanyi (Hungary)
50. Don Luigi Sartori (Italy)
51. Fr. Eugenio Melandri (Italy)
52. Fr. Paul Valadier, S.J. (France)
53. Don Vittorio Cristelli (Italy)
54. Bishop Bartolomé Carrasco Briseño (Mexico)
55. Fr. Philippe Denis, O.P. (France)
56. Bishop Samuel Ruiz (Mexico)
57. Teresa Berger (Germany)
58. Fr. Renato Kizito Sesana (Kenya)
59. Don Leonardo Zega (Italy)
60. Fr. John Sye Kong-seok (Korea)
61. Fr. Paul Cheong Yang-mo (Korea)
62. Fr. Edouard Ri Jemin (Korea)
63. Jacques Dupuis, S.J. (Belgium)
64. Luigi Lombardi Vallauri (Italy)
65. Fr. Jim Callan (USA)
66. Monsig. Luigi Marinelli (Italy)
67. Reinhard Messner (Austria)
68. Fr. Marciano Vidal (Spain)
69. Josef Imbach, O.F.M. (Italy)
70. Don Franco Barbero (Italy)
71. Fr. Cipriano Carini, O.S.B. (Italy)
72. Juan José Tamayo (Spain)
73. Don Vitaliano Della Sala (Italy)
74. Rev. Mary Ramerman (USA)
75. Rev. Ludmila Javorova (Czechoslovakia)
76. Bishop Felix Maria Davidek (Czechoslovakia)
77. Rev. Christine Mayr-Lumetzberger (Austria)
78. Rev. Adelinde Theresia Roitinger (Austria)
79. Rev. Gisela Forster (Germany)
80. Rev. Iris Muller (Germany)
81. Rev. Ida Raming (Germany)
82. Rev. Pia Brunner (Germany)
83. Rev. Angela White (Austria and USA)
84. Fr. Edward Cachia (Canada)
85. Fr. Clodovis Boff (Brazil)
86. Fr. Bill Callahan, S.J. (USA)
87. Fr. Johannes Metz (Germany)
88. Fr. Pedro Arrupe, S.J. (Spain)
89. Fr. Alvaro Arguello (Nicaragua)
90. Fr. Jacques Pohier, O.P. (France)
91. Archbishop Oscar Romero (El Salvador)
92. Bishop George Robinson (Australia)

Acknowledgments

I WISH TO ACKNOWLEDGE THE BRAVERY and integrity of my brothers and sisters fighting for values of justice and compassion in society and in the church, with special regard for the martyrs of the Americas. The ninety-two members of the Wailing Wall for starters, but also the fierce journalists who pursued truths about pedophilia and its cover-up and are still doing so. Also those like Penny Lernoux, who pursued the truth of what has gone on in the South American church; Jason Berry, Gerald Renner, Gordon Urquhart, Michael Walsh, and Maria del Carmen Tapia for their investigation into the scary sects so beloved by two papal administrations. And Garry Wills and James Carroll for their willingness to tell ecclesial truths. Consider George Orwell: "During times of universal deceit, telling the truth is revolutionary."

I also want to thank my agent, Steven Hanselman, for his wise guidance and dogged determination and the people at Sterling Publishing, including Michael Fragnito and Kate Zimmermann, for their support and guidance, as well as my editor, Greg Tobin. All of them helped to make this a better book. Thanks is also due David-Roger Gagnon for his assistance with endnotes research and Michael Duffy for feeding me excellent critical articles along the way. I wish to thank Jim Miller for introducing me to Sister Jane and Sister Jane for her time and presence for our interviews, as well as for her courage in her vocation; the same to Ludmila Javorova for hers.

As usual, I also wish to acknowledge those persons I cite in the endnotes on whose shoulders I stand and think. Also, Debra Martin for her prayers from the ashram and John Congar for his encouragement along the way. I also acknowledge those pedophile survivors and members of SNAP who are committed to let their truth be told so that grace might flow again, along with all those working to give birth to the visions and teachings of Jesus whether within or without what we currently recognize as church structures.

Notes

Introduction

xv   **For example, he wrote in 1962**: Cited in John Allen, *Pope Benedict XVI: A Biography of Joseph Ratzinger* (New York: Continuum, 2005), 174.

xv   **"The Pope was stunned . . ."**: Garry Wills, *Papal Sin: Structures of Deceit* (New York: Doubleday, 2000), 96f.

xv   **The most serious detective work**: David A. Yallop, *In God's Name: An Investigation into the Murder of Pope John Paul I* (New York: Bantam, 1984). An updated edition appeared in 2007.

xv–xvi   **"This was the kind of . . ."**: Wills, *Papal Sin*, 97.

xvi   **"The ghetto, which came into being . . ."**: James Carroll, *Constantine's Sword: The Church and the Jews* (New York: Houghton Mifflin, 2002), 375.

xvii   **In his role as head**: This is a very conservative number—it corresponds to the persons named in the Appendix. There are many more, and of course it is a running number since people are still being silenced and dismissed.

xx   **Cardinal Joseph Ratzinger has envisioned**: Peter Seewald and Joseph Cardinal Ratzinger, *Salt of the Earth: Christianity and the Catholic Church at the End of the Millenium* (San Francisco: Ignatius Press, 1997), 16.

Chapter 1

3   **"He was compelled to spend . . ."**: Allen, *Pope Benedict XVI*, 14.

3   **"It was a riveting adventure . . ."**: Ibid., 71.

3   **"when Ratzinger wants to strike . . ."**: Ibid.

4   **"This book leaves a sour taste . . ."**: Rupert Shortt, "A Layman's Guide to the Pope: Help and Hindrance to Understanding Benedict XVI on His Visit to Britain," *Times Literary Supplement*, September 8, 2010.

5   **"Ratzinger's reading of the war . . ."**: Allen, *Pope Benedict XVI*, 32.

5   **"that might have seriously hindered . . ."**: John Cornwell, *Hitler's Pope: The Secret History of Pius XII* (New York: Penguin Books, 2000), 315.

5   **Only one Roman Jew survived**: Cited in ibid., 317f.

6   **"In this light . . ."**: Allen, *Pope Benedict XVI*, 30.

6   **He bragged how in 1943**: Wills, *Papal Sin*, 16.

6   "Having seen fascism in action . . .": Allen, *Pope Benedict XVI*, 3.

7   In 1919, a communist uprising: Quotes in this paragraph from ibid., 4f.

7   Jews also were blamed for: Ibid., 8

7   "rock-solid Catholic ethos . . .": Ibid., 2.

7   "The truth, however . . .": Ibid., 15.

7   "This was once . . .": Ibid.

8   "He made no public opposition . . .": Ibid., 17.

8   "in light of Ratzinger's later conclusions . . .": Ibid., 19.

8   "based on a selective reading . . .": Ibid., 27.

9   "the Reich members . . .": Ibid.

9   One commentator notes that the: John Cornwell, *Hitler's Pope*, 152f.

9   "It is striking . . .": Allen, *Pope Benedict XVI*, 17.

10   But, as Ann Douglas has: See Ann Douglas, *The Feminization of American Culture* (New York: Knopf, 1977). Douglas shows the serious link between popular media and sentimentalism. See also Matthew Fox, "On Desentimentalizing Spirituality," in Matthew Fox, *Wrestling with the Prophets* (New York: Jeremy P. Tarcher/Putnam, 1995), 297–316.

11   "Everyone at the table laughed . . .": Bill Cummings, *Monk Talk: Faith Is Sanctified Imagination* (unpublished ms., Maryland, 2010), 39.

12   "Bullies go for admiration ...": Stephanie Pappas, "Behind Bullying; Why Kids Are So Cruel," http://news.yahoo.com/s/livescience/behindbullyingwhykidsaresocruel, April 9, 2010.

12   Yet bullies, despite their aggressive behavior: Ibid. The author observes: "Bullies, too, fall victim to their own behavior. They have higher risks of delinquency, substance abuse and psychological problems" (Ibid., pp. 1–2).

Chapter 2

13   A great church event occurred: John W. O'Malley, *What Happened at Vatican II* (Cambridge, MA: Harvard University Press, 2010), 1.

13   Nevertheless, he rose to considerable: Allen, *Pope Benedict XVI*, 55.

14   "The age of absolutism gave . . .": Ibid., 65f.

14   "It was a Magna Carta . . .": Quoted in Tom Roberts, "Battle Lines in the Liturgy Wars," *National Catholic Reporter*, February 19, 2010, 6.

14   At the time Ratzinger: Ibid.

15   "powers in Rome handpicked . . .": John Allen cited in ibid.

15   "They don't listen . . .": Ibid.

15   The Nijmegen Declaration said: Allen, *Pope Benedict XVI*, 67.

17   "Under the strain, university service . . .": Ibid., 114.

17   "A young, friendly, communicative scholar . . .": Cited in Shortt, "A Layman's Guide," 4.

17–18   "a shift in character . . .": Ibid.

18   "an extraordinarily strong . . .": Allen, *Pope Benedict XVI*, 118.

18   Before then he had: Ibid.

18   Regensburg was a brand new: Ibid., 116.

18   Ratzinger's own words: Ibid., 117.

19   "he sold his soul . . .": Ibid., 47.

19   "It's all about seeking . . .": Personal correspondence.

19   "those who, like Ratzinger,": Allen, *Pope Benedict XVI*, 121.

19   "As Ratzinger took on . . .": Ibid., 87.

19   "the best means of . . .": Ibid., 62.

19–20   "Truth is not arrived at . . .": Ibid., 63.

20   "most of the reforms he urged . . .": Ibid., 68.

20   In Bonn and Munster: Ibid., 104.

20   "His attempt to present . . .": Shortt, "A Layman's Guide," 1.

20   "while only a minority . . .": Penny Lernoux, *People of God: The Struggle for World Catholicism* (New York: Viking, 1989), 42.

20   This, Lernoux feels, helps to: Ibid.

21   For example, he gave the following: Allen, *Pope Benedict XVI*, 130.

21   "The Germans know how . . .": Lernoux, *People of God*, 43.

21   "Höffner and Ratzinger were . . .": Ibid.

21   Meeting in Rome at a gathering: Ibid.,44.

22   "violent condemnation . . .": Ibid.

22   The Brazilian bishops held together: Ibid.

22   "Perhaps because the Brazilian bishops . . .": Ibid.

22   The German-Polish alliance in: Ibid., 66f.

22   Carl Bernstein wrote a cover story: Carl Bernstein, "The Holy Alliance," *Time*, February 25, 1992, 28–35. Says Bernstein: "The key Administration players were all devout Roman Catholics—CIA chief William Casey, Allen, Clark, Haig, Walters and William Wilson, Reagan's first ambassador to the Vatican. They regarded the U.S.-Vatican relationship as a holy alliance . . . the teachings of their church combined with their fierce anticommunism . . ." (p. 31).

22   They produced a document: Leonardo Boff and Clodovis Boff, *Introducing Liberation Theology* (Maryknoll, NY: Orbis Books, 1988), 86.

23   "No matter how many . . .": Lernoux, *People of God*, 92. See also 90.

23   Ronald Reagan and Pope John Paul II: Ibid., 74.

23   In a personal interview I had: Lernoux told me another, very chilling, story at this last meeting (she died about six months later in 1989 of cancer). She told me how she was writing an article on the cardinal of Colombia and his relation to the drug cartels when she received a phone call from the cardinal's secretary. She was told: "We know when your daughter leaves and returns from school." With that, Penny and her husband packed up and with their daughter left Colombia after living in South America for twenty years. The Cardinal's name was Alfonso Lopez Trujillo and in 1990 he was elevated to be president of the Pontifical Council for the Family in the Vatican.

24   "This Polish pope . . .": Quoted in Allen, *Pope Benedict XVI*, 124.

24   "Medellin must seem like . . .": Ibid., 143.

24   His objections to this grassroots movement: Ibid., 139.

24   "The essay amounted to . . .": Ibid., 154.

24   He calls theology of liberation: Ibid., 157.

24   "Around the world . . .": Ibid., 158.

25   "The dictators of Latin America . . .": Quoted in ibid., 173.

25   The Vatican, as long as it chooses: Ibid., 159.

25   "This transition demonstrates . . .": Ibid.

25   "as the social reality . . .": Ibid., 133f.

25–26   "Ultimately, he alone had . . .": Ibid., 134.

26   Allen admits that his: Ibid.

26   Ratzinger wrote in 1984: Ibid., 140f.

26   One Latin American archbishop would: Ibid., 155.

27   "does not fit into accepted categories . . .": Ibid., 154.

27–28   "The theology of liberation . . .": Quoted in ibid., 156.

29   "The move was a signal . . .": Ibid., 165.

29   Allen talks of: Ibid., 171.

29   I believe that wherever: I have necessarily discussed shame and aggression among men in some detail in my book *The Hidden Spirituality of Men: Ten Metaphors for Awakening the Sacred Masculine* (Novato, CA: New World Library, 2009).

30   "Bringing the gospel into contact . . .": Allen, *Pope Benedict XVI*, 173.

Chapter 3

33   "The diabolical actions . . .": Ruth Bertels, "Father Bernard Haring—Part One" at http://www.takingfive.com/fatherbernardharing.htm.

34   "no one had done more": Ibid.

34   He issued the following statement: Bernard Haring, *My Witness for the Church* (Mahwah, NJ: Paulist Press, 1992), 82.

34   "Both Stecher and Haring are . . .": Ingrid Shafer, "To Bernard Haring: A Personal Tribute," July 4, 1998 at http://www.usao.edu/~facshaferi/haring1.htm. Shafer had lunch with Haring six weeks before his death.

34–35   "Theologians, especially those . . .": Haring, *My Witness*, 180.

35   "I no longer recognized the Karol Woityla . . .": Ibid., 218.

35   "We stand not under naked legalism": Ibid., 89.

35–36   "Despite a certain trend towards conservatism . . .": Bernard Haring, *Free and Faithful in Christ: Moral Theology for Clergy and Laity* (New York: Seabury, 1979), 4. Haring considered this book his most seminal work.

36   And he separates moral theology: Ibid., 6.

36   Haring recognizes: Ibid., 11.

36   The priestly class must be cleansed: Ibid., 12.

36   In the New Testament, Haring finds: Ibid., 21.

36   Ever critical of legalism, Haring: Ibid., 19.

37   Haring challenges the church: Ibid 78f.

37   He very much acknowledges the failure: Ibid., 158.

37   Haring calls for repentance: Ibid., 159.

37   "the church ought to be . . .": Ibid., 158.

37–38   He calls on the church: Ibid., 78f.

38   Shortly before he died Haring was interviewed: Haring, *My Witness*, 232.

38   Still more I have known: Ibid., 232f.

38   Time and again in Africa: Ibid., 234f.

39   What would you know view: Ibid., 24f.

40   In your book *War Memories*: Ibid., 20–24.

40   I know from other theologians: Ibid., 90f.

40   Before the Council everyone who: Ibid., 94.

41   He finally wrote them a letter: Ibid., 132f.

41–42   "The spectacular rise of liberation theology . . .": Harvey Cox, *The Silencing of Leonardo Boff: The Vatican and the Future of World Christianity* (Oak Park, IL: Myerstone Books, 1988), 10.

42   "Liberation theology was the herald . . .": Lernoux, *People of God*, 96.

42   "In contrast to the cardinal's . . .": Ibid., 97.

42   "By 1973 the church . . .": Ibid., 94f.

43   "knew nothing about Latin America. . . .": Ibid., 92f.

43   The basis of Gutierrez's "analysis . . .": Ibid., 93.

43   When Ratzinger attacked Gutierrez: Ibid., 100.

43   "The bishops expressed appreciation . . .": Ibid., 101.

44   "The cardinal had set everyone off . . .": Ibid., 103.

44   The phantom chase culminated: Ibid., 106.

45   Cox maintains that: Cox, *The Silencing*, 11.

46   "Rome is jealous of the vibrancy . . .": Lernoux, *People of God*, 108.

47   "He had gone, he said . . .": Cox, *The Silencing*, 8.

48   "The greatness of Saint Francis . . .": Leonardo Boff, *Saint Francis: A Model for Human Liberation* (New York: Crossroad, 1984), 51.

49   "In the early church . . .": Ibid., 52f.

49   "This was the way of Jesus . . .": Ibid., 63.

49   "The gospel seriousness of Francis": Ibid., 157.

49   "Liberation always comes . . .": Leonardo Boff, *Faith on the Edge: Religion and Marginalized Existence* (San Francisco: Harper and Row, 1989), 90f.

49–50   "Liberation always comes at a price": Ibid., 97.

50   Theology's task is not: Leonardo Boff, *Ecclesiogenesis: The Base Communities Reinvent the Church* (Maryknoll, NY: Orbis Books, 1986), 60.

50   "The primitive church, in its essential": Ibid., 63f.

51   "It is not enough to point to the": Ibid., 88f.

51   "[T]he institution of the Church . . .": Leonardo Boff, *Church: Charism and Power: Liberation Theology and the Institutional Church* (NY: Crossroad, 1985), 84f.

51   "The institutional church, faced with . . .": Ibid., 54.

52   "The church [is] almost neurotically . . ." : Ibid., 55.

52   Jesus "did not preach": Ibid., 146.

52   "The founders of the church . . .": Ibid., 152f.

53   "The earth has arrived . . .": See Leonardo Boff, *Ecology and Liberation: A New Paradigm* (Maryknoll, NY: Orbis Books, 1995).

53   "the pope's approach . . .": http://www.thirdworldtraveler.com/Heroes/Leonardo-Boff.html.

Chapter 4

55   "A short wisp of a man . . .": Penny Lernoux, "Brazil: The Church of Tomorrow," APF Newsletters of Penny Lernoux, *The Nation*, March 15, 1977.

57   "Rodolfo knew he was . . .": Ibid.

57   "abandoned children are considered eyesores . . .": Ibid.

57   "in which the people only receive . . .": Ibid.

58   "the more persecution the church suffers. . .": Ibid.

58   One of the best-known churchmen: Dom Helder Câmara was called "the prophet of the Brazilian church." In 1952 he formed the National Conference of Braziian Bishops (CNBB) which became "the principal motor for social change in Brazil, and indeed all Latin America." (Lernoux, *People of God*, 122). Câmara stood up to the military in Brazil for twenty-one years and challenged the power of the First World over the Third World. He was repeatedly threatened with death, was blacklisted by the Braziian press, and banned from radio and television for nine years. He was also a poet.

58   "to put ourselves at the front . . .": Lernoux, "Brazil."

58   Lernoux comments: Ibid.

59   "I can't sign this document . . .": Alan Riding, "Vatican Acts to Discipline Cleric in Brazil," *New York Times*, September 27, 1988.

59   "My attitude is a reflection . . .": Ibid.

59   "It is important to state . . .": Bishop Pedro Casaldáliga, "Another Way of Being Church," July–August 1997, http://www.sedos.org/english/20_10_97.htm.

61   "You want me to talk with you . . .": Bishop Pedro Casaldáliga, *Prophets in Combat: The Nicaraguan Journal of Bishop Pedro Casaldáliga* (Oak Park, IL: Catholic Institute for International Relations, 1987), 80f.

62   Bishop Casaldáliga prays that: Ibid., 95.

62   He challenges the church: Ibid., 99.

62   He reminds his listeners: Ibid., 101.

62   Dom Pedro knelt: Ibid., 108f.

63   "A prohibition was issued . . .": Miriam Therese Winter, *Out of the Depths: The Story of Ludmila Javorova, Ordained Roman Catholic Priest* (New York: Crossroad, 2001), 212.

64   "Felix was truly not typical . . .": Ibid., 36.

65   "He earned those accommodations . . .": Ibid.

65   "These clandestine activities . . .": Ibid., 66.

65   The men who were incarcerated with him: Ibid.

66   "especially stressed creativity . . .": Ibid., 80.

66   They were preparing students: Ibid., 93.

66   "He was spontaneous . . .": Ibid., 108.

66   "Society needs the service . . .": Ibid., 110.

66–67   In 1970 he gave a lecture: Ibid.

67   Felix explained that, sacramentally: Ibid., 121.

67   "The unanticipated betrayal . . .": Ibid., 123.

67   He said it was "a matter of conscience": Ibid., 125.

67   A total of seven women were: Ibid..

68   At the same time Rome: Ibid., 200.

68   "The priests themselves have never doubted . . .": Ibid., 201.

68   "They resent the implication . . .": Ibid., 201f.

68–69   "He suffered so much . . .": Ibid., 174f.

69   "I have been a priest . . .": Ibid., 240.

69   "It was so unexpected. . . .": Ibid., 217, 227.

69   "Christ made no distinction . . .": Ibid., 235.

69–70   She asks the questions: Ibid., 234.

70   Ludmila bears witness to the fact: Ibid., 253.

70   In Rochester, New York: For more about this story, see the Web site http://www.spirituschristi.org.

Chapter 5

75   My life's purpose for forty years: See, for example, Marcus J. Borg, *Meeting Jesus Again for the First Time* (San Francisco: HarperSanFrancisco, 1994). In this short book he has not one but two chapters on Jesus and wisdom.

78   Affirmative comments came: Father Schillebeeckx told me that he read it three times. "It was respectful," he said. "But only an American would have written something so blunt."

85   allowed the clique: Yevgeny Yevtushenko, "We Humiliate Ourselves," *Time*, June 27, 1988, 30.

85   To deny or ignore what is going on: For this and the analysis that follows, see Anne Wilson Schaef and Diane Fassel, *The Addictive Organization* (San Francisco: Harper & Row, 1988).

92   To seek out scapegoats is an "obscene practice": Anthony Stevens, *Archetypes* (New York: William Morrow, 1982).

99   Alice Miller has worked in Germany: Alice Miller, *For Your Own Good* (New York: Farrar, Straus, and Giroux, 1985).

102   Perhaps there is a hint: Matthew Fox, *Sheer Joy: Conversations with Thomas Aquinas on Creation Spirituality* (New York: Jeremy Tarcher/Putnam, 2003), 417.

Section Three

104   One bishop, Bishop Morelli: Lernoux, *People of God*, 133.

Chapter 6

106   **For years rumors have circulated**: "An affiliation of a Justice on the highest court in the land to an organization that, for all appearances, is nothing more than a right-wing cult should arouse not only suspicion, but an investigation," notes one commentator (http://www.counterpunch.or/whitney01172004.html). "For many years unconfirmed reports have linked Supreme Court Justices Scalia and Thomas to Opus Dei. In March, 2001, *Newsweek* reported that the wife of Justice Scalia, 'attended Opus Dei's spiritual functions'" (http://www.counterpunch.org/carmichael01302006. html). "A Senate staffer confirmed that the Judiciary Committee received numerous 'notes and letters' stating that Judge Samuel Alito is a member of Opus Dei" (http:// www.counterpunch.org/carmichael01302006.html). In Washington, speculations about ultaconservative jurist Robert Bork (a convert to Roman Catholicism) being Opus Dei are common as are reports that senators Sam Brownback and Rick Santorum are Opus Dei members (http://www.counterpunch.org/carmichael1013022006.html). John Allen reports that FBI director Louis Freeh's brother was Opus Dei and his sons attended an Opus Dei school, but he dismisses most of the other reports alluded to above in John L. Allen Jr., *Opus Dei: An Objective Look behind the Myths and Reality of the Most Controversial Force in the Catholic Church* (New York: Doubleday Image, 2005), 145. However, he does not give evidence of this except his own meetings "off the record" with Opus Dei higher-ups, every one of whom he seems to trust to tell the truth. In general his book reads like a starry-eyed story, and he ends it by saying: "my own sense is that things inside Opus Dei aren't so bad" (387). But try telling that to the thousands of persons fighting for gospel values in South America, for example, whose lives were and are ruined by Opus Dei prelates. Or the millions of persons deprived of healthy base communities by the work and ideology of Opus Dei. Allen ignores the work of Lernoux and of Urquhart and dismisses Walsh and glosses over the revelations of Maria del Carmen Tapia. This book lacks requisite critical detachment and is a sad apologia for Opus Dei. It fails to critique the reality of fascism in Spain and beyond past or present and the sorry version of 'theology' Opus Dei presents to their adherents (in fact, Opus Dei does not produce theologians but only canon lawyers and those in unbelievable numbers). He never mentions Pinochet and the role of Opus Dei in his many murders of church people, nor does he treat the scandal of Calvi hanging from the bridge following his meeting with Opus Dei operatives. He talks about finances by examining Opus Dei in the United States, but in fact Opus Dei has been far less active in the United States than in Europe and Latin America (though that is changing rapidly).

106   **"The secret organization Opus Dei . . ."**: Personal correspondence, October 21, 2010.

107   Andrew Greeley, a respected sociologist: Cited in Lernoux, *People of God*, 320.

107   Opus Dei is a highly secretive organization: Allen, *Opus Dei*, 270.

107   Under Pope John Paul II: Michael Walsh, *Opus Dei: An Investigation into the Secret Society Struggling for Power within the Roman Catholic Church* (San Francisco: HarperSanFrancisco, 1992), 7.

107   Walsh found it "sinister" that: Ibid.

108   "priest-dominated, narrow in outlook . . .": Ibid., 10.

108   "Its fundamental tenet . . .": Ibid., 37.

108   Students became: Ibid., 41.

108   "What was odd was Escriva's insistence . . .": Ibid., 56f.

108   There were three classes: Ibid., 57.

109   "It is difficult not to think . . .": Ibid., 79.

109   "Father knows best": Ibid., 106.

109–110 Such practices might begin with: Ibid., 110f.

110   "As I have not ceased . . .": Ibid., 116.

110   Confession to an Opus Dei priest: Ibid., 116f.

110   A Jesuit priest and clinical psychologist: Ibid.

110   Obedience of heart and mind: Ibid., 118.

111   Panikkar believed that Opus set: Ibid., 133.

111   "Freedom of conscience leads to . . .": Ibid., 137.

111   "The affair of the Roman documents . . .": Ibid., 141.

111–112 American Archbishop John Foley: Ibid.

112   Opus Dei has inserted itself: I have my own story to share. The Monday after Ratzinger was made pope I received a call early in the morning from Chris Matthews's *Hardball* television program to be on that evening to discuss the pope, since, they said, "we know you have an alternative view on him." I declined the invitation. They called every hour for several hours. Finally I asked, "How much time will I get?" They replied: "Thirty minutes." I agreed to be on the program and went down to the TV station in Oakland at 4 p.m. They hooked me up to the program on the East Coast and the lady at the other end said, at 4:25: "Are you ready, Father?" "Yes," I said. At 4:27 she got on and said, "I'm sorry, Father, but you are not going to be on the program. There is not time to do your rich story justice." I replied: "This is not about me but about the new pope. You people bothered me all morning and then you promised me a full thirty minutes." Her reply: "Sorry, Father, but you are not going to be on the program." I said: "This is a political act." She hung up.

        The young man in the studio who had hooked me up said, "I have had this job for eight years and I have never experienced anything like this before." I said, "Welcome to the land of Opus Dei." When I shared this story with a friend I said,

"Chris Matthews should change the name of his program from *Hardball* to *Softball.*"
"No," my friend replied. "From *Hardball* to *No Balls.*"

112   Says a Vatican correspondent about the prelature: Lernoux, *People of God*, 316.

113   More recently we had a follow-up phone conversation: Phone conversation, October 17, 2010. Name withheld for security purposes.

113   He was later identified as an "important" CIA agent: Lernoux, *People of God*, 318.

113   Penny Lernoux established: Ibid., 131f.

114   "all those who go around . . .": Ibid., 143f.

114   In Bogotá, Colombia, the elite: Walsh, *Opus Dei*, 143.

114   "Opus Dei has nothing whatever to do . . .": Ibid., 144.

114   Another apologist writes: Ibid., 144f.

114   "The truth is more complex . . .": Ibid., 146.

114   "its strong endorsement . . .": Cited in Lernoux, *People of God*, 319.

114–115 Currently, instead of the brave churchmen: See http://www.catholic-hierarchy.org/diocese/dqod0.html.

115   In the United States Opus Dei bishops: For more on Opus Dei see Opus Dei Awareness Network at http://www.odan.org/index.htm and Octopus Dei at http://www.octopusdei.org.

115   Walsh presents a strong case: Walsh, *Opus Dei*, 187.

115   His widow said he had been in touch: Lernoux, *People of God*, 317. David Yallop also goes into considerable detail about the relationship of Calvi's death to the $1 billion debt of the Vatican bank in Yallop, *In God's Name*. He cites an Oxford professor who was once a member of Opus Dei as saying they are "sinister, secretive and Orwellian." Yallop says their goal is clear: "the take-over of the Roman Catholic Church" (p. 303).

115   "Alienation of children from their families . . .": Walsh, *Opus Dei*, 163.

116   One mother said of her daughter: Ibid., 164.

116   People who leave Opus endure: Ibid., 171.

116   This is very close to: Ibid., 173.

116   "Opus is the doyen of the neo-conservative movements . . .": Ibid., 176.

116   The right-wing movements: Ibid., 179.

117   "the process of turning [Josemaria] Escriva de Balaguer . . .": Ibid., 195.

117   Written before his canonization: Ibid., 199.

117   Amazingly, 40 percent of the testimony: See ibid., 202f. See also Kenneth L. Woodward, "A Questionable Saint," *Newsweek*, January 13, 1992, 58f.

117   "It is, I firmly believe . . .": Walsh, *Opus Dei*, 199.

118   In it she calls Opus Dei: Maria del Carmen Tapia, *Inside Opus Dei: A True, Unfinished Story* (NY: Continuum, 2006), xiii.

118   Among her charges are that: Ibid., 5.

118   "intellectuals from the sciences . . .": Ibid., 192, 194.

118   Opus Dei is very eager to recruit: Ibid., 215.

119   There is a "constant sexual . . .": Ibid., 217.

119   Escriva had an "obsession . . .": Ibid., 197.

119   There is restriction of reading materials: Ibid., 256.

119   A cultic worship of Father Escriva: Ibid., 245.

119   "increases the power of the directors . . .": Ibid., 317f.

119   The most significant area of silence: Ibid., 318.

120   Many who leave, based: Ibid., 319.

120   "Opus Dei silences critical minds . . .": Ibid., 321.

120   Tapia was herself held: Ibid., 251.

120   She was subjected to what: Ibid., 254.

120   She was forbidden to step: Ibid., 257.

120   "moment arrived when I doubted . . .": Ibid., 267.

120   At one particularly harrowing meeting: Ibid., 270.

121   "I began to shake . . .": Ibid., 272.

121   At her final interview: Ibid., 277.

121   After her escape, Tapia: Ibid., 284.

121   "Slander and defamation were used . . .": Ibid., 313f.

121   Tapia calls the experience: Ibid., 314, 316.

121   "totally unheard-of behavior . . .":   Walsh, *Opus Dei*, 14.

121   This despite a line in his maxims: Ibid.

121   Tapia does not exempt herself: Tapia, *Inside Opus Dei*, 322.

122   Beating of one's body: Ibid., 259.

122   Escriva "did not . . .": Ibid., 309.

122   "saintly before the multitudes . . .": Ibid., 310.

122   "during the last years of his life . . .": Ibid., 313.

122   "A fascinating and disturbing book . . .": Cited on the back cover of ibid.

122   "a long hard look . . .": Ibid.

122   "all who wish to see religion . . .": Ibid.

124   "My astonishment is infinite . . .": Walsh, *Opus Dei*, 169.

Chapter 7

126   "the greatest fundraiser . . .": Jason Berry, "Money Paved Way for Maciel's Influence in the Vatican," *National Catholic Reporter*, April 28, 2010, 1.

126   "magnetic figure in recruiting . . .": Ibid.

126   "members are not allowed . . .": Nicole Winfield, "AP IMPACT: Vatican Probes Group Tied to Scandal," Yahoo News, September 25, 2010.

126   The facts are these: Jason Berry, "Money Paved Way."

126   "I had arrived at the Legion . . .": Ibid., 3.

126   Nothing was done: Jason Berry and Gerald Renner, *Vows of Silence: The Abuse of Power in the Papcy of John Paul II* (New York: Free Press, 2004), 2f.

127   Maciel met Raúl's mother in 1977: Jason Berry, "How Fr. Maciel Built His Empire," *National Catholic Reporter*, April 13, 2010, 5.

127   Raul sought $26 million: Rachel Zoll, "Alleged Son of Legion's Priest—Founder Sues Order," Yahoo News, June 21, 2010, 2.

127   It was not only Ratzinger who protected: Berry, "Money Paved Way," 6. A Polish friend of mine tells me that this cardinal is currently creating havoc in Poland as he is pushing the integrist agenda, namely the marriage of church and state, while the populace wants none of it.

128   "Cardinal Sodano was the cheerleader . . .": Ibid., 9.

128   Father Richard John Neuhaus: Barry, *Vows of Silence*, 202.

128–129 Former U.S. ambassador to the Vatican: Ibid.

129   "cause for hope in a time . . .": Ibid., 203.

129   Indeed, when an American journalist: The incident is reported also in Berry and Renner, *Vows of Silence*, 290f., 295.

129   Indeed, Ratzinger told a Mexican bishop: Ibid., 218, 220.

129   For many years abuse was: Richard McBrien, "Some Back Story on Renner, Berry and the Legionaries of Christ," *National Catholic Reporter*, June 14, 2010.

130   Maciel's "life was arguably the darkest chapter . . .": Jason Berry, "Money Paved Way."

130   The assets of Legion of Christ: Tim Johnson, "Mexico Hit Hard by Vatican's Repudiation of Legion's Founder," McClatchy Washington Bureau, May 11, 2010, 1.

130   Perhaps his stubbornness is partially: Lernoux, *People of God*, 249.

131   He holds a post in nine Vatican: Al Baker, "Ex-Boston Cardinal Gets Plum Post in Rome," *New York Times*, May 28, 2004, p. A4.

131   "the poster boy": Peggy Noonan, "How to Save the Catholic Church," *Wall Street Journal*, WSJ.com, April 17, 2010.

131   "He has also become the poster boy . . .": Ibid.

131   Governor Keating later quit: Berry and Renner, *Vows of Silence*, 305.

132   "What we have experienced . . .": Ibid., 293.

132   "Where love reigns, there is no will to power . . .": Aernout Zevenbergen, *Spots of a Leopard: On being a man* (Cape Town, South Africa: Laughing Leopard Productions, 2009), 144.

132   "where there is fear . . .": Iyer Raghavan, *The Moral and Political Thought of Mahatma Gandhi* (Oxford: Oxford University Press, 1978), 138.

133   "It's almost been said that if you vote . . .": Lernoux, *People of God*, 249.

133   "perceived by the bishops . . .": Ibid., 225.

133   Eighteen different ballots in all: Ibid.

133   "His view of bishops' conferences . . .": Ibid., 251.

133   In 1986, during a graduate ceremony: Ibid., 252.

133   "the papal enforcer in church communities . . .": Ibid.

133   Because Law, like Ratzinger: Ibid.

134   "even though the bishops' conference . . .": Ibid., 362.

134   "The catechism project was not popular . . .": Ibid., 251.

134   Law adopted the agenda of Cardinal Ratzinger: Ibid., 251f.

134   "Law is more interested in sexual issues . . .": Ibid., 251, 252.

134   Law established the Communion and Liberation: Ibid., 251.

135   "the Italian version of Opus Dei": Ibid., 45.

135   "another cardinal with historic ties . . .": John Allen, *Opus Dei*, 251.

135   When Law was made a cardinal: Ibid., 251f.

135   "militant interventionism in temporal matters . . .": Gordon Urquhart, *The Pope's Armada* (London: Bantam, 1995), 25.

135   "He has an Opus air . . .": Lernoux, *People of God,* 324.

135   "CL openly proclaims . . .": Ibid., 324.

135   "spirituality was reduced . . .": Ibid., 328.

135   CL has been called: Urquhart, *The Pope's Armada*, 6.

136   "The movement has caused havoc . . .": Ibid.

136   "John Paul's open support . . .": Lernoux, *People of God*, 325.

136   "underlie every utterance . . .": Urquhart, *The Pope's Armada*, 27.

136   Giussani's perspective is called both: Ibid., 27f.

136   Like Pope John Paul II and Cardinal Ratzinger: Ibid., 261.

136   Giussani finds the root for all: Ibid., 58.

137   "in Catholic thinkers of the past . . .": Ibid., 290.

137   "a retreat from the conciliar view . . .": Ibid.

137   "They rejected Vatican II's call . . .": Ibid., 173.

137   "the institution is infallible . . .": Ibid., 65.

137   "These are views which would shock . . .": Ibid.

137   A "crusading righteousness" follows: Lernoux, *People of God*, 346.

137   "as a new justification for the papacy . . .": Urquhart, *The Pope's Armada*, 69.

137   "You should trust Communion and Liberation . . .": Lernoux, *People of God*, 334.

137   CL is a "bitter and vociferous" opponent: Urquhart, *The Pope's Armada*, 272.

138   "burst forth in their full fury": Ibid., 74.

138   "Some movements imagine . . .": Ibid.

138   Another Spanish group accused CL: Ibid., 75.

138   "in addition to members . . .": Ibid., 143.

138   Most welcome to Ratzinger's worldview: Ibid., 143.

138   "CL's greatest ally": Ibid., 140.

138   "hierarchical Church in which authority . . .": Ibid.

138   "devalues reason . . . They are militantly": Ibid., 10.

138   They also fit a mold: Ibid.

139   CL now enjoyed support: Ibid., 79.

139   "sent shockwaves through the church . . .": Ibid., 68. For lack of space I am not treating the Neocatechumenal Way in the body of this book. It is highly secretive but boasts 1.5 million followers in 106 countries, supports seventy seminaries, and is called "the most powerful neoconservative movement in the Church." The founder, Kiko Argüello, is "the nearest thing to a televangelist that we have in Spain." After his conversion from agnosticism "like a good convert, he became more papist than the pope." Key to his catechesis is sexuality. Homosexuality "is a sickness that can be cured." He rejects condoms ("25% fail"). He encourages having as many children as possible—members average five children per family. Pope John Paul II was an ardent admirer of Kiko, and his personal secretary, Stanislaw Dziwisz (now a cardinal), is their champion. Kiko's army includes 3,000 priests and 1,500 seminarians. They organize many "religious demonstrations" that are in fact political ones, and they decry the separation of church and state. Kiko is "one of the most powerful men in the Catholic Church." See Jésus Rodríguez, "Kiko, la Cólera de Dios" (Kiko, the Wrath of God), *El País*, June 29, 2008, http://church-mouse.Ianuera.com, May 17, 2010.

139   "With the movements . . .": Urquhart, *The Pope's Armada*, 68.

139   "The founders of the new movements . . .": Ibid.

139   This time Cardinal Ratzinger spearheaded: Ibid., 70.

139   "we see certain kinds of movements . . .": Ibid., 79.

140   "all of which were well established . . .": Ibid., 173.

140   "the total obedience the new movements . . .": Ibid.

140 CL possesses "staggering wealth": Ibid., 330, 329.

140 "a watershed in the battle against secularization": Ibid., 318.

141 He famously decreed: Ibid., 187.

142 "Protestants are not churches": "These ecclesial communities . . . cannot, according to Catholic doctrine, be called 'Churches' in the proper sense." Approved by Pope Benedict XVI, June 29, 2007, http/www.vatican.va/romancuria/congregations/cfaith/documents.

142 Mohammad was "evil and inhumane": Ratzinger is quoting Emperor Manuel II Paleologus: "Show me just what Mohammed brought that was new, and there you will find things only evil and inhumane." http://www.vatican.va/holy-father/benedict-xfi/speeches/2006/September/documents/hf-ben-xvi-spe-20060912-university-regensburg-en.html.

142 Thich Nhat Hanh is the Antichrist: A personal conversation with Thich Nhat Hanh at Historic Sweets Ballroom, Oakland California, September 13, 1999. When he told me this I replied simply: "I have read your book on Buddha and Christ and believe me you know more about Christ than they do." With that he tapped me on the leg (we were sitting next to each other in a circle of twenty of his monks who had gathered to lead many in a night of teaching and chanting) for a long ongoing time.

142 yoga must not be practiced: "Some Aspects of Christian Meditation," *Origins* 19, no. 30 (December 28, 1989).

142–143 The council had emphasized the role: Urquhart, *The Pope's Armada*, 12f.

143 Cardinal Ratzinger made it a special priority: Ibid., 13. Notice the word "integral" as in *integriste*.

143 "Whereas the council marked the coming of age . . .": Ibid., 411.

143–144 "Perhaps, as the architect of Restoration . . .": Ibid., 412.

144 "If the Second Vatican Council introduced . . .": Ibid., 411.

144 Urquhart comes to the conclusion: Ibid., 413.

Chapter 8

147 "In response to the choice . . .": Sister Jane Kelly, P.B.V.M., *X Rated Nun: Woman of Integrity* (Lincoln, NE: iUniverse, 2006), 112.

147 Then she volunteered the following: Ibid., 113.

148 "The interview turned into . . .": Ibid., 107.

149 "How prophetic these words . . .": Ibid., 94.

150 "It literally blew my mind . . .": Ibid., 95.

150 "For two years . . .": Ibid.

150   **Eight days after she went:** Ibid., 96.

151   **In her book on the entire:** Ibid., xvii, 96.

152   **The response to her going:** Sister Jane Kelly, P.B.V.M., *Taught to Believe the Unbelievable* (Lincoln, NE: iUniverse Star, 2003), 28.

154   **On May 18, 2001, Ratzinger:** Patsy McGarry, "Pope Engineered Cover-up of Child Sex Abuse, Says Theologian," irishtimes.com, April 20, 2010, 1.

154   **We know that many:** Rosemary Radford Ruether, "Silenced Discussion," *New York Times*, April 18, 2008. "During the 25 years when he headed this office [CDF] (1981–2005), Cardinal Ratzinger cracked down on progressive Catholic thought, closed down seminaries dedicated to educating priests in the context of the issues of poverty and injustice, and, again and again, progressive bishops were replaced with conservative ones . . . At least 71 major thinkers and pastoral leaders were censured during this period, often repeatedly. The effect was to create a deep chill on freedom of expression in Catholic thought. Catholic education is the poorer as a result."

154   **"There is no denying the fact . . .":** Hans Kung, "Open Letter to All Catholic Bishops," Irishtimes.com, April 16, 2010, 3.

154–155 **The person who was Ratzinger's deputy:** Dinesh Ramde and Eric Gorski, "Church Abuse Victim Sues Pope, Senior Vatican Officials," www.huffingtonpost.com, April 2, 2010.

155   **Murphy wrote Ratzinger:** Nicole Winfield, "Vatican Axed Trial for Priest Accused by Deaf Boys," Yahoo News, March 25, 2010.

155   **Jeff Anderson, the lawyer:** Amy Goodman interviewing Jeff Anderson, "Attorney Uncovers Docs Implicating Vatican in Sexual Abuse Coverup," *Democracy Now*, April 29, 2010 (http://www.democracynow.org/2010/4/29/attorney_uncovers_docs_implicating_vatican_in).

155   **"it is my conviction . . .":** Gillian Flaccus, "Future Pope Resisted Defrocking Priest," msnbc.com, April 9, 2010.

156   **"Cardinal Ratzinger was more concerned. . .":** Ibid.

156   **Boston priest John Geoghan molested:** Peggy Noonan, "How to Save."

156   **This church tribunal:** Matt Sedensky, "Vatican waited years to defrock Arizona priest," http://news.yahoo.com/s/ap/20100403/ap_on_re_us/us_church_abuse, p. 2.

156   **"There's no doubt that Ratzinger delayed . . .":** Ibid., p. 1.

157   **"The tragedy is that the bishops . . .":** Ibid.

157   **"did not report a single case . . .":** Shawn Pogatchnik, "Pope's Irish letter faces critical Catholic world," http://news.yahoo.com/s/ap/20100319/ap_on_re_eu/eu_church_abuse, p. 3.

157	**Bishop James Moriarty of Kildare**: Nicole Winfield, "Irish Bishop Resigns, Says He Didn't Report Abuse," Yahoo News, April 22, 2010; Shawn Pogatchnik, "Pope's Irish Letter Faces Critical Catholic World," Yahoo News, April 2, 2010; Shawn Pogatchnik and Verena Schmitt-Roschmann, "Irish Bishop Resigns, Apologizes to Abuse Victims," Yahoo News, April 2, 1010.

158	**"but was spurned"**: Phillip Pullella, "Wikileaks bares even tiny Vatican's diplomatic soul," Yahoo News, Dec. 11, 2010.

158	**"the cover-up of abuse during"**: Mary Raftery, "Missing chapter of child abuse must be published," *Irish Times*, Dec. 7, 2010.

158	**"The only issue for the Vatican"**: Frances D'Emilio, "Cables show Ireland irked Vatican on sovereignty," Yahoo News, Dec. 11, 2010.

158	**"The church's combination of temporal authority . . ."**: Fintan O'Toole, "The Truth Is That Child Abuse and Cover-up Are Not Primarily about Religion or Sex. They Are about Power," Irishtimes.com, April 20, 2010.

158	**Hoyos has said he had the approval**: Tom Heneghan, "John Paul Backed Praise for Hiding Abuse: Cardinal," Yahoo News, April 20, 2010.

159	**"In what other institution . . ."**: Ibid.

159	**The head of a newly formed**: Verena Schmitt-Roschmann, "Munich Diocese Faces 'Tsunami' of Abuse Claims," Yahoo News, April 2, 2010.

159	**"emphatically 'asked' to assume"**: Conny Neumann, "Was Munich's Vicar General Forced to Serve as Ratzinger's Scapegoat?" Spiegelonline, April 19, 2010.

159	**Hullermann continued to work**: Conny Neumann and Peter Wensierski, "Archbishop Ratzinger Failed to Deal with Suspected Pedophile Priest," Spiegelonline, Nov. 29, 2010.

159	**"even failed to take the problem"**: Dietmar Hipp, Frank Hornig, Conny Neumann, Sven Robel, Peter Wensierski, "Did Archbishop Ratzinger Help Shield Perpertrator from Prosecution?" Spiegelonline, March 23, 2010.

160	**One German bishop, Walter Mixa**: Melissa Eddy, "Walter Mixa, German Bishop, Offers to Resign over Abuse," www.huffingtonpost.com, April 22, 2010.

160	**In the Ettal Benedictine boarding school**: Vanessa Fuhrmans, "German Bishop Admits Slapping," *Wall Street Journal*, April 17, 2010.

160	**"one of the worst hit in Germany"**: Mark Hallam and Nancy Isenson, "German study finds systemic cover-ups in catholic priest abuse cases," http://www.dw-world.de/dw/article/0,,6294220,00.html, December 20, 2010.

160	**Recently a German woman who**: Personal correspondence, October 10, 2010. Name withheld to protect the innocent.

162	**In Belgium reports are**: Leo Cendrowicz, "Belgium's Catholic Church Repents—Too Little, Too Late?" *Time*, September 15, 2010.

162   In other instances a priest: Alessandra Rizzo and Bradley Brooks, "Predator Priests Shuffled around Globe," MSNBC.com, April 14, 2010.

163   We have already seen: Five award-winning film documentaries have told the story of specific sex abuse scandals by priests. See "5 Most Damning Films about Catholic Child Abuse," *The Week*, April 27, 2010 (http://theweek.com).

163   "I could not continue to be": George Robinson, *Confronting Power and Sex in the Catholic Church* (Collegeville, MN: Liturgical Press, 2008), 21.

164   "We can no longer accept secret . . .": Paul Collins, *The Modern Inquisition: Seven Prominent Catholics and Their Struggles with the Vatican* (New York: Overlook Press, 2002), 106.

164   "It strikes me that there is widespread fear . . .": Ibid.

164   You have silly talk about: Frances D'Emilio, "Vatican Tries to Quell Uproar over Gay Comment," SFGate.com, April 14, 2010.

165   "Those of good conscience . . .": "Mexico Rejects Church Criticism of Sex Education," SFGate.com, April 16, 2010.

165   "are at much greater risk . . .": Maria Szalavitz, "How Not to Raise a Bully: The Early Roots of Empathy," http://www.time.com/time/printout/0,8816,1982190,00.html, p. 2.

165   "you can enhance empathy . . .": Ibid., p. 3.

165–166 Mary Gordon, founder of Roots of Empathy: Ibid.

166   "one day, they just don't like . . .": Stephanie Pappas, "Behind Bullying: Why Kids Are So Cruel," http://news.yahoo.com/s/livescience/behindbullyingwhykidsareso cruel, p. 2.

167   "Bullies play a well known game": William K. Black, "What Aspect of Dealing with Bullies Did Obama Fail to Learn as a Child?" *The Huffington Post*, Dec. 8, 2010.

167   "Maciel wanted to buy power . . .": Berry, "Money Paved Way," p. 7.

167   Another ex-Legionary commented: Ibid., p. 6.

167   "deliberately flouted anti-laundering": Victor L. Simpson and Nicole Winfield, "Vatican Bank mired in laundering scandal," Yahoo News, Dec. 12, 2010. More about Vatican finances is sure to be revealed in June 2011 when Jason Berry's book on the subject, *Render Unto Rome: The Secret Life of Money in the Catholic Church*, is published.

168–169 Fintan O'Toole comments on clerical abuse: O'Toole, "The Truth Is."

169   "for me the church is not": Teófilo Cabestrero, *Mystic of Liberation: A Portrait of Pedro Casadáliga* (Mary Knoll, NY: Orbis Books, 1981), 141.

Section Four

172   **Included in this struggle are:** Cited in O'Malley, *What Happened*, 114.

172   **"the Vatican, as it has":** Cabestrero, *Mystic of Liberation*, 187.

Chapter 9

175   **"power was the issue":** James Carroll, "Celibacy and the Catholic priest," http://www.boston.com/bostonglobe/editorial_opinion/oped/articles/2010/05/16/celibacy_and_the_catholic_priest/, May 16, 2010.

176   **"The Pope alone . . .":** Garry Wills, *Papal Sin*, 163.

176   **The late and esteemed Father Bede Griffiths:** Dom Bede Griffiths, OSB, "The M-word," The Tablet, August 11, 1990 (available at http://www.vatican2voice.org/8conscience/magister.htm, April 4, 2010).

177   **Cardinal John Henry Newman:** John Cornwell, "The Papal Hijacking of Cardinal Newman," *Financial Times*, September 17, 2010. Cornwell is author of *Newman's Unquiet Grave: The Reluctant Saint* (London: Continuum, 2010).

178   **"The commendation of Peter . . .":** Robert W. Funk, Roy W. Hoover, and the Jesus Seminar, *The Five Gospels: What Did Jesus Really Say? The Search for the Authentic Words of Jesus* (San Francisco: HarperSanFrancisco, 1997), 207.

178   **Of course, Jesus did not speak Greek:** Ibid., 36.

179   **"In a world where identity . . .":** John Dominic Crossan and Jonathan L. Reed, *In Search of Paul* (San Francisco: HarperSanFrancisco, 2004), 280. Also see 278f.

180   **"I do not see any means . . .":** Cited in O'Malley, *What Happened*, 88.

180   **"I know this from having seen it . . .":** Noonan, "How to Save."

180   **"long after the apostolic age":** Greg Tobin, *Selecting the Pope: Uncovering the Mysteries of Papal Elections* (New York: Sterling, 2009), 68.

181   **"Most bishops would be in favor . . .":** "Prophetic Voices," in www.voiceofthefaithfulcatholicchurch.

181   **"In responding to sexual . . .":** Ibid.

182   **"By class, temperament, cultural bias . . .":** Bruce Chilton, *Rabbi Paul: An Intellectual Biography* (New York: Doubleday, 2004), 139.

182   **"Uniformity is a caricature of unity . . .":** Lernoux, *People of God*, 12. It seems there is a movement afoot to reduce the whole church to a "Polish model," comments Italian writer Giancarlo Zizola, which could prove to be "one of the worst mistakes in church history" (p. 14).

184   The issue to bring alive: See Fox, *The Hidden Spirituality of Men.*

185   "We are all meant to be mothers . . .": See Matthew Fox, *Meditations with Meister Eckhart* (Santa Fe, NM: Bear and Co., 1983), 81, 74.

186   "Readers today think exclusively . . .": Bruce Chilton, *The Way of Jesus: To Repair and Renew the World* (Nashville: Abingdon Press, 2010), 139.

186   "All ways lead to God . . .": Fox, *Meditations with Meister Eckhart*, 64.

187   It is a dangerous thing to leave out: I treat the divine feminine in my book *One River, Many Wells: Wisdom Springing from Global Faiths* (New York: Jeremy P. Tarcher/Putnam, 2000), chapters 6 and 7, and the sacred masculine together with the sacred marriage of the two in my book *The Hidden Spirituality of Men*, 221–276.

Chapter 10

188   "Christianity has betrayed Jesus": Howard Thurman, *Jesus and the Disinherited* (Richmond, IN: Friends United Press, 1981), 98.

188   "What has been passing for Christianity . . .": Cited in Thomas Kiernan, *A Treasury of Albert Schweitzer* (New York: Philosophical Library, 1965), 123.

190   Divinity is not oblivious of history: Today's science also honors our bodies. See Matthew Fox, *Sins of the Spirit, Blessings of the Flesh: Lessons for Transforming Evil in Soul and Society* (New York: Harmony Books, 1999).

190   My research teaches me that the symbol: See chapter on Light in Fox, *One River, Many Wells*, 50–79.

193   "The same Spirit that hovered over . . .": Quoted in Fox, *Sheer Joy*, 291.

195   "The religion of Jesus makes the love-ethic . . .": Thurman, *Jesus and the Disinherited*, 89.

197   Now we can get on with: Cf. Ernest Becker, *The Denial of Death* (New York: Free Press, 1973). Becker confesses how indebted he is to Otto Rank for his main thesis. See Matthew Fox, *Wrestling with the Prophets*, 199–214.

198   The Dalai Lama claims: See Matthew Fox, "Service and Compassion," chap. 17 in *One River, Many Wells*, 377–403.

199   In this time of ecological destruction: See Matthew Fox, *The Coming of the Cosmic Christ* (San Francisco: Harper and Row, 1988).

Chapter 11

202   Five Pentecosts ago: The story of this visit and the ninety-five theses is told

in my small book *A New Reformation: Creation Spirituality and the Transformation of Christianity* (Rochester, VT: Inner Traditions, 2006).

205 **"Ecumenicity and interfaith hopes"**: John Shelby Spong, *A New Christianity for a New World* (San Francisco: HarperSanFrancisco, 2001), 225.

205 **"one of the great righteous"**: David Gibson, "Pope's High Praise of Holocaust-Era Predecessor Sparks Jewish Ire," Politics Daily, November 22, 2010. The article comments on the "constant friction" between the pope and the Jewish community, including his support of a Holocaust-denying bishop and his restored version of a Latin Rite mass that prays for the conversion of Jews "that in the past sparked pogroms against European Jews." It is no secret that Pope Benedict is seeking to canonize Pope Pius XII. See also: Christopher Hitchens, "The Pope's Denial Problem: By reconciling with extremist bishops, Benedict embraces the far-right fringe," *Newsweek*, February 9, 2009: "What makes the present case so alarming is that concessions are being made to Holocaust-deniers and anti-Semites," one of whom lectured German bishops "on the doctrinal need to stress the general responsibility of Jews for deicide."

208 **"transfer the realities of the past . . ."**: Peter Kingsley, *A Story Waiting to Pierce You: Mongolia, Tibet and the Destiny of the Western World* (Point Reyes, CA: Golden Sufi Center, 2010), 142.

208 **"just as civilizations have to come . . ."**: Ibid., 81f.

210 **And the greatest numbers gathered**: Chilton, *Rabbi Paul*, 111f.

211 **"I am proposing a post-modern physics"**: David Bohm, "Postmodern Science and a Postmodern World," in Charles Jencks, *The Post-Modern Reader* (London: St Martin's Press, 1992), 390.

211 **"no Christian thinker before or since . . ."**: Chilton, *Rabbi Paul*, 207.

211 **Therefore a catholic Christianity**: I can recommend in particular the important work of Joel Primack and Nancy Abrams in their books *The View from the Center of the Universe* (New York: Riverhead Books, 2006) and *The New Universe and the Human Future: How a Shared Cosmology Could Launch a Global Society* (New Haven, CT: Yale University Press, 2010). I treat the issue of cosmology also in my chapter "Father Sky" in *The Hidden Spirituality of Men*.

213 **our work with the Cosmic Mass**: For more on the Cosmic Mass, see www. thecosmicmass.info. See also www.ecstaticdance.org.

214 **The Dalai Lama's most recent book**: The Dalai Lama, *Toward a True Kinship of Faiths: How the World's Religions Can Come Together* (New York: Doubleday, 2010).

216 **"Christianity was a fractured movement . . ."**: Chilton, *Rabbi Paul*, 112.

216 **"The Gospels emerged a generation after . . ."**: Bruce Chilton, *Mary Magdalene: A Biography* (New York: Doubleday, 2005), 34.

216 "Primitive Christianity was an oral movement . . .": Ibid., 51.

216 "Christianity became highly philosophical . . .": Ibid., 80.

217 "focused on the unique authority . . .": Ibid., 105–109.

217 "didn't think of themselves . . .": Ibid., 104.

218 If the early church had followed: Elisabeth Schussler Fiorenza, "Word, Spirit and Power: Women in Early Christian Communities," in Rosemary Ruether and Eleanor McLaughlin, *Women of Spirit: Female Leaders in the Jewish and Christian Traditions* (New York: Simon and Schuster, 1979), 30. It boggles the mind that Cardinal Ratzinger calls himself a theologian but as far as I can surmise has never once studied with a woman theologian or even read one scholarly work by a woman theologian and practices a willful ignorance of theology.

218 "Women, in this egalitarian movement . . .": Fiorenza, "Word, Spirit and Power," 31.

218 "Christian egalitarian creed was formulated . . .": Ibid.

218 "Jesus, Mary, and the other disciples . . .": Chilton, *Mary Magdalene*, 49f.

219 "Mary is the indispensable character . . .": Ibid., 52.

219 "Women in Jewish antiquity . . .": Ibid., 60.

219 "He becomes . . . an expert . . .": Ibid.

219 "*The Testament of Job* completely overturns . . .": Ibid., 60f.

219 Remember too that in Acts 21:8–9: Ibid., 61.

219 "Ancient Jewish literature permits us . . .": Ibid.

219 In the early Christian movement: Fiorenza, "Word, Spirit and Power," 32–33.

220 "We have no reason to assume . . .": Ibid., 34.

220 "The texts indicate that these women . . .": Ibid.

220 "Phoebe thus had . . .": Ibid., 36.

220 "Paul's letters indicate that women . . .": Ibid., 37.

221 "Paul regards prophets . . .": Ibid., 39.

221 "Paul takes for granted that women . . .": Ibid.

221 Prophets established "schools" . . .: Ibid., 39, 41.

221 "Women were prominent in the church . . .": Ibid., 51.

221 "unknown to the general public . . .": Chilton, *Mary Magdalene*, 112f.

221–222 "Christians wanted to appear . . .": Ibid., 113, 111.

222 As I write this an amazing new insult: John Hooper and Haroon Siddique, loc. cit.

222 "abject horror at the Vatican's decision . . .": John Hooper and Haroon Siddique, "Catholics angry as church puts female ordination on par with sex abuse," http://www.guardian.co.uk/world/2010/jul/15/vatican-declares-womens-ordination-grave-crime.

222   The document has also come under fire: Nicole Winfield, "Vatican: Ordination of Women A 'Grave Crime'," http://www.huffingtonpost.com/2010/07/15/vatican-ordination-of-women

222   "the new rules make no mention . . .": Ibid.

222   The dominator paradigm is passé: See Riane Eisler, *The Chalice and the Blade: Our History, Our Future* (San Francisco: Harper and Row, 1987). How sweet it would be if all the curialist cardinals were to study this book in depth. Maybe some conversions might ensue!

223   "Paul is a mystic . . .": Crossan, *In Search of Paul*, 283, 280. Crossan also recognizes the role of women in the early church. See xii–xiv and 110–123.

223   awaken lay Christians to be the mystics: Consider my recent book, *Christian Mystics: 365 Meditations and Reflections* (Novato: New World Library Press, 2011) to assist in that recovery.

224   What we call "art as meditation": See Matthew Fox, "Deep Ecumenism, Ecojustice, and Art as Meditation," in Fox, *Wrestling with the Prophets*, 215–242.

Chapter 12

226   A new term has been coined: Tom Roberts, "The 'Had It' Catholics," *National Catholic Reporter*, October 11, 2010.

227   The Brazilian church has raised: Lernoux, *People of God*, 134.

229   Nationwide 174 Catholic schools: Kathy Matheson, "One-Time flagship Philly Catholic school closing," YahooNews, June 14, 2010. Once the largest Catholic school in the world, with six thousand students, Cardinal Dougherty shut its doors in 2010.

234   Implement the ninety-five theses: All ninety-five theses can be found in Matthew Fox, *A New Reformation* (Rochester, VT: Inner Traditions, 2006), 61–68.

236   One journalist has observed that if: Hendrik Hertzberg, loc cit.

237   Share elements of monastic: A creative professor of religious studies at East Carolina University has created a one-month experience in monastic living for undergraduate students with amazing results. See Calvin Mercer, *The Monastic Project: A Manual for Instructors*, July 31, 2010, privately published and available for free. Contact: mercerc@ecu.edu.

Index

About the Author

Matthew Fox is a spiritual theologian and an activist. He was a member of the Dominican Order for thirty-four years and holds a doctorate (summa cum laude) in the History and Theology of Spiritualities from the Institute Catholique de Paris. Seeking to establish a pedagogy that was friendly to teaching spirituality, he established the Institute in Culture and Creation Spirituality, which operated for seven years at Mundelein College in Chicago and twelve years at Holy Names College in Oakland, California. For ten of those years at Holy Names College, Cardinal Ratzinger (now Pope Benedict XVI), as the Catholic Church's chief inquisitor and head of the Congregation of Doctrine and Faith, tried to shut the program down. Ratzinger silenced Fox for one year in 1988 and forced him to step down as director. Three years later he expelled Fox from the order and aborted the program. Rather than disband his amazing ecumenical faculty that included artists, scientists, activists, and teachers from many world spiritual traditions, Fox started the University of Creation Spirituality in Oakland and a unique doctor of ministry program, which drew workers of all professions who were committed to deepening their relationship between their work and spirituality. He was president there for nine years.

Fox is author of twenty-nine books on spirituality and culture which have received many awards and have been translated into forty-four languages. He is recipient of the Courage of Conscience Award from the Peace Abbey (other recipients include His Holiness the Dalai Lama, Mother Teresa, and Rosa Parks) and is currently a visiting scholar with the Academy for the Love of Learning in Santa Fe, New Mexico. He is working with inner-city youth in a program called YELLAWE to reinvent education from the inner city out, a program based on his book, *The A.W.E. Project: Reinventing Education, Reinventing the Human*. When Cardinal Ratzinger was made pope, Fox went to Wittenburg and pounded ninety-five theses at the door in protest and called for a "New Reformation." Fox lives in Oakland, California, and he lectures, teaches, writes, and serves as president of the nonprofit he created in 1984, Friends of Creation Spirituality. His website is www.matthewfox.org.

Bruce Chilton has been called "one of the world's truly great New Testament scholars." In addition to authoring many scholarly articles, his books include *Rabbi Jesus, Rabbi Paul, Mary Magdalene: A Biography*, and *The Way of Jesus: To Repair and Renew the World*. He is the Bernard Iddings Bell Professor of Religion at Bard College and an Episcopal priest at the Free Church of Saint John in Barrytown, New York.